WE WERE CHILDREN THEN

*This book is gratefully dedicated
to all of the men and women
who have
so generously shared
their memories and wisdom
with us.*

WE WERE CHILDREN THEN

THEN

Stories from the Yarns of Yesteryear Project

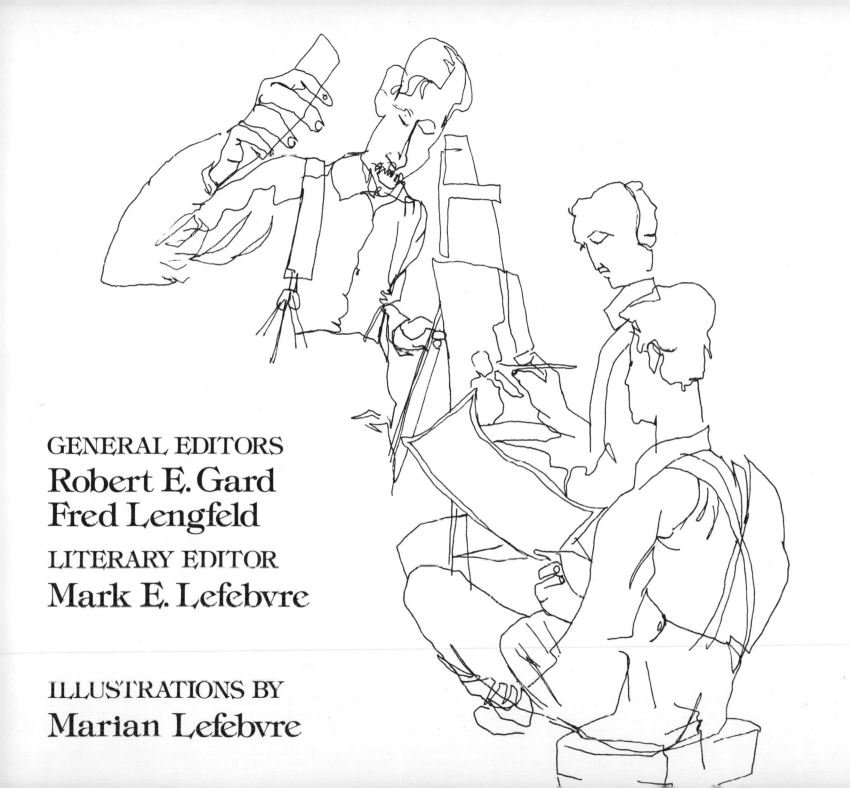

GENERAL EDITORS
Robert E. Gard
Fred Lengfeld

LITERARY EDITOR
Mark E. Lefebvre

ILLUSTRATIONS BY
Marian Lefebvre

First Edition
ISBN 0-88361-041-8
Library of Congress Card Number 76-22961
Copyright 1976 by the Regents of the University of Wisconsin. All rights reserved.
Illustration Copyright 1976 by Marian Lefebvre. All rights reserved.

Published by Wisconsin House Book Publishers in association with University of Wisconsin Extension:
Arts Development, Programs on Aging and the Revolutionary War Bicentennial Commission of Wisconsin.
Printed in the United States of America by Straus Printing & Publishing Co., Inc., Madison, Wisconsin.

ACKNOWLEDGMENTS

Grateful acknowledgment is made to the Revolutionary War Bicentennial Commission of Wisconsin; to University of Wisconsin Extension: Programs on Aging and the Executive Committee of Arts Development. Special acknowledgment is hereby given to Ann Ostrom, Programs on Aging, for her efforts on behalf of the Yarns of Yesteryear Project and to the persons who gave generously of their time to read and judge the manuscripts: Jim Batt, Frank Custer, Jill Dean, Doris Platt and Susan Smith. Special acknowledgment is made to the Wisconsin Regional Writers and to WHA radio, especially Norma Simpson, Accent on Living Programs, who took a deep personal interest in broadcasting the material written by the contestants.

Two persons are chiefly responsible for the success of Yarns of Yesteryear, the contest from which the stories included in this book were drawn: Clarice Dunn and Gen Lewis gave their full time during a two-year period to the interesting work of receiving the manuscripts and to answering hundreds of letters from contestants. Clarice Dunn made more than twenty-five radio broadcasts over the State Radio Network reading from the manuscripts.

Lastly, acknowledgment is made to *Wisconsin Trails* magazine where "The Ragamuffins" by Lois Pink has appeared and to *Farm Wife News* which printed "It's Potato-Sprouting Time, Remember?" by Margaret Damp.

CONTENTS

INTRODUCTION   xv

1 GROWING UP   1

MUD PIE MEMORIES   *Mrs. Clara Hanson*   3
GRANDMOTHER'S "RUMPLE KAMMER"   *Mabel Schroeder*   3
YESTERYEARS ONCE MORE   *Mrs. Olga L. Gest*   4
WERE THE GOOD OLD DAYS ALL THAT GOOD?   *Daisy McAdams*   7
A YARN OF YESTERYEAR   *Mrs. Leonora Dohm*   8
DISCOVERY—ERA 1900   *John Parker*   10
THE OLD SALOON   *Dick Sigl*   11
OUR CLOSE CALL   *Mrs. Martin Paust*   12
AN UNUSUAL BUGGY RIDE   *Mrs. O.L. Campbell*   13
PLEASANT ASSOCIATIONS   *Cecelia Herreid*   14
THE IMMIGRANT BECOMES RICH   *Clara A. Damm*   14
THE EMIGRANTS   *John Parker*   17
YARNS OF YESTERYEAR   *Mary Knobloch Bodenburg*   19
YARNS OF YESTERYEAR   *Blanche B. Lindblad*   22
CHA-KAH-LOW-BEE-NAH-KEE KEE-NAH   *Arthur Scott Buchanan*   24

2 SCHOOL DAYS   25

AN EARLY RURAL SCHOOL   *Evelyn McLean*   27
THE ONE-ROOM SCHOOLHOUSE   *Mrs. John Schumacher*   28
WERE YOU THERE?   *Florence A. Petersen*   29
AN 1892 FIRST READER   *Melba Baehr*   31
COUNTRY SCHOOLMA'AM   *Elizabeth Herritz*   32
THE KEROSENE LAMP   *Mrs. Esther V. Beran*   34

SPRING FRESHET   *Helen Hill*   35
PUNISHMENT WITH A TOOTHBRUSH   *Jennie Erb Joos*   36
DISTRICT PICNIC   *Mrs. Alvin Deischer*   37
THE LEARNING BUSHES   *Mary R. Nelson*   39

3 REMEMBERED PLACES   41

JONES ISLAND   *Josephine Budzisz Klotz*   43
OLD WILLIAMSBURG   *Arthur H. Maegli*   44
FIFTY YEARS AGO . . .   *Jack Fritz*   46
THE MYSTERY OF MISSING VOLUME "M"   *Mrs. Ray Ensenbach*   48

4 DAILY LIFE   51

THE FARM CELLAR, WINTER   *Ruth Burmester*   53
GRANDMOTHER'S SUMMER KITCHEN   *Melba Baehr*   55
THE OLD-FASHIONED HERB GARDEN   *Ruth Bunker Christianson*   56
GRANDMA WAS A GOOD "COOKER"   *Loreen Jacobson*   57
MOTHER'S OLD IRON COOK STOVE   *Mrs. Melvin Getlinger*   59
YE OLDE KRAUT CROCK   *Ida Carstensen*   61
MAKING SAUSAGE   *Mary Gmoser*   62
MAKING LYE SOAP   *Cyrilla Muller*   63
SPRING HOUSECLEANING   *Estella Bhryn*   65
THOSE WONDERFUL YEARS OF TAKING TURNS   *Frieda M. Lease*   66
IT'S POTATO-SPROUTING TIME, REMEMBER?   *Margaret Damp*   67
YESTERDAY'S BONUSES   *Mrs. Mildred S. Hanson*   69

5 WORKING   71

THE DRESSMAKERS   *Catherine Otten*   73
AUNT JOLEE'S FEATHER-STRIPPING BEE   *Alma M. Fabisch*   74

KETTLE OF GOLDEN BUBBLES   *Kathleen Knutson*   76
THRESHING TIME, 1910   *Alexa Young*   78
THRESHING ON THE FARM   *Mary McCrorey*   79
THRESHING DAY ON THE FARM   *Mrs. Tillman Dahl*   80
THE EXPERIENCES OF A COMMON LUMBERMAN   *Irving Goessl*   81
NO ORDINARY CAMPFIRE   *Samuel H. Thut*   83
MY JOB IN A SAWMILL   *Jerry F. Condon, Sr.*   84
MY FATHER WAS THE ENGINEER   *May Augustyn*   85
FIFTY YEARS-PLUS AS A RURAL MAIL CARRIER   *Clarence Rhode*   87
A FARMER'S PERSPECTIVE   *Walter R. Wright*   88

6 HARD TIMES

91

WORLD WAR I, A CHILD'S MEMORY   *Ruth Burmester*   93
WAR EFFORT   *Katherine T. Haefliger*   97
GREEN MONUMENTS   *Henrietta L. Ryall*   99
THE FOREST FIRE   *Laura Carlsen*   101

7 HEALTH

103

TONSILLECTOMY IN 1892   *Ottilie Mueller*   105
DIPHTHERIA SEVENTY-FIVE YEARS AGO   *Henry C. Spear*   106
THEN, NOW, AND INTO THE FUTURE   *Elaine A. Gardner*   106
BATHTUBS IN MY LIFE   *Goldye Mohr*   107

8 BOTH OF US

111

VOICES THROUGH THE STATIC   *Alonzo Pond*   113
SIGNS OF SPRING   *Dorothy Pond*   114
THE BIG BLAST   *Eleanor Morgan*   116
EARLY DAYS IN WISCONSIN   *Alvin H. Morgan*   117

HANGING BOBS   *Mary J. Phillips*   119
MEMORIES OF MY BOYHOOD ON THE FARM   *P.C. Phillips*   119

9 CHARACTERS   123

ONCE THESE CAME DOWN THE CITY STREETS   *Dorothy V. Walters*   125
EARLY BLACK RESIDENTS   *Clara Skoll*   126
THE KOHLMEYERS OF LOGANVILLE   *William C. Thies*   127
"WALK SOFTLY AND CARRY A BIG STICK"   *Mrs. M.M. Dunn*   129
MOTHER   *Lenore Beck*   130
ABE'S BEAR HIDE   *Dorinda Clark*   131
A CHILDHOOD FRIEND   *Mildred M. Rosenthal*   133
GRANDPA'S PRIDE   *Mrs. Otto Kangas*   134
GOD GAVE GRANDMA GERTRUDE GUTS   *Mrs. Albertus Lemmenes*   135
MA   *Mrs. J.L. Tibbetts*   136
FOR THE PRICE OF A HAIR RIBBON   *Sister M. Susanna Neubauer, O.P.*   138
PURPLE RIBBONS   *Mabel Schroeder*   139
INSPIRATION FOR PRAYER   *Roderick MacDonald*   140
MEET MY UNCLE BART   *May Augustyn*   142
AN INCI-DENTAL CHILDHOOD   *Herbert W. Kuhm*   143
MY CONTRIBUTIONS TO BUFFALO COUNTY   *Otto Witte*   145

10 GYPSIES   147

FATHER MEETS THE GYPSIES   *Ruth C. Lembke*   149
THE NIGHT THE GYPSIES CAME TO DINNER   *Maurine H. Leischer*   151
JUST PASSING THROUGH   *Charlotte Knechtges*   153
HALES CORNERS FAIR   *Emily E. Hunt*   155

11 ENTERTAINMENT & HOLIDAYS 159

A GOOD SHOW TOWN *Mrs. R.E. Wolfgram* 161
SMALL TOWN CINEMA *Elizabeth I. Philleo* 163
LET'S GO TO WASHINGTON PARK, PAPA *Dorothy V. Walters* 164
THOSE GOOD OLD DAYS OF WINTER *Lucille Boneske* 166
THE RAGAMUFFINS *Lois Tucker Pink* 168
THE CHRISTMAS I REMEMBER BEST *James A. Jones* 170
THE CHRISTMAS HOLIDAYS, IN CHURCH
  AND ON THE FARM, IN THE 1890s *Elsie A. Schutz* 171
CHRISTMAS EVE 1897 *Jessie Gaebele Bauer* 172
TRIPLE DUTY CHRISTMAS TREE *Sister M. Adrienne Downey, O.P.* 173

LIST OF CONTESTANTS, 1974-1975 175

INTRODUCTION

THE YARNS OF YESTERYEAR PROJECT —
HOW IT ALL BEGAN
Clarice Chase Dunn

When Professor Robert E. Gard in January 1974 asked me to conduct a statewide creative writing contest for senior citizens, I hesitated. As I was already developing an oral history project for Wisconsin Regional Writers Association, I certainly didn't need an additional assignment. Then I remembered what my octogenarian neighbor had said the day before.

"Some people think all us old-timers like to do is play cards."

Our *National Observer* had been left in his mailbox by mistake, and he had walked the quarter mile to deliver it in person. Over coffee we talked of many things: the lumbering industry in the Chippewa Valley, threshing days on the pre-agribusiness family farm, the melodious songs of the World War I era, and contemporary topics ranging from vegetable gardening to politics. Leaving, he apologized for taking up so much of my time. I assured him that I had been enriched by his ideas and his reminiscences.

Perhaps I should undertake this new project.

"How much time is involved?" I asked Professor Gard.

"Oh, not a great deal. Get out a brochure. Find a competent judge. Award prizes at Wisconsin Regional Writers Spring Conference at Beaver Dam in May. That's about it. We probably won't get more than fifty entries."

Then he told me that University of Wisconsin Extension Arts and Programs on Aging had been working cooperatively to expand and enrich programming for senior citizens. Creative writing seemed a logical sequel to the Oral History project initiated in 1972. Wisconsin Division on Aging had provided funding for the contest and Wisconsin Regional Writers had pledged assistance. Historical Wisconsin, with emphasis on recollected folkways as a bicentennial tie-in, would be the theme of the contest.

I agreed to take on the project.

As I worked on the brochure, the idea kept building that even if only fifty senior citizens did enter the contest, their manuscripts would have tremendous value: value to the writer as a creative experience, value to the reader as an addendum to Wisconsin history.

Response to the contest was immediate, enthusiastic, and widespread. A week after the publication of the brochure, manuscripts began arriving at contest headquarters. Some were written on yellow-lined paper; others were professionally prepared. Many came from hospital beds and nursing homes. Recent retirees still in the mainstream were happy to have this opportunity to develop a new interest. Letters attached to the manuscripts expressed appreciation for this invitation to write about the past as it affected them.

Since the brochure had not stated that contestants were limited to one manuscript, many found the first try so rewarding that they sent in additional entries and the contest closed with over 300 manuscripts from 274 contestants from 129 localities. Because of this overwhelming response, three judges were needed to read and evaluate the manuscripts. We were extremely fortunate in getting Frank Custer, local history buff and feature writer for the Madison *Capital Times;* and Jill Dean, Editor, and Susan Smith, Associate Editor of *Wisconsin Trails.*

From the receipt of the first manuscript, it was obvious that this was not an ordinary contest. There was evident a hunger for communication, a sense of gratification that the day-by-day experiences of ordinary men and women were considered important enough to write about. The volume of correspondence was such that the need for secretarial help became urgent. Genevieve Lewis, teacher, journalist and secretary, volunteered her services.

We had assumed that the contest would be over with the awarding of prizes at WRWA Spring Conference. It wasn't. Remember the magic pudding pot in the old fairy tale? It kept right on making pudding because no one knew the prescribed words for turning it off. Contestants did not regard the contest as a one-time event but as an ongoing activity and nothing could turn them off.

They asked for criticism of their work, suggestions for next year's contest, and information about other contests. They wanted to join writers' groups.

Personnel in senior citizen centers asked for help in starting writing clubs and the first creative writing workshop for senior citizens was held at the Colonial Club at Sun Prairie.

Then in October 1974 the statewide correspondence became nationwide. *Modern Maturity* magazine published an article written about the contest by Janet Schlatter of Madison, Wisconsin. Letters requesting detailed information on how to organize such a contest poured in from almost all of the fifty states. They came from bicentennial committees; state, regional and local historical societies; groups working with the aging, and various civic organizations. Almost two years later, these letters continue to arrive. Professors Lengfeld and Gard had indeed hit upon an idea whose time had come.

Because the manuscripts give an intimate picture of dooryard Wisconsin over the past eight decades, their value to historical fiction writers is obvious. Consequently, the entire 1974 collection was put into the archives of the Wisconsin State Historical Society for research purposes. The 1975 collection is housed in the archives of the Wisconsin Academy of Sciences, Arts and Letters.

Another contest spinoff is the Yarns of Yesteryear radio series, carried on Norma Simpson's Accent on Living program (Wisconsin Educational Radio Network). Only one broadcast featuring the manuscripts was planned, but public response from all over the state was such that twenty-two programs have been aired.

When it became obvious that the contest had inspired nationwide creative writing activity among senior citizens and could no longer be handled by one person, Genevieve Lewis was made co-director of the contest for 1975.

The 1975 contest was not just a repetition of the previous year. Many contestants had become seriously interested in writing and the range of topics was amplified. In 1974 happy themes predominated; in 1975 much grim personal history was narrated. Doris Platt, Supervisor of Museum Education, Wisconsin State Historical Society, and James Batt, Executive Director of Wisconsin Academy of Sciences, Arts and Letters joined Jill Dean and Frank Custer as judges.

The contestants, 659, from 271 communities, became more closely identified with the Wisconsin Regional Writers Association which now furnishes all of the prize money. Individual WRWA members do outreach work with senior citizens in their own communities, and the WRWA Round Robin program has been expanded to include a senior citizen category.

The idea of a bicentennial book of Yarns of Yesteryear reminiscences came in response to the many letters from Accent on Living listeners who inquired as to the source of the manuscripts. Listeners assumed that the manuscripts were already in book form and requested the name of the publisher.

"Can't the manuscripts be circulated throughout all of the libraries in the state?"

"Why can't every senior citizen center have xeroxed copies of the collections?"

"Schoolchildren should have access to these stories."

We do not as yet have the funds to accede to these requests. We do have this volume, *We Were Children Then*, a bicentennial gift to the nation from the men and women who have lived and worked and achieved, and whose lives have become part of the fabric of history.

In this year of 1976, Yarns of Yesteryear lights its third candle as the nation lights two hundred. Perhaps it is the concurrent celebration that has intensified interest in the contest. Perhaps that is why the queries continue.

1 GROWING UP

MUD PIE MEMORIES
Mrs. Clara Hanson

In the days gone by when I was a youngster, we didn't have many toys. I liked dolls best and had a few, but nothing like the beautiful ones to be had today. However, we learned to pretend and use what was at hand. The first I remember of "Playing House" was in an old cook shanty in our yard. Our table was a large chopping block and our dishes were mostly broken crockery. My older sister, Gladys, was not short on imagination. Morning glory vines climbed over the shack, so the open flowers became our telephone, one bloom for the receiver and one for the transmitter. We tried to be very "grown-up." Later my sister had to be Mother's helper in the house as we were a large family. Then my younger sister, Bernice, and I moved our playhouse into an old wooden corncrib. It had about five or six partitions about a foot above the floor. So you see we had many rooms and furnished them with anything we could scare up. The room nearest the door was of course the kitchen and here most of our activity took place. Mud pies, how we loved to make them! After a rain, when the sun had dried things off, we would tell Ma that we wanted to go "over east." That meant the further end of the farm where there was a small water hole. We would walk down the lane, stopping to wade in every pool of water we could find. Soon we would come to what we were looking for. Where water had deposited very fine dirt particles and they had dried, we found our "chocolate." We would scrape up some "bars" for our frostings and chocolate syrup. If we found sand, that was our brown sugar. Burdock was plentiful and that became our rhubarb. Then back home to "bake." Such cakes, pies, bread and cookies you'd never believe. A corncob made a dandy rolling pin and put a nice design on each cookie. For very special occasions, we would go to the woods behind us and bring flowers and pretty leaves to decorate with. We prepared many a meal, but our eating was only imaginary.

Our brother would come galloping up on his "horse" and tie it outside. It was only a tobacco lath with a twine but rather wild just the same. Of course, brother came in for "lunch." Once we invited our older sister for dinner. What a feast we prepared, but we couldn't eat a bite because everything was made of mud. While we played, we changed our names. I was Ethel and she was Grace. We also had two imaginary companions named Ella and Milla. That was a deep secret, but what fun we had.

We would walk quite a distance for flowers for our vases. There were many spring flowers in the woods back of our playhouse and later we would find wild phlox and sweet william along the roadside. As time went on, we had to learn to work and had less time to play. One day a storm came and blew the old crib over on its side. That was the end of our playhouse. All left for us was a big clean-up job.

My sister and I are senior citizens and grandmothers now, but I still cherish the memory of the carefree days when we were a couple of kids.

GRANDMOTHER'S "RUMPLE KAMMER"
Mabel Schroeder

A trip to Grandmother's attic or "rumple kammer" was a soul-satisfying experience to a four-year-old girl— me. The attic was over the kitchen wing of the house. A heavy plank door off the laundry and storage area led to the steep narrow stairway. Grandmother helped me up the first steep step and gave me a boost up the last very steep step. Old Mooie the blue-gray Maltese cat followed slowly.

The attic was comfortably full but clean and orderly. A large window at one end made it bright and cheerful. While Grandma rested in the rocking chair with the broken arm I sniffled and snuffled like a puppy at the bunches of herbs hung from square-headed nails near the chimney. There were big bunches of dill which smelled like the pickles Grandma made. The bundle with the tiny white flowers was camomile. It made fragrant tea and was used on cuts to prevent blood poisoning, so Grandma had told me. Spicy smelling smaller bundles were marjoram, basil and "bonen-kraut." Then there were bunches of nose-tickling tansy. These kept ants out of the pantry. Near the window stood a small wooden cask filled with shiny flax seeds. These ran through my fingers and hurried back to their places. They made me laugh. The flax seeds smelled like clear, cool water.

Grandmother had opened the cloth-covered box with the leather hinges and was looking through the tiny rolls of cloth scraps saved from sewing. I didn't like the black and brown sateen. It smelled like hot iron, an acrid smell.

I dug around among the little rolls until I found the blue and pink sprigged dimity. Grandma told me again about the pretty dresses Mama and Aunt Ottelia wore to Great Aunt Visa's wedding. But she couldn't remember which one had been Mama's, the pink flowered or the one with blue roses. The dimity smelled like the apple trees in Grandma's back yard.

Mooie had finished her investigations, and, having found no evidence of mice, she now rubbed against Grandma and purred loudly.

While Grandma picked up her pieces of gray calico, closed the lid of the box and pushed it back to its place, I asked again to hear about the hump-backed trunk which stood way back under the eaves. Patiently, Grandma told me about the time she had used the trunk. It was when she had gone to a place she called "Out West" to take up land for Uncle August in the Dakotas. She said there were no trees out there and the water tasted "shreklich," but the wheat and flax fields were beautiful.

Before leaving the attic Grandma filled one pinafore pocket with hickory nuts and put a bar of lye soap in the other. I hitched myself down the clean scrubbed stairs on my seat, step by step.

Grandma opened the side door and Mooie and I sat down on the big flagstone outside the door and cracked a few hickory nuts before giong home to Mama and to my afternoon nap.

YESTERYEARS ONCE MORE
Mrs. Olga L. Gest

Do you remember those years? Were they good to you? Undoubtedly there were both good and bad to all of us. Naturally, we would rather remember the good things that happened to us, than to remember the bad ones!

I am seventy-two years old and a resident of a nursing home. Two of the things that I enjoy doing are reading about the true things that have happened to other people, and writing about events in my life.

Having been a reporter for three different newspapers, I have had many unusual experiences. For instance, there was the winter that we had the ice storm.

Everything in our town was covered with ice. When I called in the story to the nearby big city newspaper, thinking that it would make an interesting story, I was told that it was not anything unusual, because the weather was like that all around in this area!

And there was the time when one of the big city newspaper reporters called and told *me* about something that happened to a man who used to live in our village. He had committed a murder in another state! I was asked to find out all I could about his personal life while he was in our town.

When I was a kid, it seemed that we had more snow in the winter than we have now. We sure used to enjoy rides in sleighs pulled by horses. There were heated bricks to keep our feet warm. And how we used to cry when our folks wouldn't let us ride on the runners of the sleighs!

I can remember when I went to country school about sixty years ago, we used to have spell downs. We would "choose sides" and the two teams would line up on each side of the schoolroom. The teacher would pronounce the words and we would try to spell them correctly. The person who spelled all of his given words correctly was the winner.

We also had "flash card" drills, in addition and subtraction. We would choose sides and the teacher would show cards like this: $4 + 3 = ?$; $10 + 8 = ?$; $6 - 2 = ?$; $14 - 9 = ?$ Whoever gave the answers correctly and stood up the longest was the winner.

In the 1925-35 era, home talent plays were popular. Our grade-school mother's club was very active. And one year we put on a play called "The Spinster's Club." I had great admiration for the woman who directed the play. She had found this one-act play, "The Spinster's Club," which was very amusing, but wasn't long enough for an evening's entertainment. So she found another one-act play. With the two of them, she had a two-hour's program. One of the plays had nine women and eight men in it. I was "Poor Aunt Bess." When the play ended, all the ladies were paired off with a boyfriend, except me. So someone led me to the front of the stage and said, "Is there anyone in the audience who will marry poor Aunt Bess?" And a man, way at the back of the auditorium, stood up and said, "I will." And he marched up the center aisle and came and stood beside me on the stage. I might add that I was quite tall and thin, and the man was short and fat. When the audience heard the man speak, they turned in their seats to see what had happened. His response and walk up the aisle surprised and amazed everyone. That part had been added by our director.

I was born and raised on a farm, and during the years of about 1915-25, a popular pastime was parties in the homes. We would roll up the rugs and dance to music by a violin and a guitar, or accordion. My brother could play an accordion without having taken any lessons.

There was a creek running through our farm and many times I would go wading in it. There used to be bloodsuckers in the water, and they would cling to my feet. These had to be pulled off! Ugh! But that was the only way they would come off. Sometimes we had to put salt on the pests to get them off.

Here are a couple of accidents that happened to me. Once, when I was wading in the creek, I stepped on a sharp stone and cut the underside of the big toe on my left foot. I still have that scar. Another time, we were playing blind man's bluff. I was it, and had a cloth tied around my eyes. I opened my arms real wide and went forward. Instead of catching a person, I hit a tree. I must have made a hard contact, because my nose was broken! My parents didn't take me to the doctor to have it set. As a result, I now have a small, sharp bone sticking up near the bridge of my spectacles.

When I was attending high school, my girlfriend and I rented a room from a lady in town. I had quite a lot of hair on my arms. People used to tell me that someday I would be rich because of it. But I didn't like the way my arms looked, so I bought some hair remover and put it on my arms. Then I swung my arms around to dry them. Some of the hair remover fell on the bathtub. It ate the enamel off the tub in many places. As a result, I had to buy my landlady a new bathtub!

In the town where I lived when I was married, there was a woman who was bedridden with arthritis. Faith healers were popular at that time. This lady was suffering from a lot of pain, besides being disabled. So she hired an ambulance, a driver, an assistant driver, and a woman companion to take her to a faith healer in Michigan.

She was on a stretcher and was placed in the front part of the hall, just below the stage waiting for her turn to be "healed." The sick people who were on the stage became healed after the healer put his hands on them and did some talking. What do you think happened to the lady from our town? Do you think she got healed? Well, you guessed it: she never even got up on the stage!

When I was about twenty years old, we wore hats when we went to church and to other places. I had a lot of hair and wore it in a braid around my head. I needed a large-sized hat, because of my hair style, and because I had a "knowledge bump" on the back of my head. Whenever I wore a hat, I would be in misery because it was tight and the hairpins would hurt my scalp.

Then bobbed hair came into style. I wanted to bob my hair, but my husband didn't want me to. I was unhappy because my head would hurt me so much. One day I went to the barber in our town and had him cut my hair so that it was just above my shoulders. When I got home, my husband was mad at me and I looked terrible! So the next day, I went back to the barber shop (there were no beauty shops in our town then). The barber cut my hair shorter and singled the back of my head. It made me look much better, and my hat didn't hurt me anymore when I wore it. When I had my hair cut against my husband's wishes, would you call that Women's Lib?

When I was a kid on the farm, we used to go "Jul Bukking." That is a Norwegian term, which translated means "Christmas Clowning." We would dress up in some crazy outfits, including masks, and then call on our neighbors to see if they would know us. We would dance and sing too. Of course we always got treats at each home.

I can remember when gypsies used to travel from one house to another in horse-drawn covered wagons. They would be looking for food, but presumably would take anything that they could put their hands on. My parents used to say to me, "If you don't behave, we will let the gypsies take you." I was very scared and would run and hide whenever I saw them coming.

These are my "Yesteryears." I hope that you have enjoyed reading them as much as I have enjoyed writing them.

WERE THE GOOD OLD DAYS ALL THAT GOOD?
Daisy McAdams

You must have heard or spoken of those good old days—way back when you and I were young. Well, as I now sit and think of those bygone days—they *sure were good*.

Of course we had our ups and downs. Our food was good and wholesome, not already drained of much of its goodness before we got it. Remember the delicious bread Mother used to make? You could smell the goodness when it was baking and you could hardly wait for a slice with the crunchy crust and good butter on it. Boy, you certainly called that *good* bread. What you get today is like a hunk of cotton, wimpy and stretchy. The meat also, so much of it has been rid of its natural goodness. You at times do not know just what kind of meat you are eating. Such is the type of most of the foods you get today.

In my day, we walked to our work, rain or shine, as the wage we received would not allow for a five-cent trolley car ride. Also in those good old days, if we had a dollar in our pocket we felt at ease, as the good old five-and-ten store had plenty of things we needed.

And we had our good old family doctor, who came in snow or rain, night or day, hitched up his horse to the buggy and with his little satchel on the seat beside him, would come when you called. The little sugar pills, with medicine on them, that he left for you did more good those days, than the stuff you get today.

There were the good old five-and-ten-cent movie shows. First the five-cent silent picture with printed words and then along came the movie with voice. We used to buy our tickets and then stand in line until the door opened and we were ushered in. At times we had to stand for quite some time but we did not mind even though we got the smell of onions or garlic or of stale tobacco. We had good movies and enjoyed them.

There were places called saloons where they sold beer and whisky and other drinks. We never had much disturbance, but would see someone stagger in and out at times. The old curfew bell rang at nine o'clock each night and we younger folks had to be off the streets. One felt safe in walking the streets, day or night, in those good old days. There were few automobiles as there were only a few who could afford one. The bicycle was popular and there also was the tandem bicycle.

In the early '90s I worked for three dollars and fifty cents a week and then twelve-and-a-half-cent hourly wage in the first factory I worked. We still walked to and from our work. Can you see us paying five cents each trip? Oh no, but we still saved a bit from those wages. But even so those were good old days. Little folks would get a penny to spend for a stick of candy or maybe you bought a large white wax gum heart that always had a picture on it.

Some of your food you bought from someone who made trips to your home. Remember the coffee and spices that someone would bring? You bought coffee and he would give you a coupon which you saved and when you had enough of them you could go down to the coffee stand and turn them in for beautiful dinner dishes, glassware, or other things. All those lovely things, and you could choose what you wanted.

We went to Sunday School each Sunday and we were never allowed to spend money on Sunday or go to a show so we would get the old flatiron and Dad's hammer and a large tin milk pan and a bag of hickory nuts and crack nuts until we had plenty, and that took some time. We also had black walnuts which were *so good*. But awful hard to crack and sometimes we would pop a large pan of popcorn and pour melted butter over it and sprinkle on some salt.

Well, we had ample and were good and healthy and the work never hurt us, as I have been enjoying all this for the past ninety years and I still work all day in the O.T. room, at the home. I'm living in these latter years, so work hurts no one and it is good for you and you still have time to look back to those good old days, which *were* all that good.

A YARN OF YESTERYEAR
Mrs. Leonora Dohm

Today, after three days of sub-zero weather, water pipes in the well froze, leaving me without drinking water; after drawing water from the cistern in the basement and heating it on the stove to do the dishes, I reminisced.

Mother was a perfect housekeeper, proud of the whitest wash in the village. No detergents, she used Gold Dust Powder and homemade soap. After machine washing, white clothes were boiled on the kitchen stove. Mom always wore aprons and never worked outside without her sunbonnet. Dad earned our living while Mom saved for a rainy day. She was the handyman, replacing small windowpanes, puttying loose ones and doing other small repairs. We were a healthy family, but measles, chicken pox, whooping cough, we had 'em, but seldom had the doctor. When we were listless or feverish, Mom consulted the book, *Chat With the Family Doctor*, studied the symptoms and treated us accordingly. We had few books, but another one often used was *The Business Guide*. It held a wealth of information. My parents were married in 1895 and father had bought this book in 1888 for one dollar; perhaps he used it to figure hired men's wages. It was the fourteenth edition so must have been popular.

Dad was an independent laborer with a team of heavy workhorses. He hauled wood, stones, gravel, used the wagon in summer and sleigh in winter. He played cards and checkers with us evenings. He loved auctions, often started the bidding, sometimes ending up with odds and ends for a quarter. Once he bought a saddle which Mom used to sole the family shoes, and a neat job she did. One cold frosty morning someone's shoes needed tacking so Mom asked my sister to fetch the shoemaker hammer from the summer kitchen. The frosty-white large round head intrigued my sister; she stuck out her tongue to lick it and got stuck. She found it easier to put it on than to pull it off. I too got a surprise once. I saw an open beer bottle on the summer kitchen table and tilted it up to get the last drop. I got it, but it wasn't beer. A neighbor had borrowed kerosene and returned it in a beer bottle. Ugh, I can taste it yet. If I'd used my nose first it wouldn't have happened.

My sister brought the family joy with her talents. A straight "A" student through high school, while a senior she won the state championship in Palmer Method handwriting and typing. Later she won many awards as an artist, was good with needle and tatting shuttle, sewed yards of tatted lace in her graduation dress and wrote the Homemaker's Creed. My brother loved hunting and fishing and worked with father after completing school. I was the homebody, helped mother, learned to crochet, piece quilts and braid rugs. Mom's folks lived a half mile up the road. Daily I used brother's bicycle to visit them and play with grandfather.

The home I grew up in never had plumbing. Soft water was pumped into the summer kitchen and heated in the wood stove reservoir. The pump always had to be primed. The well-water pump, just outside the kitchen door, supplied drinking water for family, horses, cows and chickens. We pumped water into a wooden half-barrel for animals and kept a granite pail with dipper in the kitchen sink near the washbasin. The sink had no drain so wash water in the basin was thrown out the back door.

The woodshed, connected to the summer kitchen, was full of wood Dad cut, hauled, sawed, and split during winter. Near the woodshed stood the outhouse, larger than most, provided four seats, small, medium, and large to accommodate all ages. Outhouses remind me of the farmer that wrote to Sears, Roebuck to send him ten rolls of toilet paper. In reply he received a letter saying "On page 400 of our 590-page catalogue you will find number and price of merchandise you asked for." Farmer wrote back, "If we had your 590-page catalogue we wouldn't need your toilet paper." Neither did Mom buy toilet paper; old catalogues were recycled via the privy. Years later when my husband and I removed our farm outhouse, we took snapshots of us standing in the doorway with a catalogue, providing proof today for our grandchildren of the good old days.

Our home was heated by a wood cook stove in the kitchen; the wood heater in the parlor was used only on Sunday for company. Sis and I slept upstairs in a bedroom heated by a pipe from the parlor heater. Needless to say there was no dillydallying when going to bed. Kindling and kerosene were readied in the evening to start the morning fire. The stove was out long before morning. When lamps were blown out, it was bedtime.

Cars, electricity, radio, TV we knew not. We coasted downhill in moonlight, had sleigh ride parties, house parties and dancing. Father played the accordion, the hired man jigged and we ate popcorn. Later Dad bought a player piano and fifty music rolls. I started music lessons.

Neighbors got together to butcher, make sausage and have quilting bees. Spring meant soap boiling, smoking hams and bacon. Dad and his team worked on the road several days to pay off poll taxes. Highways were repaired by the taxpayers. No concrete, just gravel or dirt roads. Spring thaw meant ruts and mud puddles.

We had plenty of exercise at home: the washing machine was turned by hand, the pump handle worked up and down, the wooden butter churn turned round and round — when cream wasn't the right temperature it took forever. What a thrill to hear the splash, splash of the cream turn into the clunk, clunk of butter. Then a delicious drink of sweet buttermilk we shared. Mom made the skimmed milk into cottage cheese.

Our lawn was the favorite gathering place of neighborhood children. We played Croquet, Drop the Handkerchief, Pump, Pump Pull-away, Hide and Seek, and Andy Andy Over the Outhouse. At parties we romped with Farmer in the Dell, Stagecoach, and Fruitbasket Tip Over. Other favorites were Hide the Thimble, Skip Come a Lu My Darling, and Musical Chairs. We never owned a football or basketball, but we did play baseball.

Folks sometimes asked Dad, "Do you live on the corner with all those children?" He told them the children did not all belong to him.

We walked several miles to church and school as we had to pay to drive across the toll bridge.

Earlier years we had no movies but Dad loved to take us to Ringling Brothers Circus. He enjoyed that as much as we did.

Thank you Dad and Mom for the memories!

DISCOVERY—ERA 1900
John Parker

The river ran through our town. The main street was just a dirt road and the horse-drawn vehicles crossed the stone bridge to Dr. Skinner's drug store, Peabody's grocery, Stapp's dry goods and Miss Liebenow's millenary shop. In the evening old man Pippen leaned his ladder against the lamp posts and lit the kerosene lamps. We ran through the spray of the sprinkler wagon as it passed to lay the summer dust. A dam impounded the millpond to run the gristmill below. In the winter the butcher filled his icehouse for summer use. From the dam we fished for bullheads and red horse and in the sandy shallows caught castle builders. We divided the water above the dam with a board and there was a wonderful cave behind the falling water. We waded in the pond for frogs' eggs that turned to pollywogs and when the bloodsuckers got on our legs, we pulled them off and smashed them on a rock with a stone to see the blood squirt. In the spring we followed the fish-spearing party. Sucker Trap walked up the center of the creek with a torch of rags soaked in kerosene, and if the guards gave a warning whistle on the approach of old Tut the game warden, he doused the torch in the water and everyone ran for a safe hiding place in the darkness.

Miss Clark was our grade school teacher and give us firm and efficient punishment with a hickory stick. We called her "Grannie Clark." We had spelling bees, mental arithmetic and contests in reading like "Theosophus Thistle the thistle seed sifter, sifted three thousand silver, slippery thistle seeds." Professor Roads came in for singing class. He carried a tuning fork which he struck sharply on the desk and hummed up and down the scale until he had a "C" or a "G" and then said, "Now sing." We had a choice of "Old Oaken Bucket," "The Ivy Green," "Spring Song," and others, but our favorites were "Marching Through Georgia" and "Columbia the Gem of the Ocean."

Our school yard was divided by a high board fence: boys on one side—girls on the other. We had wonderful games at recess, such as Bull in the Ring and Bombay Leap Frog. In Bombay Leap Frog, you jumped over the one that was down in a ritual that went: "flat hand," "left and right-hand mail carrier," "knuckle twist," "bumps" and "ride and spur the mule." The one who failed the ceremony had to bend down to be the next mule.

We could not get close enough to the world around us. There were fields and woods to explore. Climb the tallest tree to see what was in the redtail's nest with the huge hawks screaming a protest in the blue sky above, dig into the clay bank to see what was at the end of the kingfisher's tunnel. We climbed saplings in the swamp to the top, and when they bent over, we rode the branches to the fern-covered ground below. We sprinkled stale beer on the oak trunks to attract and catch big night moths. For excitement — see who could get closest to the buck sheep in the pasture before he attacked and who could reach the split-rail fence before he knocked you flat. But the real thrill was to mount the cowcatcher in front of the engine when the evening train stopped, and the awesome dash through the dark countryside to the next village. We walked two miles to the lake to swim, and watched the bees at the farm going out to the fragrant clover fields with the merry singing bobolinks, and farmer Ed told us about the wonderful organization of the bee colony. The treadmill that ran the buzz saw fascinated us. Two horses were tied to a wooden stall with a moveable plank floor. When the brake was released the horses slid down and had to walk uphill to keep in place.

After school was out we found work running errands, hoeing gardens, picking potato bugs and weeding the long rows in the sugar beet fields. In a job where you helped to get out the weekly newspaper, you learned to set type, one letter at a time, upside down and from left to right. When the composing stick was full of type it was transferred to a twenty-inch tray which made a column. Six columns made one page. The pay was one dollar a week from seven until six. Friday was printing day and George would get a couple of men from Bau's saloon to run the big press. It operated by a wooden handle attached to the flywheel. They got twenty-five cents each— enough for ten beers.

We were older now and discovered girls and went to dances and did the barn dance and the rye waltz. One Sunday afternoon Em's pa let her take the horse-drawn surrey to go swimming, and on the way to the lake the girls sang the latest songs—"Hiawatha," "Red Wing," and "I Wonder Who is Kissing Her Now?" Tessie Ann swam out of her swimming bloomers and had to stay in the water until the boys went to dress behind their clump of bushes. When we got to the surrey the horse was balky and wouldn't budge. We twisted his tail, blew into his ears and thought of building a fire under him. But we got him started by kicking him on all four legs at once, then rushed to get into the rig before he stopped again. We were late for supper and had to rush to evensong to enjoy the new mantle gas-burning lamps that replaced the old Rochester kerosene wick lamps that hung from the ceiling. We rose to sing the last hymn, "Softly Now the Light of Day, Fades Upon my Sight Away," when the pressure failed and the lights went out and left all the people standing in the solemn darkness of the quiet church.

Time wears away the carefree days. Summer ends. The winter woods knee-deep in snow and empty fields eternal secrets keep!

THE OLD SALOON
Dick Sigl

Do you remember those good old days? The jolly good purveyor with the big belly and the schnurrbart from ear to ear. His trousers were loose, but couldn't fall from the shoulder suspenders covered with the prominent four-pocket vest. His gold watch chain dangled with a fob of the times.

His blue-striped shirt was visible from the shoulder to the elbow only, and what you could see of his collar covered a size nineteen neck. That was a real diamond stuck in the tie.

When his eighteen-inch black armbands were pulled back you could detect the VSDB penny cufflinks, worth a dollar then.

Can you remember the cheek-to-cheek smile when you ordered the biggest beer in town and laid down a V-nickel? There were no ladies present. So you walked over to the "Men's Stand Up" while you ordered a little three-ounce Guckenheimer, one-hundred-proof, to show that you were a he-man.

On the way you could feel the fumes of the pot-bellied stove, ten feet from the corner. And you could see the lumberjacks hunched around the poker table with the private compartments for the stud players.

The piano emitted the strains "Elauterbach Habic" and "Sweet Adeline" as your body warmed up to the good old days. You puffed on the Cuban cigar as you forgot that Mamma needed some P&G soap and a barrel of flour.

Maybe a little shot of Lash's Bitters would be good for your kidneys and liver. And maybe it will cure biliousness and dyspepsia. At least that's what the sign says.

You clear your throat and aim for the spittoon, or thereabouts. Somehow, you edge over to the end of the mahogany and fill your gut with blood wurst and rye bread before you go home to eat.

That jolly good fellow offers you a nightcap 'cause it's too early to go home, and even takes a little snit with you "for old time's sake." You sip it down and are so proud of your heritage that you buy another one back for the house.

They were six for a quarter then, seven in a pinch. And in those days all good fellows shared their blessings.

Time went on. But the clock stood still. You didn't have to worry about losing your driving license. There were none. Old Dobbin knew the way home.

When your pants were finally full and your gold certificates were gone, you didn't even need a nickel for a cab. Your jolly good friends would bundle you up and throw you in the cutter. They would loosen the reins, and Dobbin would take you home where Mama and the children prayed the rosary that you would never forget "those good old days."

Do you remember those good old days? I do.

OUR CLOSE CALL
Mrs. Martin Paust

I was born in Milwaukee, Wisconsin, on June 22, 1882.

While growing up we had no radio or television those days for amusement. We had to make our own fun, through family affairs, picnics, church-going, school affairs, ball games, playing musical instruments like the piano and violin.

I remember one incident very clearly. I always say it was "our close call."

My father was very religious and very strict. Many evenings we children would sit on the front porch and sing choirlike. Neighbors would come over and gather around to hear us. But when the clock struck nine, Pa would come out and say, "Children, it's bedtime." We would run into the house and up to our bedrooms. He never had to tell us twice!

When I was fourteen years old, my sister Della and I successfully pulled a trick on my father I never forgot. One evening he took us to church. After the sermon he stopped to talk to some members of our church. Della and I continued on towards home. About halfway we passed a dance-hall saloon and stopped to hear the music and watch the dancers through an open door. Forgetting the time, we looked up the street and were shocked to see my father coming, but we didn't think he saw us. We ran across the yard, into the house through the back door, and scampered up to our bedroom. We hurriedly took off our shoes, crept into bed and pulled up the down-filled quilt over us. It was just nine o'clock!

Right after that Father came upstairs to our bedroom. When he opened the door he said to my mother, "Oh, they're in bed. I thought I saw them near the saloon." My mother, who must have heard us, said nothing. I am sure she thought listening to music and watching dancing could not be called a sin. After all, we were in bed by nine o'clock.

After everyone was asleep, we got up, undressed, and put on our night clothes. We had a good laugh under the covers about "our close call."

AN UNUSUAL BUGGY RIDE
Mrs. O. L. Campbell

As a girl in grade school in a farming district of western Wisconsin, I had many buggy rides, because that was our only means of transportation. With either one horse hitched to a one-seated buggy or two horses hitched to a two-seated buggy, which was an open-air rig, we went to church and to town to buy our supplies, or to visit neighbors or on other errands.

I usually walked to and from school, which was nearly two miles, but if the weather was stormy or if my father happened to have errands which would take him close to the school, he would often stop and take me home.

But on one occasion which I can't forget, my father came to the school to take me home, and as he had an errand which would take him close to the home of one of my schoolmates (a girl who was one of my special friends in the school), he asked her to ride with us. This time the two-seater buggy was used, with two horses doing the pulling. My father sat in the front seat, driving, and we girls sat in the back seat, which was some distance from the front of the buggy.

The road was rather narrow, with trees on each side, but we didn't have to worry about any traffic, coming or going. A car wouldn't have tried to pass us, because there were very few automobiles in the country at that time, none that I knew of in our neighborhood.

So, it was a very quiet ride. The weather was nice on this day and we were enjoying both the ride and the freedom from school after being inside most of the day.

Suddenly, either the horses started going faster, or the buggy struck a stone in the road, and my girlfriend and I were tossed right out onto the ground, together with the buggy seat we had just been sitting on. This startled us so that we could hardly think for a minute. Then we realized that my father was going on without us, not noticing that we had fallen out. This was very embarrassing for me, and I was angry at first, to think we were not even missed. But I finally called to him, and he came back, put the seat in again and we got in to finish our ride home. All he said was, "I guess I didn't have the seat fastened in this time." (I suppose he had been hauling something in the back of the buggy and just forgot to see that the seat was fastened.)

It took some time for me to get over this, but the good part of it was that neither of us were hurt (except our feelings), and after all these years (it must have happened nearly sixty years ago), I still remember this incident vividly. I'm sure my father wouldn't have wanted this to happen, and he probably felt bad too, but he was a man who never said much nor showed just how he felt. I'm sure he must have been more careful thereafter, in seeing that the buggy was altogether safe to ride in.

PLEASANT ASSOCIATIONS
Cecelia Herreid

When I was a little girl about six years old, my parents used to take me along on their occasional calls upon their countryside neighbors. In almost every home that we visited, there was a grandpa sitting in a rocking chair or a grandma sitting by her spinning wheel either carding the fleecy wool or spinning it into strands of yarn. As soon as we came indoors upon our arrival, I was taken into their warm, friendly hospitality and entertained by their charming conversations. What I could never quite understand was how they could know that I had a doll and a doll carriage with a pink parasol on it, and that I sewed the doll's dresses, and that I sang a lullaby when I lay my doll to sleep. I wondered how they could know all of these things. They even hummed the lullaby which Mother had taught me and then asked me what the first line of the song was and if I would sing it for them. I knew it so well that I sang it right away just like this: "There cometh the dove on beautiful wings as white as snow flakes are. He cometh to me and leaneth on me to hear my darling's prayer." Then they sang all the rest of it.

They always patted me on the head while I sat by their side and the sensation was so pleasant it made me drowsy, just like my patting Tabby my cat on her back made her drowsy, so drowsy that she purred.

It is now eighty-four years since I was that little lassie. Though we have grown old and live apart, we still enjoy life and like to participate in the activities of society in so far as we are able. We feel that we have an inherent claim upon the forbearance of our younger relatives and friends and associates. We like to be recognized as one of their number.

THE IMMIGRANT BECOMES RICH
Clara A. Damm

This true story begins a hundred years ago in Germany, when my mother was born in Pomerania. A few years later, my father was born in Remscheid, the Rhineland area of Germany. They were destined to meet in Racine, Wisconsin, marry, adopt the U.S. for their country, have children and live the good life of American citizens.

My mother was orphaned when about eight years of age and lived with various relatives, never for any length of time. At the age of fifteen, she was fortunate enough to become a maid in the household of the pastor in that rural area. This, indeed, was a position of prestige for an orphan girl, as ordinarily they were sent to the potato fields, or to tend the geese. There were books to read in the parsonage, and my mother read everything she could get her hands on—especially those books telling about the United States of America.

As soon as she could save enough money for passage, she was on her way, arriving in Racine in 1898, living with a cousin and family, and working as a maid at the Drexel Hotel. There was no time for night school to learn the English language, so the daily newspaper became her textbook and friendly co-workers were her teachers. She spoke English well after a few years and was very discouraged with other immigrants who would speak the language of their homeland in their daily lives, hoping others would, also. She would often tell them, "Speak English, *this* is your country!"

My father did not have a happy childhood in the Ruhr Valley of Germany. He had a stepfather at an early age, who had no time for a stepson. His mother was busy with the other brothers and sisters, so fond memories of his parents are dim, but those of his grandmother he cherished. At the age of fifteen, he went to work in the foundry where his stepfather was also employed. The work was hard and the pay was low. He never saw his pay, as it was turned over to the family coffers, which was the custom in Germany at that time. He broke his arm in a fall when quite young, but it wasn't considered important enough to see a doctor, hence a crippled arm that he cannot bend at the elbow. This arm kept him from serving in the German army. When he was about twenty-one, with his grandmother's encouragement he was able to come to the United States, traveling with an aunt and uncle. His grandmother even "borrowed" a decent shirt for him (he thinks from his stepfather), so that at least that part of his dress would be acceptable.

In 1903, in Racine, the marriage of these two immigrants took place, and they pooled their few resources, which were mostly love and grit, and established a home in a small upper flat on the north side. Two children were born to them, my brother in 1904 and I in 1907. The midwife charged five dollars to deliver my brother, and seven dollars to deliver me. Prices were indeed going up.

Times weren't very good and foundry workers' wages in those days were very low. We do not recall a "deprived" childhood, as there was always much love and companionship, and plenty of plain but nourishing food. We never had a babysitter. Our social life with our parents consisted mostly of visits to other families for all their celebrations. I recall waking from sleep on a bed just loaded with everyone's outer garments. Some clothing was nice and soft, but much was rather coarse and rough. We were at the party together, and that's what mattered. We never had a car, so coming home from the party meant a "horseback" ride on Dad's shoulders, when I was very young and sleepy.

Sunday afternoon visits to Dad and Mother's friends were fun, too, because we usually stayed for supper and thoroughly enjoyed someone else's fried potatoes and baloney together with especially tasty homemade dill pickles. We must have had some sweets too, in the "Good Old Days," but they weren't important enough to remain in my memory.

Occasionally, in the summer, we would have a most enjoyable ride on the open air trolley from one end of the line to the other. This was real fun!

In 1914 our folks had accumulated enough money for a down payment of five hundred dollars on a home costing twenty-two hundred dollars. It was wonderful! Everyone was happy! Gaslights, inside toilet and bathtub and even a gas hot-water heater and tank in the bathroom! No more heating water on the kitchen stove for that weekly bath! Also, the house was brick and had a basement—two very important status symbols.

We had three stoves in this little house—one in the kitchen, a combination stove using either wood or gas; another large, upright, coal burning iron monster stood in the dining room, giving enough heat for the entire downstairs area. It had much nickel plate on it that always shone ,and the isinglass in the doors gave us interesting reflections of the fire going on inside. The third stove was in the largest upstairs bedroom. This was an absolute necessity as the frost would come through the walls in the wintertime, and even the featherbeds couldn't keep us warm. It seemed we had stovepipes running all over.

The only work my father ever had was in the foundry, and it was dirty and dangerous. The work was very hard, and there were no lockers for street clothes, or showers to clean up before going home. Every evening after dinner, my mother would string a line from one corner of the kitchen to the other and hang up all the clothing my dad wore that day. It was damp from sweat and grimy from foundry dirt. That "foundry smell" permeated our little house, but Dad's clothing had to be dry for the next day's work. Much later, when a furnace was installed in the basement, we were thankful the drying line could be transferred downstairs.

Then came 1917 and the war years. Dad was already too old to serve his country, but we did our part by buying thrift stamps which eventually grew into savings certificates. We learned to eat and enjoy the dark bread made from the only flour available.

In 1918 my brother graduated from the eighth grade with honors, but there was no money for further education. He applied for a working permit but the principal wouldn't okay it, hoping our parents would send him to high school. Mother then went over his head to the superintendent of schools and was asked, "Do you need the money this little boy will be earning?" and she answered yes. So, he went to work and his earnings went into the family coffers. My brother felt deprived of an education.

In 1920 I graduated from the eighth grade with honors, and again high school was out of the question, even though many tears were shed. I was enrolled in the local business college for secretarial training and bookkeeping, so that I, too, could soon enter the labor market and bring home my earnings. I, too, felt deprived of a high school education, but I was grateful for what I had.

The mortgage was paid off on our home during the years my brother and I were working, as Dad couldn't do it on his molder's wages. The highest wage he ever received was two dollars and sixty-five cents a day!

In 1928 my brother married in June and I in November. Then came the Great Depression of the thirties, and it was necessary for our parents to remortgage the home.

In 1936, Dad developed glaucoma in his right eye and had to leave the foundry, as he was ill and losing his sight. In 1939 the eye was removed. Two months later Mother died. My husband and I moved in with Dad to try to salvage the home and stay with him until he was well enough to return to work. He never did, and we stayed.

Years passed and his general health improved, but he agrees that the "Good Old Days" weren't all that good. It's the sixties and seventies that brought about legislation to make Social Security benefits and supplemental Social Security benefits available to him. Now, at age ninety-five, he can pay his own way. He feels he is rich! His children, now sixty-eight and seventy-one, can go to high school or college if they wish, free.

Where, but in the state of Wisconsin in the United States of America could this immigrant become rich?

THE EMIGRANTS
John Parker

After a long, tedious sea voyage and many starts and trials, we came with our parents to this place in the new land, which the owners got by deed when Millard Fillmore was President of the U.S., about 1850, three hundred acres at one dollar and twenty-five cents per acre. The small tenant house sat upon a moraine knoll, and the surrounding hills reminded us of the Yorkshire hills and moors which we had abandoned. The meadow ran down to the marsh and bog and the oak forest extended to the shores of the clear spring-water lake.

There was no bathroom or toilet. Everyone had to go out back regardless of the weather—no icebox or telephone. Television and radio had not been invented yet. We were isolated except for the neighbors. We acquired a horse named Florry and a cow called Bossy and someone gave us a little pig to raise. The neighbors helped us to put in some crops. The corn was put into the ground with a planter, worked by hand — two slats with steel points on a hinge and a canister to hold the corn. When open, the corn came out at the bottom. The ground was marked in squares, and the rhythm of the planting was: step-jab-open-close-step. The wheat was sown by taking a handful from a bag on the shoulder and scattering it as you walked.

Our new world was filled with strange birds and wild flowers. Mrs. Taylor showed us the birds she called "lazy bird," "fire bird," "butcher bird" and the dark brown breasted, sweet singing orchard oriole, with its swinging nest in the apple tree, made of neatly woven dried grasses; "angel birds" we called the plovers in the meadow for the way they raised their wings above their backs, and toward evening, the grouse drumming in the forest. We would make believe it was the Indians coming, but no one dared go into the dark woods to find out. She named the flowers in the marsh and bog—the curious fly-eating pitcher plant with its umbrella blossom; the delicate pink orchids, Calapogon, Arethusa and snake-mouth Pogonia; jack in the pulpit and lady slippers. The ovenbird called, "teacher, teacher," among the maidenhair ferns around the mossy ancient oaks.

Some evenings we had Bible readings out of the Old Testament, and Elsie and her brother came over to listen. The boys liked the stories about David and Goliath, Jonah and the Whale and Noah's Ark. Elsie wanted the ones about Ruth in the Fields, Susanna and the Elders and finding the baby in the bulrushes.

Some days Mrs. Fine, with her fuzzy hair in a silk kerchief, would stop by with her horse-drawn store on wheels: dry goods, pins and needles, thread and yarn, and linen crash for kitchen towels. The cloth was sewn in a continuous piece, which went over a wooden roller on brackets. By pulling the towel around the roller, you had a dry spot for your washed hands.

Soon the nesting plovers had left the meadow and it was haying time. The hay was cut by hand with a scythe. The flat rake had wooden teeth front and back that flopped over and left a pile of hay. It dug into a bumblebee's nest and the bees stung old Florry, who ran for the barn and smashed the rake into pieces and the hay was then raked up by wide wooden hand rakes.

The wheat was harvested with a cradle scythe, swung by hand, then spread on the wooden floor and threshed with a flail made of wood. The wheat was spilled from one basket to another and when the chaff was blown out by the wind, it was taken to the mill and ground.

The corn was cut by hand with a long-handled knife, and the ears were husked with a sharp wooden husking pin that fitted the fingers like a glove. The vegetables were put in the root cellar, under sand, and the cabbages hung by the roots from the ceiling. Then, when the days got cold, it was time for pig-killing day. We helped build a large fire under a big iron kettle full of water, hanging from a tripod. In the afternoon we were sent on an errand and when we returned Piggy was missing. The next days were busy ones. An oak barrel was filled with water and enough salt was added to float an egg. The hams were put into the brine to cure. Head cheese was simmering on the kitchen stove, to be poured into bread tins to cool and turn to jelly. Slabs of bacon were made and meat was ground and mixed with sage, marjoram and summer savory to be made into sausage.

We were now ready for the coming winter. There was no thermometer, but we knew when the nights were cold — the water pail in the kitchen was frozen over by morning.

No overshoes, but our shoes were rubbed with beef tallow. We walked a mile and a half through the snow to the one-room schoolhouse, which was heated by a large cast-iron stove—five feet long and two feet high and wide and burned four-foot lengths of cord wood at a time.

The winter was severe and one day tragedy struck, and the head of the house was gone. Our neighbor loaded our belongings on his wagon and we moved to a cottage in the village two miles away.

That was the year that William McKinley was President of the United States, and when the battleship Maine was sunk in Manila Bay, war was declared against Spain. The slogan for recruiting men for the army was "Remember the Maine." But in June Teddy Roosevelt's Rough Riders defeated the Spanish army at San Juan Hill and the same day, the U.S. Navy destroyed the Spanish fleet at Santiago di Cuba Bay and the war was over, and the United States annexed the island of Cuba from Spain.

There were a few gold coins left from the original cache, and we were told to be sure to get twenty-one shillings for the guinea.

We hated to go to Peabody's store for groceries, because as soon as we entered, old Peabody would yell at us, "Two-cent cake of yeast; pound of rolled oats," so that we had trouble remembering what we were sent for.

It rained one such day and we stepped into Dr. Skinner's drug store out of the rain. It was a fascinating place. The front windows were decorated with large glass bottles, two feet high, filled with blue, green and red liquid. The shelves were lined with patent medicines: "Pinkhams Elixir for Pale Women," "Nervine" for debilitated men, "Emulsion of Cod Liver Oil" for growing children and "Castoria" for constipated babies. Dr. Skinner sat at his desk, looking like a long-nosed owl, with his pince-nez at the very end of his nose. Mrs. Skinner and friends were talking. Mrs. Wilson said, "Alda Robbins's hat would fry eggs."

Mrs. Skinner said, "Oh, it's starting to rain again."

Everyone looked out, but it was only Patsy Kinney's horse that was tied to the hitching post outside the open door. Dr. Skinner said, "You boys go home now. The rain has stopped."

On Sunday we went to morning prayer at nine and evensong at seven and learned to sing the psalms in plainsong, the ancient nonmetrical chant melody. Reverend

Le Mon came on Communion Sunday and always marked the label of the bottle of wine to see how many sips the old janitor took between his visits. One night at choir practice at Paul's house, his Aunt Gertie said, "I'll skip across and get more hymn books."

The student minister said, "I'll go with you."

Paul said, "Let's follow 'em and see if he kisses her in the vestry room."

We were giggling when we got back and Mrs. Peabody tried to kiss Paul, and he hit her with a pillow and broke her glasses.

School studies were getting harder now, and discipline was strict. There were no organized school athletics, but we played ball games like One Ole Cat and rougher ones like Bull in the Ring and Duck on a Rock. A feud developed, and a gang fight was held in a thicket by the river, but the principal discovered it, took the names of the leaders and punishment followed.

Soon school was out and we were free from old Prof's tyranny, and suddenly it was summer. Many changes came and it was the three of us against the adult world about us.

President McKinley was assassinated. Then came Theodore Roosevelt, William Howard Taft and the idealistic Woodrow Wilson who would keep the country out of the war raging in Europe. But soon the United States was in it, and the brothers made the return trip across the sea to the Old Country to help make the whole world safe for democracy.

YARNS OF YESTERYEAR
Mary Knobloch Bodenburg

In 1880 my paternal grandfather set out in two covered wagons to travel west from a Dutch settlement in Pennsylvania. Little Melvina was the youngest of eleven brothers and three sisters. One evening they camped north of Pittsburgh where the Allegheny and Ohio rivers meet. The little seven-year-old girl ran to pick wild flowers. Grandmother was busy preparing the evening meal by the flaming campfire. A son was sent to find Melvina as there were still a few Indian groups in that area, which worried Grandmother. The all-night search for the little girl was fruitless. All they ever found was her pink gingham sunbonnet near the Ohio River's edge. Their aim was to find and join two of Grandfather's brothers in northern Indiana, so they sadly continued their journey westward and they settled in Carroll County, Indiana, near Camden. My father still had the urge to travel, so he borrowed a horse from an older brother and rode westward alone. In Kansas he bought a team and wagon and also a white wild mare, which he brought back to his Indiana home.

As we grow older memories of events in our childhood seem to become more vivid. I have seen the three-room log cabin where I was born. I clearly remember the day we moved to a larger farm near an old covered bridge near Rock Creek. That creek still flows lazily south through Carroll County, Indiana, down to the Wabash River.

It was early spring and getting towards evening as Papa turned the team into the farmyard of our new home. He untied the frisky colt from its mother's side and led the cow and heifer to the barn. They had followed us twelve miles, tied to the end-gate of the wagon. Mama reminded him to handle her two setting hens carefully when he removed them from under the wagon seat. My sister shouted with glee as we saw lamplight shining from the big farmhouse, "O Mama, Grandma and Grandpa are here too. There is their buggy and Old Babe over by the hitching post." The table was set in the large kitchen and Grandma welcomed us all with a "Hurry up! and wash the dust off your face and hands, supper is all ready." We could smell the odors of home-cured ham, hominy and gingerbread. They had been there all day, setting up the big bed for Mama and Papa and they had put together the two trundle beds for the five children. The evening was full of surprises for us, peeking into the front room where Mama's organ stood in a corner. Two parlor chairs and a small marble-top table, shiny and new, were a surprise for Mama. The pantry shelves held our good dishes on the top, and our old gray flowered ironstone china on the lower shelves, with the big tin bread pans and old black iron kettle.

Those were happy years for me as I remember walking down the back lane to attend the little red one-room school, along the new barbed-wire fence. Then over the stile we went—three wooden steps up and three down—to a path to the dusty road. Neighbors' children joined us. We all carried our noon lunch in tin pails. The girls wore calico and gingham dresses down to the tops of new button shoes. I remember reading all the books in the cupboard, used then in all country schools. We all drank from the same tin dipper. I learned my ABCs from the large chart by the teacher's desk.

It seems that Mother was always sewing by lamplight in the evenings. Daytimes I helped her knead bread with flour from our own wheat, which Papa had taken to the old gristmill to grind in late August.

I carried the wood ashes from the old round wood heater and the kitchen range to a barrel near the smokehouse. Mother poured water on those ashes to make the lye to cure the corn into hominy to add to cracklins (grease to make our homemade soap). We made that soap in the big black, copper lined butcherin' kettle out in the back yard.

In late August we picked all the apples in the orchard to make our yearly supply of apple butter. Cousins and aunts came to help peel apples and cut them into quarters. They were cooked outdoors, too, in the big kettle. Grandmother was always there to stir and season it with just the right amount of cinnamon and apple cider. Two small brothers carried broken rails from the old fence to keep a slow fire going under the kettles.

In late October when the field corn was all picked and in the big corncribs, we children shelled the corn from the largest and best ears to make hominy in the two large crockery jars. Mother used some of the liquid lye and water to soak the shelled corn to take off the outer husks from the grains. Then it was soaked in cool water for a week. Then boiled and cured with salt and a little alum to keep it crisp. Sometimes we put it into crocks to set in the milk trough in the milkhouse. Twice a day we pumped fresh water in a wooden trough from the old wooden pump into the milk trough to keep the milk and butter fresh. I can still see the two old tin skimmer ladles we used to skim the cream off the top of the day-old milk. The old wooden churn with its upright stick dasher was a real burden to my sister and me. Sometimes it took more than an hour of up and down pushing before the golden globules of butter would appear. We knew we would soon have a big batch of good golden country butter. We washed and worked the butter with a wooden paddle in a big wooden bowl with cold water to clear out all the buttermilk. Then mother pressed it into wooden molds, and it was cooled again in the cold milk trough and put in flat crockery jars. When we turned it out for table use on a dish, there was always imprinted on the top a picture of a sheaf of wheat or a flower.

It was such fun for me to follow my father in the deep furrow behind the plow. There I often found Indian arrows or a nest of new cottontail bunnies in the spring. I learned to ride and jump fences with the white mare from Kansas. We were a busy happy family and I could hitch the team to our carriage and drive to town when I was ten years old. There, at the Golden Rule General Store, I turned in a half bushel basket of eggs for ten cents a dozen and received yard goods of flannel or cottons, for us to sew.

Once in late summer a band of gypsies camped near the covered bridge and Mother lost several of her early capons. The gypsies knocked on our door for three days but we girls hid and stayed indoors. We had heard that they would take girls away from home and leave in the night. Father gave them some corn for their horses and Mother gave them apples and eggs.

On wintry nights when our school work was done, we helped Mother tear apart old shirts and dresses into strips for carpet rags. Then we could eat the good, Russet winter apples we had put away in a barrel in the smokehouse. The smokehouse was filled with jars of fried down sausage, smoked hams and shoulders, as we always butchered eight or ten hogs on butcherin' day. I remember I helped my aunt scrape out the small intestines to be filled with sausage and we rubbed the hams every day for a week with salt, brown sugar and saltpeter before they were smoked and hung from the rafters.

July and August were busy times for my sister and me. We cut boiled sweet corn off the cobs and dried it in the sun on a sheet on the shed roof, and we pared and sliced the best early apples and dried them in the sun also. Then they were stored in muslin bags and hung in the old summer kitchens ready to be cooked at any time.

When I was twelve years old and Father and Mother had eleven children, we moved from Indiana to northern Wisconsin. Father had sold our two farms and the horses and even my little red hen and her chicks which I loved so much. We were headed for Phillips, Wisconsin, and had to change trains in Chicago. Our tickets called for transportation from the Pennsylvania Railroad Station to the Soo Line Railroad Station. Father and Mother and my brothers were put in one carriage and all of us sisters and one brother were put in another carriage. The cab driver took us to the wrong station by mistake. My father and mother were about to board the Soo Line train when they realized that we had not arrived. They supposed our carriage was right behind theirs. This was a trying time. Father located us by telephone and we were brought to the right station. We all arrived at Phillips at six o'clock in the morning on March 28, 1906. There had been a big snowstorm. We were met at the station by an old friend from Indiana and he took us to a hotel where we had breakfast. We hadn't eaten since noon of the day before. As we drove west on W we had to go over a real high bridge over Wilson Creek. The wind was so strong we thought it would blow us over the side of the bridge. We all were so frightened. Mother started to cry and we girls cried too.

We finally bought a large farm close to town. I attended the Price County Normal School and taught in District Number 1, Town of Worcestor.

YARNS OF YESTERYEAR
Blanche B. Lindblad

The creak of the century-old rocker mates with an old woman's bones. She dreams, and it's yesteryear, and she's a child—reliving a simple, better time . . . There are no words like *ecology*, *Women's Lib*. "Neat" isn't a superlative: it means long stockings, pulled tightly. There's no fuel shortage; the round stove belches soft coal smoke.

Grandma is wanted, needed — for mending, peeling tomatoes, advising. Electric gadgets don't exist, nor food additives, hurting noises. The rash of violence is absent. Women are covered; men swear some, chew plug tobacco, and admire—but don't molest.

A depot child, the old lady remembers. Sanborn, Wisconsin. The D.S.S.&A. Railroad, like the Northern Pacific and Omaha lines, was part of a developing north country in the Lake Superior region. The logging industry flourished. Like Grimm's Fairy Tales or Lydia Pinkham, the Hind's Lumber Company was a *name*. So was Rust-Owen. The camps, she remembers—the virgin timber in the Drummond-Barnes area—camps and lumberjacks, gaiety in the saloon, next door. Immense loads of logs floating by, square stacks of lumber by the tracks. In and out of her dream, white winter peace . . .

Sanborn—a small American melting pot, in the Marengo Valley. Surrounding farms of Finnish people in the hills, friendly Croats — with only a mud trail from their Argo location, Iowans, Germans, others. A close community; ladies from the M.E. Church and St. Ann's attending both Aids. Farmers exchanging wares for supplies at the store. A school, a hotel with a pump. Later, the railroad, the depot — a life center. Dad, as agent, transferred from Superior because he craved land; after hours, Dad with a canthook, and dynamite and saw, carving out a home on his wild eighty . . .

Clocks were set by incoming trains. Mail in gray bags, cream cans hoisted aboard from the large wagon. Telegrams clicking through Dad's fingers, the wall phone cranked. Tickets, information, a dusty smell. People, making connections, invited to eat. Father Sharron, bushy-haired, brilliant, taking five eggs in ten bites. Mischa Elman, polite. Smiling folk, with time to talk.

Trains—fascinating, whistling, churning. Boxcars with bums, cargo-laden flatcars, diners, sleepers with faces. Brakemen, conductors in blue suits approving Mother's pass. The sound, "Boar—ed!" Lanterns swinging. Rides in the engine, caboose. Trains to crawl under, jump between. Section men pumping handcars. Best of all, the 10:10 night train, rocking a child's bed . . . An old one feels, hears the lullaby . . .

The depot ,rusty red, had cinders around it and they hurt bare feet. So did the wooden walk leading to the post office. (Slivers; Dad with the pinchers . . .) Upstairs, a home. Varnish over paint, portieres draped. In the parlor, a green morris chair; over the Adam Schaaf piano, the picture Frightened Horses. A skirted orange crate for a dressing table, a chammy skin for powdering. Mother, a woman of great beauty, dignity. A curling iron . . .

Music . . . The hand-wound phonograph and Galli-Curci. "Once again, once again . . . I will sing . . ." An older sister, in plaid taffeta, playing. Mother's soft alto on Stephen Foster airs. Songs from her childhood, Civil War melodies. Stories. Mother's father saying, "Children, royal blood flows in your veins — you are descendants of England's queen, and of Lord North." Mother's mother gathering the family for prayer; her father lining them up against the wall, for straight backs, and saying, "March!" The framed Declaration of Independence, two signers checked with pencil.

July Fourth! The town waking to Dad's firecrackers. A ball game, with homemade outfits. A band Dad secured, playing all day and evening until boarding a train for Nebagamon. A little girl, wearing medallions from her mother's wedding suit, forgetting her lines at the flag raising. Men proud, hats removed. Heads up, singing, "And this be our motto: In God is our trust!"

Stability. Surety . . . The old 10:10 . . . No man's heart failing him, for fear . . . A coyote, loud, nearby, but not threatening . . . The train, rocking a bed . . .

Seasons . . . Summer, and a swinging bridge over the Marengo River. Summer and the Campfire Girls. Rainbow trout, in a tub. Walking rails, picking strawberries along the grade, dodging snakes. Boulders, sand, heat, bog, bees. Grandview and Delta country, and fat berry pies. Butter from the hills, a lady calling, "Whoa!" beneath her orange umbrella. Jumping from a barn beam to hay. Catching fireflies. Cream, fresh bread, brown sugar. Honey in the comb. Laddie-dog.

Work—honorable. Slops to haul downstairs, water from a pump. Night jars to the outdoor toilet, trying not to inhale. Milk from a neighbor, daily in the dark, avoiding the rain barrel. The lawn swing, cracking, swaying; listening to night sounds. People dancing at the Woodman Hall, its floor cornmeal clean . . .

Fall. School, and a mother always waiting. Sateen bloomers and a new middy suit. Learning, loving poetry: "By the shores of Gitchie Gaumie . . ." The exciting traveling library, small art prints. Respect for a teacher with a horsewhip.

Blazing Birch Lake maples. Cottage cheese curdling on the black range. Dad working his cabbage cutter, for kraut. Dill pickles weighed from a barrel, cookies by the pound. Games. "Happy is the miller, who lives by the Dee." *Burning*, inside, when that boy's hand touched . . .

Winter was Christmas. An orange and a Hershey bar in a stocking; gifts from a rich aunt . . . Lanterns on the snow, crunching feet. A school program, with sheets for curtains.

A frozen buck in the warehouse, above freight; coal scuttles with papers beneath. Icy water pails. Breath-on-air in the bedrooms, heavy quilts with cotton bats. Buckwheat pancakes, from a sour starter, on chilly mornings. Boiling beef with onions, chicken stew, biscuits.

Mother doing applique. Mother in a beaver coat — pelts trapped by Dad. Dad, in black half-sleeves, shaving lumber in his office, for a sled. The millpond, pre-tested. Bonfires, clamp-on skates, shadows, mystery. Sore throats, and a swab on a pencil and blue vitriol. Turpentine and lard on the outside, and a sock. Dr. Andrus, from Ashland, in his sleigh.

Holiday dinners, with napkin rings, and Rogers Brothers silverware, 1847. A sister tatting. Folding long underwear around ankles. Flannel slips, angels in the snow. Long evenings. Dad, a history lover, recounting a nation's course. Puff-puffing, Standard tobacco in his pipe. Tales of his boyhood in lower Michigan. Working in a sawmill, for a few pennies a day. Training for telegraphy. A honeymoon ride in a caboose . . . Reading, trimming the lamp wick . . .

Magical spring. Apple blossoms, wet feet. A shoe-box of paper dolls, lost to the wind. Arbutus. A garden, hand-wrung clothes on the line. Sugar cookies, pieplant sauce. Dandelion greens. Violets and cowslips, and tomboy tricks at dusk. Dad at White River, fishing suckers; little fingers in the spurting holes of a water pipeline . . .

Easter, and church. A jacketed stove. A thumb, wet, turning Bible pages. The pump organ; a deep voice singing, "They crucified my Saviour . . ."

Remembering . . . A crowd. Listening to Teddy Roosevelt. A great man. *He was President!* World War I; the Flu; a child sensing the start of global tragedy. Woodrow Wilson, in a tall hat, long coat. A little sister atop a red chair, entertaining— singing, "O how I hate to get up in the *mawning.*" People of good will, clapping. Alert, looking clean . . . The smoke of the D.S.S.&A. absorbed by blue skies . . .

Absolutes: God, Country. People looking ahead; a marching pride, a "God Bless America" in hearts. A peace present; wisdom overshadowing knowledge. Dedication. Washingtons and Lincolns in overalls, at farm chores—and tapping out messages in depots.

A child's hand outstretched, eyes solemn. "I pledge allegiance . . . ." A child, blessed — each night, train-trundled. The 10:10 lullaby of yesteryear. Rocking, an old lady remembers, and dreams . . . .

CHA-KAH-LOW-BEE-NAH-KEE KEE-NAH
Arthur Scott Buchanan

When I was a young boy, a family of Indians was camped on the west bank of the Wisconsin River, and at the mouth of Moccasin Creek, just a mile north of the village limits of Nekoosa. That this area was for many years an Indian campground is shown by the Indian burial mounds nearby. Nekoosa means "Swift running water" and with the exception of Wisconsin is the only geographical Indian name still in use in Wood County.

A little over sixty-four years ago two older brothers and I had the opportunity to observe Indian basket-making. They made their living by doing what was in season. For example, in the fall, the cranberry harvest. The cranberries were raked by hand, and the Indians did most of that work. Wintertime it was hunting and trapping. Springtime was basket-making time, because nature's ingredients were at their best.

When a number of baskets were made, a large colorful shawl was placed on the ground and then the baskets were piled up on the center; the four corners were then pulled together and tied. The men helped load the bundle of baskets onto the squaw's back for her mile-and-a-half trek into town.

Announcing her arrival by beating softly on a small drum, she woke up our rabbit hound and our neighbor's raucous pet crow. When Mother opened up the front door that led out onto the porch she was greeted by the old squaw in her Potowatomie tribal language, Cha-kah-low-bee-nah-kee kee-nah. The squaw was sitting on the porch floor with the baskets spread all around her.

Thanks for the fun. I have enjoyed this much more than whittling a whistle out of an elderberry branch. P.S. Cha-Kah-Low-Bee-Nah-Kee Kee-Nah means: Come sit—smoke pipe—you buy.

2 SCHOOL DAYS

AN EARLY RURAL SCHOOL
Evelyn McLean

In November of 1916 our family moved from the village of Edgar, Wisconsin, to a cheese factory eight miles into the country.

The school I attended was two miles from my home. Every day I walked this distance unless I was lucky enough to get a ride with one of the factory patrons. For these long winter walks I was dressed as for an Arctic expedition, in long fleece-lined underwear, long black cotton stockings, high-buttoned shoes, a flannel petticoat topped by a woolen dress and a hand-knitted heavy sweater and warm coat. Since we had never heard of galoshes, my footwear was a pair of heavy rubbers. Over these were pulled a pair of knee-length leggings. A knitted stocking cap and scarf and warm mittens completed the outfit.

Often, the lunches in the tin lard pails would be frozen by the time one reached school. We would set them near the pot-bellied stove to thaw out for the noon lunch.

This was one of the few schools in the state which still held an eight-months session. Classes started at nine o'clock in the morning and closed at four o'clock in the afternoon. There was an hour nooning, and two fifteen-minute recess periods during the day.

Inside the building were double desks and seats for about fifty children. At the front of the room on a small platform stood the teacher's desk and chair. Behind the desk was the one small blackboard and over it was a rack containing maps. There were no recitation benches. The seats attached to the front desks were used for this purpose.

Children varied in age from five years to sixteen. However, these older pupils often attended only during the cold months, when there was little farm work to do. Most of the families in the community were first-generation German, Polish, and Bohemian, and still spoke these languages in their homes. Education was not considered of too much value, except for such basics as reading, writing, and arithmetic. History, grammar, and geography were merely frills to these good people. Many of the children never completed the entire eight grades of school. Usually four or six years was considered enough, though often a child went to school more years than this, covering a few months at a time. The state did not have a compulsory education law at this time.

Classes were of fifteen-minute duration. The subjects were minimal: reading, writing, spelling, grammar, arithmetic, geography, and history. There were no art, music, or science courses.

Copybooks were used for penmanship. These predated the Palmer Method used later. These books contained moral sayings at the top of the page, such as, "A stitch in time saves nine," which one copied over and over until a page was completed. Young children wrote the alphabet.

The stove stood at the back of the room between the the two entry doors. It was the duty of the older students to fill the woodbox at noon. A triangular shelf held the water pail and dipper. The water had to be carried from a neighboring farm, as the school had no well. Two children usually went for water. This was considered a privilege in the warm months, but not much fun in winter. Two outdoor privies took care of other needs.

Under one set of windows was a small, rudely made bookshelf with a few "liberry" books, such as *Heidi*, *Tom Sawyer*, and *Little Women*.

Our teacher, Daniel Wirkus, was the son of a local farmer. He had some odd ways of maintaining discipline, but they seemed to be quite effective. Just before dismissal each night those who considered themselves to have been good all day in deportment and lessons were asked to stand. Sometimes a child who dared stand when he hadn't been good would be hooted down by his mates. To all the "good children" the teacher would hand a card which read, "Good All Day." A certain number of these cards were later turned in to the teacher, and the child would receive a beautiful card with roses, forget-me-nots, or violets in vivid colors painted on it, and the words, "For a Good Child."

Another mode of discipline was to place a bad child upon a high stool beside the teacher's desk, facing the room. While this does not seem very severe, even some big pupils, larger than the teacher, after an hour or so of this punishment, became embarrassed and chagrined.

A game was played at this school during the warm months that I have never seen or heard of before or since. It was called Threshing Machine and was more popular than baseball. A line of straw hats would be placed in a row on the ground, about a foot apart. The object was to hop around the row of hats on one foot without putting the other foot to the ground, or touching the hat brim. Anyone doing this was "out." When all had had a turn, the winners lined up behind one another with legs outspread. The losers then had to crawl through this tunnel on hands and knees, and be paddled as they went through. Agile crawlers could make it often with only a few slaps received. Older boys were usually barred from the game, as they hit too hard.

However, most of the children much preferred going to school than to staying home. This was often the only time they had to play. At home most of them worked like adults, and were kept at home during fall and spring months to work in the fields. I always recall a girl named Rose who lived near the school. She had to stay home for several days and take care of the baby while her mother helped outside. At recess Rose would come down to the fence, holding the baby in her arms, and wistfully gaze across at the children playing on the school grounds.

Another time, walking home from school, I grumbled that I wished it was Friday night, so I would not have to go to school the next day. A little girl from the primer class piped up, "Oh, I like to go to school. Days when I am home I have to clean the barn."

Before the school year was over Mr. Wirkus was drafted into the army. We were embarking upon World War I. A young lady taught the last few weeks of school.

The next fall I accompanied my mother to Edgar. A flag-draped coffin was lifted from the train and accompanied down the street to the sound of marching feet and muffled drums. Daniel Wirkus had died in camp at the start of the influenza epidemic.

The next year I attended school in another district, which had a nine-months course, and more modern facilities and teaching methods. Whether I learned more or not is debatable.

THE ONE-ROOM SCHOOLHOUSE
Mrs. John Schumacher

Our teacher had a bell with a long wooden handle to call us when school started. She had walked a mile from the streetcar track and built a fire in the old wood stove that stood in the center of our one-room school. We children were put to work filling one end of the room with wood from the woodshed and getting water for drinking and washing. Now we were ready to thaw out our frozen noses, ears and fingers and begin the school day.

I am seventy-six years old and attended the one-room schoolhouse for eight years, from 1904 to 1912. We were taught reading, writing, arithmetic, spelling and music. Our library was a small cabinet on the wall with books such as *Heidi*, *Little Women*, *Black Beauty*, and *Robinson Crusoe*. A world globe hung from the ceiling. Charts and maps rolled out like window shades. The teacher's desk sat on a platform.

Our first desks were for two children. We wrote on slate boards with slate pencils while the teacher wrote out work on the blackboard with chalk.

Later we got our first lead pencils and tablets. The led was brittle and the tiny eraser broke off quickly. The tablets ended the messy job of cleaning the slate boards and gave us spitballs.

Spitballs, whispering, carving desks with jackknives, dipping girls' hair into inkwells, all led to our teacher making us sit on her desk platform. My sister Mary claims she spent most of her eight years there.

About twenty-five pupils made up the eight grades. There was much absenteeism from measles, mumps, and other illnesses. We started each day with a song. One morning we were singing "My Country 'Tis of Thee" when an ink bottle someone had left on the stove to thaw popped its cork and sent ink spraying onto our white-washed ceiling. That was the end of singing that morning. Our ceiling remained ink stained until summer when it had its annual whitewash.

On winter days we helped teacher sweep up, using snow for sweeping compound. We would sprinkle snow on the floor and sweep it around the room and out of the back door. It would not melt and it picked up dirt wonderfully.

Recess and lunch hour were spent out-of-doors, a cow pasture was our playground. We made a board serve as a bat, our ball was made of rags. Our games were Crack the Whip, Ante Ante Over, Pump Pump Pull Away. Footraces, High Jump, and Tag were popular all year around. Winter meant snowballs and snow forts.

At the end of the school year we had a picnic in the woods. Parents provided cakes, cookies, buns, lemonade and sandwiches. The eighth-grade students wrote tests to qualify for their diploma, signed by our superintendent. Mother framed each one and hung it on the wall.

I feel we got a good education, and I have always been grateful for the opportunity to attend our one-room schoolhouse.

It has been fun writing down these thoughts. I hope my memories bring a smile to other students of that era as they recall their early schooldays.

WERE YOU THERE?
Florence A. Petersen

'Twas in 1906 I entered school, carrying my lunch, my little rubber boots, and as my learning progressed, my textbooks meticulously covered with homemade cloth covers. Though much of the early training and lore have long been forgotten, somehow I do recall learning from *Stepping Stones to Literature*, the *Mother Tongue* language books, Potter, Jeschke, and Gillett's grammar, the Hamilton arithmetic, Smith's *Farm Arithmetic*, a huge brown and tan geography, Hart's American history,

Spencerian penmanship manuals, and in my teaching career the Palmer Method with its Progress pins and certificates of merit. We practiced pronouncing incomprehensible multi-syllabic words in the beige-covered orthoepy book.

Strange as it may seem, some of all this book work clicked! Didn't we learn the subjunctive mode in fourth grade? Didn't we compute the area of a parallelogram, compound interest, cubic root, the rolls of paper needed to decorate a room 15′ x 23′ x 9′ with three windows and two doors of stated dimensions? Couldn't we whiz through oral quizzes such as $6 + 2 + 5 \times 7 + 9 \div 10 - 3 \times 8$ and the like? Still, I was a bit shaky about the cubic contents of a silo and the area of a rhomboid.

Yes, we had music. "My Old Kentucky Home" vied with "Dixie," "Work for the Night is Coming," "Battle Hymn of the Republic," and the plaintive lyric beginning "There once was an Indian maid, A shy little prairie maid," who died of heartbreak and was known to us as "pretty Redwing." We knew naught of the *do-re-mi*s; part singing was unknown; the reed organ with its high top sometimes had mice in the pedals, but we sang! We even knew the third stanza of "The Star-Spangled Banner!"

Drawing, not art, occupied us, too. Little folk were not neglected. When through with the day's word cards and Beacon charts (1916 and on up), they colored stenciled replicas of the Sunbonnet Babies, the Overall Boys, and Brownies, or made their own tracings, fastening them with brass brads.

One thing that stands out over the years was the attempt to teach something of patriotism through history, music, memory work and readings, pictures such as Pilgrims Going to Church, Departure of the Mayflower, Signing of the Declaration of Independence, Washington at Trenton, The Minutemen, and, of course, practically every schoolroom had large portraits of Lincoln and Washington.

We memorized "The Landing of the Pilgrim Fathers," Miller's "Columbus," "The Concord Hymn," "Old Ironsides," "The Gettysburg Address," "O Captain, My Captain," "The Flag Goes By," "In Flanders Field," "America for Me"; we thrilled to "Paul Revere's Ride," and to James Buchanan Read's "The Revolutionary Rising," beginning "Out of the North the wild news came." For good measure some of us learned Henry Ward Beecher's oration, "The American Flag," and Patrick Henry's great words closing with, "I know not what course others may take, but as for me, Give me liberty or give me death."

We could recount the story of Molly Pitcher, debate the merits of Nathan Hale and Major Andre, and recite "The Blue and the Gray" at Memorial Day observances.

At program time we pupils were therefore not at a loss. Even the younger ones could join in Mary Howlister's stirring song, commencing with:

There are many flags in many lands,
There are flags of every hue;
But there is no flag, however grand,
Like our own Red, White, and Blue.

Parades and flag drills were numerous. A pantomime of "The Star-Spangled Banner" was popular in our area, at least. Didn't we utilize *The Memorial Day Annual* for patriotic material? On Memorial Day, with banners flying, we solemnly carried our peonies, snowballs, irises, apple blossoms, lilies of the valley, tulips, and roses to the local cemeteries. Certainly we knew where our war dead lay. Of course, we were aided by veterans, the high school, and churches.

Oh, yes, we enjoyed our history, both American and Wisconsin. Do you recall Reuben Gold Thwaites's Badger histories and the Blue Book, and in the twenties Hugh Bonar's civics outlines? We could trace military campaigns, knew of Jackson's "Kitchen cabinet," sympathized with Black Hawk, and followed the travels of Old Abe, the Chippewa Valley eagle carried by the Eighth Regiment in the Civil War; we admired Teddy Roosevelt, later fought over Robert M. LaFoleltte and women suffrage. No one could have labeled us apathetic.

Ecology is the word today. Maybe we'd never heard of it, but didn't we plant trees on Arbor Day? We kept bird calendars also. The *Arbor Day Annual* was almost a manual. We preserved wild flowers, identified trees and birds, and were not unfamiliar with "The Sandpiper," "Robert of Lincoln," "The Brown Thrush," and other nature poems.

No, we had never seen a school movie, but basket socials gladdened almost everyone — except possibly the young man who had paid for the wrong young lady's basket. He dared not show his dissatisfaction publicly; his partner might in time become his mother-in-law. Anyway, his generosity did enrich the school coffers.

Those days are gone now, but in retrospect, wasn't school fun?

AN 1892 FIRST READER
Melba Baehr

There is in my family's possession a book printed by Ginn and Company in 1892. It is Ellen M. Cyr's *The Children's First Reader*, and the purchase price was just twenty-eight cents.

From this quaint, last-century book I learned to read before I was in the first grade. The fact is, I knew most of the stories by heart long before I even set foot inside a schoolhouse.

The stories acquainted me with a number of things about the world around me, although it is not the reader I used after I started school. The many pictures in the book are charming. It is not difficult to picture the boys and girls of the last century leaving their play and opening this reader to the day's lesson. Even leaving such a fascinating game as Threading the Needle ("The needle's eye That doth supply The thread that runs so true; Oh, many a lass Have I let pass Because I wanted you.") could not have been too difficult when there was this little reader from which to learn.

The first story is about little Elsie meeting Grandpa while she is on her way to see Grace. They are going to blow bubbles. Elsie has her doll with her and is using a dustpan for a doll carriage.

Another story tells of the day Mamma took the two girls on a picnic in a pretty wood. They had a long ride on the horsecars to get there. How many first-grade pupils of today would know what a horsecar is?

The girls in the pictures wear dresses with ruffled pinafores, long black stockings and high-topped buttoned shoes. The boys are clad in knee breeches, black stockings, high-topped shoes, and straw hats. Mamma wears floor-length dresses, her hair style features a pompadour, and Papa always has a mustache.

There are stories about bobolinks, bees, humming-birds, a gray squirrel oddly named "Bunny," fireflies, butterflies, and spiders. One of my favorites was the tale of Helen, who "is a dear little girl. She likes to make others happy." She pays frequent visits to Mrs. Gray, an elderly lady who lives near her. One day Mrs. Gray gives Helen a little package of morning-glory seeds and tells her to plant them under her window. The morning-glories will grow up to Helen's window, she is told. "The blossoms will peep in at you," Mrs. Gray says. "I cannot come to say 'Good-morning' to you. The blossoms will say it for me." After the morning-glories are in bloom, Helen tells Mrs. Gray, "I say 'Good-morning' only once. Your morning-glories say it many times."

At the time the book was printed it was not many years since Indian tribes had roamed freely over the western plains and mountains, unconfined as yet to reservations. Two stories in the reader are about Indians. The pictures show their tepees, still used for habitation.

Harry lived in the far West. When his father took him to see some Indians, he found a pappose (this is the spelling used in the book) on a board, hanging on a tree. "What a funny place for a baby!" Harry thought.

Harry also visited with an Indian boy of his own age. The Indian boy was taking care of a pony. He showed Harry his wigwam, which was made of skins, and gave him a bow and arrow. Harry gave the Indian boy some pretty marbles in return.

Some words are used in the reader which are no longer familiar ones. One of them is "cars" for the parlor cars on a train. "Car" today has an entirely different meaning to a child, who undoubtedly thinks of an automobile when the word is read.

But in 1892 Charlie and Mamma ride the cars to the seashore. Charlie "likes to ride in the cars" and "how fast the cars go!" One picture shows Charlie and Mamma seated in the cars, looking out the window at the passing scenery. They see a river, little boys playing with a boat, and some horses running in a field. The horses are afraid of the engine, Charlie is told.

At the seashore the children are pictured wearing straw hats and bonnets, a sort of romper-type bathing suit with sleeves and sailor collars, and beach shoes. They find a starfish with five arms, sea mosses, sea urchins, and seashells. Then the children make sand pies. "Put on your hat, Alice," Charlie says. "The hot sun will burn your face."

Little poems are scattered throughout the volume. The one I liked best as a child came after a story about four children popping corn on a snowy day.

Snowflakes and popcorn dance about;
The corn in the house, and the snow without.
The wind peeps in at the children gay,
Blow, wind, but you can't blow our flakes away.

This little reader from the days that have gone forever is a treasured volume, enchanting in its words and pictures of a way of life that is no more.

COUNTRY SCHOOLMA'AM
Elizabeth Herritz

In the fall of 1921, I went out to seek my fortune as a rural teacher. A graduate of Sauk County Normal, I was bubbling over with ideas and plans for a successful year. My head was in the clouds; my feet, alas, would often be stuck in the mire or plodding knee-deep through snow.

My contract stated that "for the sum of $115 a month the said teacher is to teach, govern and conduct the common school of said district to the best of her ability; make reports required by law, and endeavor to preserve, in good condition and order, the school-house, grounds, furniture, apparatus, for a term of eight months between Sept. 21, 1921 and May 1922, as the district shall direct; PROVIDED FURTHER, that the wages of said teacher for the last term shall not be paid unless said teacher shall have made the report required by law."

The contract did not state that I would be required to build the fire mornings and do janitor work. That was taken for granted.

As far as I was concerned, the salary was only incidental. My aim was to impart knowledge to young minds. I would teach my favorite subject, American history, with patriotic fervor. I would teach an appreciation of the arts: a love for poetry and for the paintings of famous artists.

That first year my school consisted of thirty-three pupils, all eight grades. The daily program to be followed was given by the county superintendent. There was no place in it for the class in German I had been told by local authorities I must teach. I managed to squeeze it in late in the afternoon several times a week. German was still spoken in the homes.

There was no well at the school and the pupils had to carry water in pails from my boarding place a quarter mile away. It was put into a stone jar with a spigot faucet. I insisted each child bring his own cup. By noon the water was rather warm—no ice cubes in those days.

On a warm day the children sat outdoors under the oak tree to eat their dinners which they brought in tin pails. Most of my noon hour was used to put new work on the board. I was too busy to think of my stomach and sometimes hardly touched my lunch.

Keeping the school clean was a problem. It was scrubbed twice a year—at the end of the term and during Christmas vacation. Thirty-three pupils walking along country roads brought in a lot of grime. The sweeping compound used daily helped to keep down dust. When the floors became unbearly dirty, I got busy on a Saturday, heated water and mopped up the place the best I could.

To get the wages I was entitled to at the end of the month, I had to go through a lot of red tape. I had to send a note to the secretary of the board with the request that he write the order for the payment. If he remembered to do so, his daughter brought the order to school the next morning. Then it had to go to the director for signature and his children returned it to me. Finally I could go to the treasurer's home for the money. Usually I borrowed a horse and buggy from my boarding place. From the safe in his bedroom, the treasurer took a hundred and fifteen dollars in paper bills and I received them in exchange for the order.

In 1974 I would consider it very foolhardy to travel along a country road with that much cash. In those days I thought nothing of it.

My room and board cost six dollars a week and when I got back to the house I paid my debts. The rest of the cash I put in my trunk. Very little went for myself—perhaps an extra pair of woolen stockings or high-top overshoes. Country schools had no modern workbooks and to provide seatwork I spent a small fortune. Teachers also were expected to buy books to continue their own studies.

It may sound as though I did not enjoy my work. On the contrary, I loved it. I taught in the district four years. Eight students graduated from the eighth grade—quite an honor in those days. There had been only two graduates before 1921. I was always sad when closing day came. A teachers' strike was as unheard of in the 1920s as the atomic bomb. In fact, a strike like that would have been considered a strike against God.

THE KEROSENE LAMP
Mrs. Esther V. Beran

The time was four-ten in the afternoon of a December day and I was exhausted! Twenty-four pupils, grades one through eight, had filed out of the Clay Hill country school, each going his separate way on foot.

My desk was loaded with spelling and arithmetic papers which had to be corrected before I could leave for my home in the village three miles away. Little Mary's spelling paper was on top and lo and behold she had a perfect score, an achievement for her. Ten-year-old Jim was finally learning that nine and nine is eighteen, not seventeen! Then, there was my favorite, John, who couldn't even be graded! His paper was a succession of dots, dashes and circles. Whenever possible, I sat down beside him and helped him with the tasks he was capable of mastering. His happy smile of confidence was all that I needed to make my day warm and bright.

As shadows and dusk darkened the room, I lit the kerosene lamp which rested on a bracket on the wall behind my desk. Mother had loaned it to me even though she hoped that I would leave school before dark. My way home was a three-mile trek into town. The country road

through a heavy woods was scary enough even in daylight!

When the papers were all checked and the grades entered in my class book, I attacked the chalk boards, which the older children had cleaned. The school owned no workbooks, printed units, duplicator or typewriter so problems and study questions had to be written on the blackboard.

The school board had furnished us several charts to be used for experiences and reading and they were my pride and joy! On his recent visit to our school, Mr. Jones, the county supervising teacher, had commended us on our use of the charts. So I used his suggestions and brought the question and study guides up to date. After that, I duplicated tests, an endless chore by hand!

After the next week's lesson plans were completed, I went to the hall and emptied the water pail and scoured the dipper. Twenty-four of us drinking out of a common dipper! Scandalous, but we did and seemed no worse for it!

The old potbellied stove looked so very forlorn so I dusted it fondly and shook down the ashes. Now it was ready for me to build a new fire on Monday. You see the teacher was also the maintenance man!

Everything seemed to be in order so I began to remove my coat and hat from the hooks on the wall. Just then there were steps on the porch! Mother had often warned me to keep my door locked when working late but now I knew that the door was still open! Perhaps one of the children had returned to retrieve a mitten, cap or lunch pail. No they wouldn't come this late. Then there was a gentle rap. My feet seemed frozen to the floor. My lips made no sound. Then someone turned the knob and the door opened. In the dim light I could make out the very tall shape of a man. He came forward into the room and my first thought was that Ichabod Crane had stepped out of *The Legend of Sleepy Hollow*, which the eighth-graders were currently reading. Then he moved nearer and lowered a long stick from his shoulder, at the end of which was a sack of some kind. Certainly this was no place for a tramp to stop since there wasn't even a crust of bread around.

Then the man spoke, "We saw your light, after picking up traps on the south forty. Thought mebbe you'd like a ride into town. Our horse and sleigh are waiting!" He noticed the frightened look on my face and my hesitation, so said, "Come in, Johnny, and make me acquainted with the schoolma'am." Another figure appeared in the hallway. It was little John, my dear little John, who couldn't be graded. He skipped toward me, his big smile broader than ever. He grasped my hand and put it into his father's big, strong hand.

Fright was replaced by a feeling of security as I blew out the flame in the lamp and put on my wraps. Little John took my hand again as we followed his father to the cutter.

Today, fifty-one years later, my priceless lamp has a very special spot on my desk and I am reminded often of a special relationship between the boy, his father and his teacher.

SPRING FRESHET
Helen Hill

A gently blowing south wind gave the March day a feeling of spring come at last. Little and Big Cane creeks were still fast in frozen winter sleep as I crossed their icy chests on my way to my little country school that morning. This was my favorite shortcut. I loved the nearly two miles of virgin timber hugging my narrow trail so closely all the way. It gave me time to observe, to meditate, to plan. Protected from winter winds and drifting snow I walked in comfort daily.

By seven-fifteen I had the fire built, fresh water in the drinking fountain, the flag up. A half hour later one of the mothers stopped in briefly as she dropped off her three children. After a comment on the fine morning she invited me to come for supper and spend the night. I thanked her kindly and asked for a rain check on that as the ice still let me cross.

How mistaken I was to be!

Shortly after four-thirty the pupils who went my way for a mile walked gaily and full of chatter with me to the gate leading to my shortcut. Here we called gay good-byes and parted for the day. Now I was suddenly aware of the lowering sky filled with fast flying clouds dark with snow crystals. As suddenly the sun disappeared behind the darkest ones.

Mr. Lee called to me across the pasture to "have a care. The creek opened at noon. Better not try it."

I assured him I'd be OK and went on down the slope to Big Cane. As Mr. Lee had warned—it was open and raging, roaring, foaming. A trout stream grown to river size since my morning's crossing. My usual fording place was a maelstrom of movement. I went along the banks for half a mile seeking a crossing. Great chunks of wood and ice bobbed along with chunks of undermined bank and other debris. The channel itself was greatly altered by the fast moving water. Many large trees had fallen for the same reason.

Carefully I retraced my steps wishing I'd accepted

the kind invitation of the morning. Then I came to a huge elm tree spread in all its majesty across the flood and roar, its roots still clinging to the bank's edge, the huge top apparently reaching the other shore.

Gingerly I climbed upon it easing my way along its huge trunk. The rush of foamy water dizzied me, filling me with terror. The lowering darkness did likewise, for wolves and coyotes roamed this heavy woods. Step by careful step I got to the middle of the stream where my weight suddenly caused the root end to break loose from the shore and swing out into the flood. To my consternation I now saw the top end no longer reached the other shore and I could get to neither bank now. Nor could I swim!

The fury of the water had thoroughly soaked me. My knee-high rubber boots I walked in, spring and fall, were full of icy water. My stiffly frozen skirts and coat hampered me greatly in all movement.

It was chore time at home and I knew my husband would be moving between house, barn and yard. Would he hear if I yelled? Could a woman's hysterical voice carry a mile or more through heavy woods? I was desperate. It was worth a try. Cupping my hands to my mouth and facing towards home I called his name over and over several times. Only silence answered me. There was not even an echo in this rushing, roaring wildness around me.

Again I tried to gain the bank but every move shifted the tree perilously. I was deeply frightened and had myself a good cry over a mental picture of myself landing in a watery grave, leaving no clue.

Meanwhile at home my husband, watching the wood trail's end worried about the lateness of my coming, wondered if Big Cane had opened as had Little Cane which ran through our barnyard pasture. He finally bridled our faithful horse, Jack, threw a blanket on his back and started out for the trail.

It was just dark when I saw them through my tears and never a Lochinvar could have looked so gallant as he, to me. I yelled in relief. The horse rolled his eyes and whinnied shrilly. My husband shouted "Hang on!"

At the creek's bank the horse fought against entering the roaring, icy water. After much urging and coaxing he came alongside my elm tree snorting and blowing wildly.

My husband said, "Put your arms around my neck and throw your leg over the horse's back and hang on to me." This I did and thus we rode in mad plunges out of the deluge safely onto the trail where I then got off to walk. My icy skirts made uneasy riding. My boots had to be emptied of their icy contents. Besides, it was warmer walking. We reached home just as darkness threw its black shadows over the countryside.

Spring indeed!

PUNISHMENT WITH A TOOTHBRUSH
Jennie Erb Joos

One of the (now!) amusing things to remember of the schooldays of long ago was the ghastly punishment of having to stay after school so teacher could brush out one's mouth with soap and water. Today this action would probably be classed as corporal punishment, or the teacher might find the toothbrush — or worse — turned upon her/himself.

When I began going to country school at age six, I could speak only the language of my immigrant parents —Swiss—and knew no English. It is quite a job to learn a new language and, at the same time, receive one's total current education in that language. Not only my lack of English stuck out, but a number of other things, such as weird braids, foreign-looking clothing, such as a pinafore apron over a dark calico dress, and perhaps no shoes—certainly in spring and fall.

However indifferent the teacher might have been to hastening the double educational process, my schoolmates were most helpful, including those in all grades (first through eighth), and both sexes. During recess time and lunch hour, while playing outside, they tried to help my education along by saying a word in English and indicating that I should repeat it. I never quite understood why they would shriek and roll over with laughter when I repeated the word to the best of my ability, doing—I thought — a rather good likeness of what I had heard. But one day when the teacher happened to come outside unexpectedly, the startled look on her face puzzled me, as did the sudden hushed silence of my schoolmates.

Afternoon classes went along as usual, but at the close of the schoolday the teacher stood up and announced, "All those children who have said a dirty word today, raise their hands. They will have to stay after school so I can scrub out their mouths with soap and water."

Suddenly I saw the light, as it dawned upon me what was the relationship between my repetitions of their words and the children's mirth. I raised my hand because I was pretty sure I had said a dirty word that day, as well as on plenty of other days, too. School was dismissed and everybody went home except the teacher and me. She looked abstracted and did not have much to say as she dutifully scrubbed out the mouth of the only pupil who had raised a hand. And, between tears and a moving toothbrush in my mouth, I could say nothing either, even

had I been able to speak clear English to explain the situation. I think she used Fels-Naphtha laundry soap—it did not taste very good. But by the time I had walked the three miles home, the taste of the soap in my mouth and the salt in my tears was gone.

DISTRICT PICNIC
Mrs. Alvin Deischer

I regret the passing of the little one-room country school. There was such a pleasant comradeship among the dozen or so families that comprised the district. It was a fellowship that was precious in those lean years, the twenties and thirties, when there wasn't much time nor money for pleasure.

School always closed with a picnic and everyone came. No matter how pressing farm work was, our district picnic had priority.

Preparations began a few weeks in advance, when the ladies of the board got together, and, fortified by coffee and cake, made the plans. Slips for each family were made out like this: dessert (or salad or rolls) and whatever you wish. The "whatever you wish" took care of a wide variety (and what a variety) of food. The slips were just an assurance of some of everything and not a lot of one thing. Also the store order must be made out: ice cream, lemons, sugar, and coffee. So, all things decided on, and a second cup of coffee duly enjoyed, they left feeling righteously relieved to have things for the big day well organized.

Preparations in the home, too, began in earnest, the girls looking in Sears sale catalog for something pretty (and cheap), moms checking up on favorite recipes, and the boys, disdaining worries about clothes, practicing up on their leg work and throwing arms—the reason being the big event of the afternoon, the ball game. It was the boys (and big girls) against their dads — youth versus age! And how those dads could play! Needless to remind them of last year's sleepless night after the game, a night spent rolling and groaning, and then for days aching muscles. That all came afterward — picnic day they played ball.

When the day came at last, morning's work and chores were done up quickly. The children needed no urging to help. Then with a bulging basket we were off. If you happened to be the treasurer's family, you had to go to the store to pick up the order. The ice cream was packed in heavy tin pails, two in a heavily insulated canvas container. It kept nicely frozen that way. The storekeeper also loaned us an ice cream scoop.

At the schoolhouse willing hands made light work of everything. The teacher's desk must be pushed aside, the men must get the sawhorses and tabletops from the woodshed, and put up our big picnic table in the front of the schoolroom. The women must wash off the accumulated dust, and spread the tablecloths. In the girls' hall was a little two-burner kerosene stove, and that's where the coffee was made. Annie always made the coffee. She was generous of build, generous of heart and generous of abilities. When the water in the big pot boiled she added the grounds beaten up with an egg or two, and the smell was tantalizing. Everyone got hungrier and hungrier. Maybe time has enhanced its flavor but I still say Annie's coffee was pure ambrosia.

The table groaned with its weight of goodies, as basket after basket was emptied. The little ones galloped in and out of the schoolhouse, too excited even to play. At last everything was ready. The children filled their plates first, then the rest of us. We ate leisurely and long, enjoying this relaxing time with friends.

Last of all the ice cream was opened, and although we all always declared we were "just too full," nobody failed to go around for the generous helping the treasurer meted out. Ice cream for all of us was no everyday affair, and how good it tasted!

But the best of all was the fellowship, the visiting with our neighbors. Farm work with the machinery we had in those days was strenuous and time consuming, and we didn't often take time to relax and have fellowship with one another.

Before long the big event of the afternoon began shaping up — that ball game. The very young, and the very old were spectators, the little ones ready to cheer wildly at everything, impartial to either side, and the older men more mildly interested. The teacher joined her pupils, and the hired men joined the dads, and the game began, a game as important as the world series.

Inside the schoolhouse the ladies began slowly cleaning up. Many a taste of this or that was enjoyed again, and many a recipe was shared. The neighborhood news was digested, and each pretty new apron admired.

Soon the afternoon began to end. The ball game was over and the players came straggling in, tired, hot, and thirsty. Some were in a hurry to drown their disappointment in a cool drink and refreshments, and some were grinning but with the same need for refreshments. The ice cream container was opened again, and the treasurer carefully doled it out so that everybody got some. We knew enough to leave some cake on the table to go with the ice cream, and our Annie saw to it that we all had coffee again. Of course the lemonade had to be finished too.

Slowly and regretfully we began packing up our things. The tabletop and sawhorses were put back in the woodshed, and the schoolroom put back in order. The treasurer must take back the empty ice cream containers and the scoop.

All too quickly our district picnic was over, until next year.

THE LEARNING BUSHES
Mary R. Nelson

Like the one-room schoolhouses, gone are the Learning Bushes: those borders of rocks, roots and trees, which farmers unintentionally formed when clearing their land. These strips of wilderness kept nature and civilization in balance.

Our farm lay between two of these natural museums. The north hedgerow stretched a mile along the road to the next farm. We called it the high bush. The south hedgerow or low bush, scalloped our front yard like a dust ruffle, and skirted the banks of a stony brook that fed a small pond.

As a child I was in a constant dilemma as to which bush I wanted to visit that day. They both had their seasonal attractions. The high bush hugged the spring blossoms close to its rock wall. Overhanging branches kept them secret and elusive. Bloodroot, dogtooth violets and maybells vied with young shoots of wild plums, choke-cherry and maple saplings for growing space. The south or low bush scattered its wild blossoms for all to see: huge patches of cowslips, buttercups and wild iris lay strewn in dazzling array. The pussy willows along the brook marked a path to cattail marshes. In both hedgerows the insects alone offered more than a scientific laboratory. What a revelation to see a large luna moth emerge from a cocoon.

We learned patience from those hedgerows. You do not pick blossoms if you wish the fruit. You do not take the eggs if you want to see and hear birds. You do not cut off a sapling if you care to have a tree.

Although Mamma left us pretty much to ourselves to learn from the bush, there was one job she always did herself. In late June when the air was thick with the scent of all nature in bloom, Mamma knew it was time. A mysterious smile lit her face and we knew we were to have our yearly treat. Mamma went to pick the elderberry blossoms. She didn't trust anyone else to pick just the right flower clusters. As soon as Mamma plodded through the high thistle, burdock and stinging nettle to get to the elderberry bush, Catherine, our oldest sister, began to mix and beat the batter for elderberry blossom fritters that Mamma would make. Leona hurried to bring the deep fryer. Even before Mamma arrived with the bushel basket full of blossoms, my mouth began to water.

Somewhere I had heard the phrase, "The odors of heaven," and when the blossoms were in the kitchen, the odors of heaven filled our house.

Once more Mamma picked over the flowerets and washed them. When one by one she dipped them into batter and then into the hot oil that intensified the aroma, I could barely stand the waiting. But the learning bushes had taught us patience and soon enough the platter of lacy fritters was sprinkled with powdered sugar and our feast began. Mamma believed in educating our taste buds, but these elderberry blossom fritters were also a spiritual experience. Catherine said it was food for the gods, but I wanted to say something original. I tested more fritters. All I could say was more, more. Mamma chided, "If we take all the flowers there will be no jam or wine."

It was the same with wild roses. As much as we loved to pick bouquets, we knew that leaving the flowers to mature would give us rose-hip jam. As lingering as the flavor of the elderberry blossom fritters was, that lasting was the taste of rose-hip jam. Long after you had finished a snack and rolled your tongue around your mouth, the flavor was recaptured. And you longed for more. But through every window in the house you had a view of part of the learning bushes to remind you of the lesson of patience. So we deferred immediate gratification and slowly acquired wisdom.

The lesson of moderation was further taught to me and my sister Helen: we were told not to overeat on chokecherries. What we didn't know was how much is too much. But after eating a lard pail full, we were in no condition to ask. We fought for breath. It took Grandma Wallace all night to feed us pure cream by the spoonful before we fell asleep without gasping for air. The game of just one more was never played with chokecherries again.

Now there is nothing left of the learning bushes. The chokecherries bloom no more along hedgerows. For myself I am not so sad: I can aim the camera of my memory on any distant event to relive my childhood experiences, but for the children of today I mourn. In spite of the sophisticated learning devices schools have, where can today's young ones experience direct contact with nature? Along my hedgerows I had my wayside shrines, grottos and private chapel. An enormous old box elder's branches sagged over the rocky pews of my chapel. There were three sections of bird choirs. I liked the oriole's best. It was here I saw creation in the making.

But now it is all gone and again I ask, where will the children of today learn to feel the relationship of earth, man and God?

3 REMEMBERED PLACES

JONES ISLAND
Josephine Budzisz Klotz

My birthplace was a unique strip of land known as Jones Island, a part of Milwaukee, accessible by rowboat. Settlers were mostly Kashubian immigrants, an ethnic group that will long be remembered as friendly, hardy, merry people. Most of them earned their livelihood by fishing in Lake Michigan, which reminded them of their homeland. We had a family of seven girls and two boys. Fishing was a family project. My oldest sister ran the engine of our fish tug which was named after her, "Mamie." The girls strung fish nets and at times we all helped bait fishhooks with minnows for certain kinds of fish. At the docks were fish shanties and reels for drying nets. The fish tug would come in from the lake loaded with its catch, the fish would be cleaned, packed in ice, and shipped to another city if not sold at the dock. The nets were reeled up to dry, then packed in boxes to be reset in the lake for the next catch. Stormy weather was costly to the fishermen, torn nets were mended. Sometimes other than fish were brought in, once it was a loon, another time Father caught a water moccasin — both were donated to Washington Park Zoo. The empty reels were often used by kids for gymnastic antics.

The island consisted of homes, saloons, fish shanties, sheds, outhouses, butcher shop, bakery, grocery store and clubrooms. Beautiful trees and vegetation were abundant. Chickens and ducks were plentiful. The river was one boundary and Lake Michigan the other. The lake front did not have any protective breakwaters and sometimes the lake was really wild and the waves treacherous. The island was a tourist attraction and picnic area for city folk. Smoked fish and beer were common refreshments. Many well-known art instructors brought their classes here to capture the unforgettable scenes.

In our home during winter months we slept under featherbeds made with wild duck feathers. We had a wood-burning stove in the kitchen and from its oven came some of the best white bread and raisin bread ever made. Mother made her own jelly and did a great deal of canning. She prepared fish in many ways so no one ever tired of it. We also had smoked fish and at times we had "domers" which were fish that were cleaned, seasoned and stuffed with onion, wrapped in paper and baked on the dome of the boiler of a fish tug as it headed homeward. Our parlor had a big black and shiny metal coal heater. The front part of our house was a saloon. Many times customers could not resist the aroma of Mother's cooking and there was always enough to share. On one corner of the bar was a free lunch. Lake crabs in season sold for ten cents a dozen.

We all had plenty of assigned chores; since we had kerosene lamps there were chimneys to clean and shine with newspapers, wood boxes to fill; Father needed help to saw wood with a crosscut saw. He would tell us to ease the saw along and not press down, then we had to chop the wood. The wood was picked up in the river or on the lake shore. We took turns washing glasses and cleaning the huge mirror in the saloon, and cleaning the tables and chairs. These tables were wood with iron legs and an undershelf on each corner for beer glasses.

Our school consisted of several barracks staffed by teachers from the city who came across the river in rowboats, and sometimes in winter when ice filled the river the city fire tug would be called upon to bring the teachers across. Our playground was the shore of the lake and we would build sand castles and tunnels. As we grew older, we went across the river to finish our schooling. On days when the river would begin to fill up with ice we were excused early so we could get home. Men would push big cakes of ice away from the boat with pike poles.

Most of us were able to row or scull boats at an early age. Sometimes we were stranded across the river and we would yell "Yoo-Hoo" at the top of our lungs to attract the attention of someone to come and get us.

Many tragedies occurred, such as a boat being lost for several days and finally returning covered with ice. The men told harrowing tales of eating raw fish for survival. I also remember a father and son team fishing and the son came back alone because his father was caught in the nets and drowned as he was setting them. My father, brother and a workman lost their lives when their boat was apparently struck by lightning during a sudden squall in summer.

We had big wedding celebrations and masquerade balls, with prizes. On St. John's night families gathered at the lake, made a huge bonfire and drank beer.

The Coast Guard station was located at the harbor. There were long piers extending to the lighthouses at the end and it was an adventure to walk along the pier, often very risky when windy or covered with ice.

The Islanders lost their settlers' rights after a long court battle and were forced off because the early settlers never acquired legal deeds or descriptions of their land. The city of Milwaukee later bought the site from a steel company for its sewerage plant. I still lived there when this project was started and remember going underground with engineers while this was all in the experimental stages.

Hopefully Jones Island may always be remembered as a quaint seafaring community of Kashubes, and though I am fully American, I am proud of my heritage. It is ironic that today the island is a tank city, sewerage plant, car-ferry dock, and now in the process of developing a fisherman's park — very sad to think that the real settlers, the fisher folk, were forced off.

OLD WILLIAMSBURG
Arthur H. Maegli

At the turn of the century I as a boy lived on the then north side of Milwaukee that was jocularly known as Williamsburg. The name is no longer used as it was forgotten a long time ago. This was a predominantly German settlement and our family pattern was that of a rather clannish people, living in peace and quiet. In looking back I do not hesitate to say it did develop a happy life.

This era was marked by general stores that sold merchandise in bulk or open lots. There were a few exceptions, such as baking powder or soda, certain canned materials, plus foil-wrapped tobaccos.

In autumn my father and the entire family made great preparations to withstand our vigorous winter. One of the heavier jobs was to clean, polish and hang the storm sash — only after the glass sparkled. My mother would have it no other way. Another big job was to erect the smokehouse which we called "Mr. Smokey." The walls had been stored in four sections during the summer. We raised the sides and bolted them together, clapped on the ventilated roof, and then hung the door on the rusted hinges. The fuel that was used was a hardwood sawdust, chosen because it did not readily burst into flame, which was not wanted, and also because it smoldered evenly and provided the ultimate in flavor. Consequently it became my job to haul the sawdust from the nearby sawmill; several wheelbarrows sufficed.

In fall our entire neighborhood was dotted with smokehouses in operation, filling the air with a mouth-watering odor.

In early October a butchered whole beef and hog was purchased from the friendly butcher down the street. The entire family working together ground and processed the meat into various sausages such as summer, liver and knockwurst. After grinding, it was spiced with herbs and spices unknown now, then re-run through the grinder into sausage casings. The bacon sides, hams and butts were placed in a brine solution until it attained the wanted point; just how my father determined this I do not recall. Then the sausage and meat were hung in the smokehouse, the sawdust was ignited; the smoldering fire heated the material gently until it had absorbed the full flavor, smoke-tinged.

Then the smoked sausage and meat were removed to the attic and hung along the side wall. I can still smell the delicious odor. However, the sight of swaying sausage never failed to arouse a chuckle in me. For as time went by the odor did become a bit pungent so we opened the windows briefly and the draft set the sausages in motion.

We also prepared sauerkraut. From our garden innumerable heads of cabbage were sliced on a special cutter to the desired degree of thickness. Then it was pressed into a barrel as my father seasoned the mass with salt by the handful. When the barrel was almost filled the drumhead was placed loosely on the cabbage and then weighed down with a stone as big as my head.

Soon the fermenting cabbage became sauerkraut.

The resulting odor excited the appetite, and sometimes we children ate a handful raw. It was delicious.

Another effort was producing apple cider. In our back yard we grew Wolf River apples. These apples were huge tart, red-cheeked beauties and very juicy. We picked bushels of them. To produce the cider we ran them through a hand-powered grinder that separated the juice from the pulp. The liquid then was poured into a crockery container. Certain crocks received sugar, some did not. Soon nature provided soft cider for the children. Strangely enough, hard cider also resulted — that remained in my father's private domain.

We had several cherry trees. They were of the early Washington type: light red and very juicy. The home-made cherry pies that my mother made were in an unequalled class. Did you ever smell a baking cherry pie in a wood-burning oven? Many quarts of cherries were canned. The balance went into wine.

Our homestead lacked a central heating system. The kitchen stove was a "Lindeman Hoverson," a wood-burning flat topped range designed for heating and cooking. It was equipped on its side with a reservoir for heating water, and a massive oven.

The sitting room was akin to our present day family or living room, and adjoined the kitchen. It was heated by a monstrous nickel-plated "Live Oak" heater. Topped by an ornamental mounted knight in armor, its insinglass doors reflected the cherry fire glow. The fuel, a hard coal, was delivered by team. Two burly teamsters carried the coal in hampers on their shoulders and dumped it down the portable chute into the coal bin in the cellar. The process was noisy and very dusty.

The basement was referred to as the "Gemuse Kellar," a German term meaning vegetable cellar. In it was stored all the edible material for winter consumption. On racks, cabbages, apples, rutabagas were stored without touching each other to prevent spoiling. Shelves were filled with canned goods, fruits, vegetables, juices, berries and pickles. In a huge bin were home-grown potatoes. In the corner stood the sauerkraut barrel with the cabbage fully fermented. I cannot adequately describe the odor except to say it was heavenly. Away from this area was a wood-burning stove that was placed in service only in the most severe weather. This stove and the kitchen stove used wood for fuel. A cord of maple slabs was delivered to our curb, and we carried them to the cellar via an opened window. As the pieces were too wide for the stoves we split them in halves or thirds.

It is difficult to remember the old days without connecting it with certain odors. Making sauerkraut, grinding apples, the smokehouse odor, and that of the gemuse kellar are now so old-fashioned as not to be compatible with our present day of ease. But as with memories all this must pass away.

FIFTY YEARS AGO . . .
Jack Fritz

I can remember as a child living in Clearwater Lake, Wisconsin, where my folks had a forty-acre farm, with some land facing the lake. We had kerosene lamps to light up our rooms and in the front room we had a large potbellied stove where we burned large pieces of wood. I recall the great influenza epidemic of 1918 which had spread throughout the United States, taking a heavy toll of lives; I was down with it and nearly one in every family here in this small town had died of this sickness. We did not have the medicine we have today to fight this illness and we just had to live or die with it.

Our winters here were bitter and rough and sometimes we would hitch up our horse to the cutter and ride to Eagle River which was about six miles away; we would always have a deer rifle and a lantern with us when we rode around as at times timber wolves would swoop out of the timber to follow the horse, and at times we would have to fire a few shots to scare them off.

Eagle River was a small town and had wooden boardwalks and the street was not paved. On the way home we used to while away the time singing these songs that were a hit at that time: "Ka-Ka-Ka-Katie" and "My Pretty Redwing." We did not have indoor toilets then and you had to venture out in the cold and deep snow to the outhouse, which was cold and sometimes drifted over with snow, but we did not mind this at all.

In Clearwater Lake there was a grocery store which was also a hardware store and post office. I used to deliver milk there every day. The store was about a mile from our home; I walked to this store in deep snow carrying our milk in a can and when I got to the store I warmed myself at the big potbellied stove which stood in the center of the store. This stove is still in this store and the store has changed hands many times but the inside still looks like it did when I was a kid out there.

There also was and still is an old depot which is a boxcar with the wheels taken off; inside this depot were two wooden benches and a stove. The Northwestern train did not stop here, unless you flagged it down, so it was not used very much.

Nearby there is a large potato warehouse which my brother helped build in 1919; in the wintertime my brother used to work as a lumberjack in Robbins which was about twenty miles from Clearwater Lake; and sometimes on a Saturday night he would join the other lumberjacks and drive to Rhinelander where they would raise cain and get drunk; the Rhinelander jail always was full of drunken lumberjacks and the next morning they would be freed to go back to their lumber camps.

At Christmas time I used to help string popcorn for the Christmas tree and we would light the miniature Christmas candles on the tree; then in the evening we would go for a sleigh ride and listen to the bells jingle on the horse's harness; this was a great adventure to all the children.

I recall helping my brother go out on the lake and cut ice with a large hand saw. Then we would haul the ice blocks home and put them in the icehouse and cover the ice blocks with sawdust. In the fall we used to drive over to see the fair at Rhinelander; it was always a very interesting affair to see and to meet old friends.

In the wintertime when my brother and I went out into the forest to cut our winter's supply of wood, we would wrap a burlap bag around our boots and tie it around our ankles; this kept our feet from getting cold. We also used to tan the deerskins and make gloves and once my brother made me a buckskin vest which I always wore and took good care of.

We always used to wait for the mail-order catalogs to arrive so we could lay on the floor near the warm stove and look at the pictures in the catalogs. Even though money then was in short supply, we enjoyed it and we saved all the catalogs no matter how old they were.

X   I used to watch my mother preserve fruit and vegetables, and put them in the old mason jars that were so popular at that time. We had a small hayfield and we would go out there and cut the hay with a scythe and my mother would rake the hay into a large bed sheet and tie it and put the bundle of hay over her shoulder and carry it to the barn where she would pile it in heaps to dry.

Outside our house there was an old water pump; you had to prime it to get the water started to run and we used to wrap burlap sacks around the pump pipes to prevent it from freezing up as the temperature sometimes got around thirty below zero.

Around Christmas time we would go into the woods and cut a four-foot fir tree and bring it home and then we would sit by the stove and string popcorn on long strings to put on the tree; we used the small miniature candles to light up the tree and it was a beautiful Christmas tree after we had it all finished.

I recall one winter's day when we had a blizzard; it snowed throughout the night and the next morning; when we wanted to go to the barn to feed our cattle, the snow was piled up to the top of the barn door, so we had to shovel our way to the barn. The snow was drifted on the road and no mail could get through so I walked to town and picked up the mail for my neighbors and our mail and on the way home I stopped in at each farm home to deliver the mail; they gave me coffee and cake and when I arrived home I could not eat anything as I was full. Sometimes I would get ten cents from my neighbors for bringing them the mail, and those days ten cents was a lot of money to me.

I remember buying a stick of peppermint candy for one cent and that stick of candy lasted me a long time; milk was six cents a quart and a dollar went a long way those days.

We used to get the Saturday Evening Post magazine each week which was five cents a copy and the Liberty magazine which also was a nickel a copy.

We always waited for the spring to arrive so we could get out and enjoy the sun and nice air of the north-woods, then we would go out on Clearwater Lake and do some fishing; I knew every foot of this lake for I spent many days on it fishing or just rowing around it.

My brother got a job as a section hand on the North-western railroad that ran between our property. I used to watch him and the crew pump the handcar down the rails to check on the rails and ties.

These certainly were happy days to me; days that I have never forgotten.

THE MYSTERY OF MISSING VOLUME "M"
Mrs. Ray Ensenbach

To the casual observer the record books in the office of the register of deeds of Washington County, Wisconsin, look dull and uninteresting. Volume "M" of deeds is over a hundred and twenty-five years old and contains a record of the purchases and sales of land which took place before the year 1850. Its cover is a little more worn, its edges more tattered than its neighboring volumes, and its ink is more faded and less legible. This ancient volume was secreted in a strange hiding place for many years. If it could speak, what a strange, exciting and intriguing tale it could tell about the early days of Washington County!

A glance at a map of the state of Wisconsin will show that Washington County is one of the smallest counties in the state, but this was not always true. Originally it extended from its present western boundary line all the way eastward to Lake Michigan, with Port Washington as its county seat.

In the horse-and-buggy days when roads were only widened and enlarged Indian trails through the woods, the staunch burghers from the western part of the county found it a long and difficult chore to get to Port Washington to transact their legal business, as the roads were muddy and rut-filled in spring, dusty in summer, and often impassable in the winter snow. They therefore petitioned that the county seat be moved to a more central location, preferably West Bend. Other villages also vied for the honor of becoming the county seat, which, after all, had many material advantages and the best opportunity for growth. This was the beginning of the rivalry for the county seat.

From 1840 to 1853 the site of the county seat was a burning question and the cause of many heated quarrels. Three elections were held, but there was always a suspicion of fraud and foul play. Eventually it was necessary to ask the legislature at Madison to solve the question. With the wisdom of Solomon, the lawmakers decided to split the county in two, with West Bend as the county seat of the larger western portion, which kept the name of Washington County. Port Washington then became the county seat of the smaller eastern part, newly created Ozaukee County. This was the end of the thirteen-year fight for the county seat, but only the beginning of the "battle for the books."

All of the records were still in Port Washington, and the authorities there refused to give them up. Armed with a writ, a West Bend group went to Port Washington to "clean up the office of the Register of Deeds." However, the Port sheriff had taken precautions to prevent the removal of the books, and they returned to West Bend empty-handed.

Feeling that the only way to get the records was to

steal them, four members from West Bend decided to loot the office of the register of deeds at night. The building was dark, and they gained entrance easily enough. After lighting a few candles they began stuffing the record books into their bags, when they were surprised by the Ozaukee County sheriff, whose keen eyes had noted the flickering candlelight in the room, and, looking through the keyhole, had discovered what was going on. He then rang the riot bell, which alerted the militia. The West Benders were roughly seized and the books were taken from them and placed in a safe hiding place. Several more attempts were made to find them, but they proved futile.

The matter of the division of Washington County was taken to the state Supreme Court, and it was only after the court decided that it was constitutional that some of the Port Washington officials decided it was impossible to "buck City Hall"—or the Supreme Court. At that time a letter was received by a West Bend attorney from the editor of the Port newspaper, stating that he knew where some of the volumes could be found. Again at night the West Benders went to the editor's home and were given some of the books, together with a clue as to the whereabouts of the others. Early in the morning they triumphantly arrived back in West Bend with their precious cargo of books.

The clue given by the editor was, "Look between the walls of the arcade building in Port Washington" for the balance of the record books. Port officials realized that the court would compel them to co-operate so they opened the portion of wall which held the books and found everything except Volume M.

But what of Volume M? After all, it contained numerous records of transactions which took place in the early days of county history; it was needed to trace the chain of title to real estate, and was irreplaceable. The fact that this volume was missing always galled the officials and attorneys of Washington County and caused bitter resentment.

May we surmise what happened to Volume M? Possibly when the other volumes were being placed between the walls of the arcade building someone grabbed Volume M as a souvenir, feeling that none of the books would ever be found and he would have a permanent and valuable memoir of the county seat quarrel. His guilt feelings must have increased when the other volumes were discovered and given to Washington County, but he probably was reluctant to acknowledge his theft. As the years went on and he grew older he decided to hide Volume M as the others were hidden — thrust between the walls of an office building. Was he a builder? A painter or plasterer? The owner of the business building in which the book was hidden? We will never know whose hands placed the book in its secret place, and if any of the old-timers knew they never disclosed their knowledge. It will always remain a mystery.

In any event, Volume M gathered dust year after year. The building grew older, and many decades later they decided to remodel it. Imagine the surprise of the workmen and officials when they found an ancient book stuck between the walls, dusted it off, and found that it was the missing Volume M! Word of the important find spread quickly and caused excitement and celebration in both counties.

The animosities and rivalries between the two counties had long since disappeared, so this prized, historic volume was immediately dispatched to West Bend under official escort and considerable fanfare.

THE FARM CELLAR, WINTER
Ruth Burmester

Many things were put into the farm cellar. In Grandmother's time a skimming rack stood along the north wall of the place in summer. On it were set a number of flat, tin pans into which the milk was daily poured. After it had stood and cooled, the cream was skimmed off and made into butter. There were no cream separators in those days. Papa once told that in those times his mother kept a barrel of soft soap near the foot of the stairs. A cat, having fallen into it one time, was rescued before she became completely immersed, but lost her fur afterward. In the remembrance and telling of this incident, he also recalled a time in his youth when his mother fell on the cellar steps, broke a shoulder. When the doctor set the bone, Papa, a small lad, fled the house at her outcries of pain (no anesthetic) and ran and ran, way out past the windmill, still hearing her screams.

In my day, the main things that were put in the cellar for winter were potatoes. When the potatoes were ready in the fall, there was a potato-digging vacation from school. It was of two weeks length; everybody had potatoes to take care of.

Well, there we were, going out to the field on Monday morning. Jessie and I had on new white canvas gloves with red wristlets; the big boys and Papa had plain brown ones. Papa had got a lot of new bushel baskets when last he went to town. (An old ledger says: "2 doz. baskets, $4.80.") They were all packed tight together, a strip of wood ran through the handles of each on the side, and James had to take them off for us, one by one, when we got to the field. The horses ran down the road, the double wagon box (with the end-gate along to-

day) jolted so that we could scarcely hang on. Lewis stood up big on the box bottom, his feet braced far apart, like a man. He sang: "Come over here, Come over here, zee Alexander's Rag-Time Band."

Papa drove the potato digger. It went wiggling and shaking along the rows, the horses straining into their collars. The potatoes dropped off behind a great chain which circulated around and around, bellying out below in the middle, and the dirt fell between the steel bars of the chain, the vines were thrown off, and off came the spuds! How big and white they looked. We hurried to finish a row, to start on a new, keeping track of the number of bushels we had filled, all the while. Soon I had thirty-two baskets, pretty good! Papa paid us two cents per basket for picking-up, and the money was our Christmas money, to be spent for gifts for other members of the family. Papa would take us to town in the sled some day in December, and we would do our shopping. Meantime our money was kept in our small iron banks, mine shaped like a little black house with red trimmings. And because the paper on which the combination was printed had been lost, I had to do a deal of twisting and turning to get the door of it open when I wanted the money out. Else I must sit and shake, shake, shake, getting the pieces to come out one by one through the top slit where I'd put my coins in.

The filled baskets of potatoes were emptied into the wagon box by James. He drove the team along the rows which had been picked clean, the horses now and then reaching down for a weed to chew in their waiting. When the wagon was full, it was driven to the north cellar window (the three-paned sash removed) and the potato chute dragged up, set with its low end protruding through the window frame, its high end up against the wagon box which had been backed (with a deal of shouting at the horses) into position. Then with flat-tined scoop-fork the menfolks would scoop up the potatoes and throw them into the top of the chute. Down they rolled, the loose dirt falling through the slats of the chute, and thus keeping so much soil from going down into the cellar.

The smell of new potatoes, freshly dug, an earthy smell, came up into the kitchen. Papa was glad the potatoes had done so well that year. During the winter (near the beginning of spring) he would take many hundred-pound sacks, sixty-pound sacks, to town to sell, or to trade for supplies. If he got twenty-five cents a bushel, he would feel he was still making money, though they sometimes got as high as thirty-five cents. The frost topped, green topped, sliced-into tubers, the scrubs, having been sorted out each time a load of potatoes was prepared for market, were dumped into the feed kettle, a mash of hot food for the hogs in winter; discarded potatoes, pumpkins, old squashes, rutabagas, pails of oats, were always steaming and cooking near the smokehouse.

Along in November, when the harvesting had been completed, the cellar was made secure for the winter by being "banked up." The menfolks brought loads of straw, piled it along the outside walls, across the sloping outside entry doors, over the two windows (especially thick along the north wall). Papa would have used some horse manure with the straw, but Mama would have none of that. Long boards were laid on top the straw, holding it in place.

Sometime in spring, in a sunny spot, a hen would make her "stolen" nest and lay eggs in this banking. On the north side, taken away of a warm day in May, the straw might yet retain under it solid spots of ice. Banking-up the cellar made the house warmer in winter, but it also made the cellar very dark. Regardless of the time of day then, one had to have a lighted lantern to go down there from inside.

"Light the lantern, Helen. Go down and fetch up a pitcher of sorghum," Mama might say of a winter below-zero morning. "We'll need some for our pancakes."

It was my job to peel the potatoes for the day. I used an old flat tin pan (one of Grandmother's skimming pans heretofore mentioned) to carry the potatoes in. And when I went down with my lantern, I swung it into all corners with vigor, to scare away any rat before I settled down to loading my pan with potatoes. If Mama sighted a rat when she was down there (to get a piece of salt pork for her baked beans) she would call in a cat from out-of-doors and shut Pussy down cellar for a few hours of mousing. Puss would "Meow!" to go out when she was ready, be waiting on the top step.

A lantern must be lit and ready before anyone started down those twisting steps. "Dear, yes, your father's mother fell and broke a bone there," Mama would caution. There were many trips down—for the bringing up of carrots (from the box of sand), for onions, cabbages, rutabagas. For jars of fruit and vegetables, the mason jars (mostly two-quart but many quart size also) filled with: strawberry sauce, raspberries, blackberries, peaches, plums, cucumber pickles, apple and beet pickles; some of the latter in gallon crocks. Mama was not one to make sauerkraut, there was none of that, but there was pickalilli, chowchow, tomatoes. Sometimes there were cherries, if the two trees in the orchard had produced that year. No beans, corn, peas. Mama couldn't make such things keep for her. Her jams and jellies she placed on the upper shelves of the pantry—the cellar was too damp.

One of my fondest recollections of the farm cellar is

the barrel of New York apples kept down there in winter. Papa always ordered one which came to him shortly before Christmas. Grandfather and Grandmother had spent some rather desperate years when they started their home in Wisconsin, early 1850s. Determined to save what few potatoes they had for "spring seed," they had wintered largely on turnips one year—a winter that sickened Grandfather for life of the vegetable. They had endured other long years waiting for their newly planted apple orchard to produce, thinking often of their old days in York State where they had grown up, and the apples and vinegar they had to use in those times. So I think that my father got into this practice because, after the railroad came through our town in 1871, his own father had followed it. At any rate, those New York apples we had at Christmas time, brought up of a winter evening, were large, red, and delicious. We had, of course, apples of our own raising, never as perfect as these, however, and by that time of the year wrinkled, softened, perhaps spotted with rot. The New York apples were a special treat, kept well until spring, if the bottom of the barrel wasn't reached long before that!

GRANDMOTHER'S SUMMER KITCHEN
Melba Baehr

Summer kitchens are no longer built into modern homes. In company with pantries, bay windows, and the screened-in front porch, they have disappeared from the contemporary American scene.

But Grandmother did have a summer kitchen in her home, and she found a multitude of uses for it. In fact, she probably considered this room indispensable to her way of life, and no doubt it was.

Grandmother's summer kitchen was joined to her regular large kitchen by a small, open-on-one-side porch, which served as a repository for stacks of stove wood in wintertime. As the summer kitchen was never heated during winter months, its cold weather purpose was that of a storage place for washtubs, washboards, kraut cutter, stone crocks, sausage grinder, butter churn, and a miscellaneous number of household items used frequently but not daily. There was even a cheese-baited mousetrap or two set out in a likely corner for unwary field mice that ventured indoors with the approach of cold weather.

As soon as warm weather arrived in the spring most of the cooking was done in the summer kitchen. This was a wise procedure, as Grandmother did all her cooking and baking on a wood-burning range. Using the summer kitchen to prepare meals left the large farmhouse kitchen cool for dining in. And with the thermometer standing in the nineties on July days this was greatly appreciated.

Grandmother cooked prodigious quantities of food for her large family. And then there were the threshing crews in the fall, extra hands to feed in haying time, besides a steady stream of visiting relatives—aunts, uncles, cousins, grandparents, and a horde of shirttail kinsmen.

The summer kitchen was redolent from early morning to late at night with a mixture of appetizing odors, from roasts, an assortment of vegetables, and breads, cakes, and pies, which came forth from Grandmother's cook stove and oven.

The stove greedily burned up a sizable pile of split wood every day as, at half-hour intervals, the lid was lifted and birch and pine were put into the firebox to add their fragrance to the boiling and baking food, as they burned to ashes.

Grandmother's sunny summer kitchen was indeed a busy place during June, July, and August, and even well into the fall, but never more so than at the canning season. Then the big preserving kettles were taken from their storage place in the cupboard, mason jars, covers, and rubber rings were arranged on the work table, and huge baskets and tubs of vegetables and fruits, crisp and fresh, often with beads of dew still on them, were brought in from garden and orchard to be prepared for canning.

Putting up these foodstuffs was hard and steamy work. Even cleaning, peeling, cutting, coring the fruits and vegetables took hours of time, to say nothing of the cooking that was needed before they were ready for the jars. But at the end, there stood the rows and rows of containers with the shimmering shades of the jade, gold, ruby, and russet colors of their contents showing through the glass. Carried down to the fruit cellar, they eventually filled the shelves before canning season drew to a close.

As the jars multiplied on the shelves we knew that wintertime was approaching, even though the days continued to be warm and sunny. The denuded fields and orchards told us the same story—that the time of warm weather could not last much longer; cold winds and snow were just around the corner.

But gradually, the warm days came to an end, and as they did, the utility of Grandmother's summer kitchen did too. One by one, its uses were moved into the farm-house kitchen.

Then one morning there was skim ice on the water pail out in the summer kitchen. This was a very obvious and convincing notice that the season of the summer kitchen had come to a conclusion for another year.

THE OLD-FASHIONED HERB GARDEN
Ruth Bunker Christianson

Herb gardens are returning. Mama's grandmother had an herb garden. I always liked to hear tell of all the good things she grew, and why she grew them. In those days, besides being used for seasoning, preserving, and medicine, some herbs were used as a cure for the mad-dog bite, others for the "king's evil," and even some to ward off witchcraft.

All Mama had in her herb garden was horseradish and rhubarb, and maybe sometimes dill if the season were right. I remember when her horseradish was once put to a peculiar use.

It so happened that Dad and his neighbor-friend were snuff-takers, much to the disgust of their church-going wives, who didn't want the preacher to find out about this wicked habit. So, in order not to let anyone see them buying the curse in a grocery store, the two men sent to Sears for it, by the roll. When one friend was out of snuff he would borrow from the other, but sometimes they were both out at the same time.

It was pretty hard to wait till the Sears order came, and one time Dad made me grind some horseradish in Mama's sausage grinder. Then he opened his empty snuff box, and soused the horseradish around in it to get any flavor that was left. Then he chewed the horseradish.

One day Dad sent me, with my little sister tagging along, to borrow a box of "Rough-on-Rats," as he and his friends called it. That was so Mama's religious relatives would not get the drift of what was going on (but I'll bet they knew!)

The day wasn't very warm, but we trudged along the mile to Mr. Walker's house. Just as we rounded the corner of the kitchen, Mrs. Walker emerged from the back door with a huge dishpan of dirty dishwater, and threw it right in our faces! Of course she hadn't expected us to come around the corner and walk straight into it, so she was pretty excited. She rushed at us with, "You get home! You kids get right home!" We thought she was mad at us, but she only wanted us to get to Mama for dry clothes so we wouldn't catch pneumonia.

At home the episode called for hot ginger tea, goose-grease rubs on our chests, and dry pinafores. All for the want of Copenhagen snuff! Dad could think of nothing else for the rest of the day, except that he must go back to horseradish.

GRANDMA WAS A GOOD "COOKER"
Loreen Jacobson

Could you make a meat loaf for your family by using thirty cents worth of ground beef and ten cents worth of ham? Grandma could, and did just that. She could turn out delectable meals three hundred sixty-five days a year.

With her rosy cheeks and beaming face, wearing a long, blue-checkered apron tied around her middle, she presided over the hot cook stove, winter and summer, like a queen. Stoking the big black monster with the right amount of kindling and wood that the boys brought in, she knew exactly how to adjust the flues to have the correct amount of heat for every type of food from crisply fried salt pork and creamy gravy to delicate angel food cake.

Grandma claimed she didn't need too many recipes. "Rule of thumb," you know.

Brushing back a stray lock of steel gray hair as she busily filled the reservoir in the stove, she said, "I don't take much truck with these recipe books. Don't need one! I like recipes I got from friends — true and tried, you know. Besides, I have a few of my own, don't forget."

Grandma managed very well without standard measuring cups or spoons. Her simplified methods of measuring were unique but effective and accurate for her. To her, a pinch of salt; enough soda to cover a dime; a rounding teacup of sugar; a kitchen coffee cup of flour; butter the size of an egg; one cup of sweet milk, running over; or one-fourth cup of shortening, almost melted, were accurate enough to be dependable.

"Grandma," I asked, "how many nut meats are ten cents worth?"

"Just what it says," she replied.

In cold weather, soup day was very special at her house. Golden yellow, swimming with carrots, potatoes, barley, and chunks of good beef floating in each bowl, soup was always served with freshly baked bread and cold milk brought in from the cooling tank in the milk house. "How," I asked, "does your soup have such a beautiful golden color?"

"Humph!" she snorted. "Nothing to it! Just enough carrots."

Only when I watched the entire preparation did I learn that the beautiful yellow color was due to eight or ten grated carrots. Often she bruised her fingers in the process, but that she never mentioned.

Since Grandma always knew how to turn out delectable food, I became ecstatic when I learned her "receipt" book was to come into my possession. At last I expected to uncover the secret of the feathery rolls she so deftly turned out; the trick of always making smooth chicken gravy; or the key ingredients in her zesty chili sauce.

By some miracle I had hoped to impress the relatives by duplicating her bountiful holiday dinners that left everyone groaning and supremely happy. Dreamer! It wasn't that simple. Accustomed to complete cookbook directions, I wasn't prepared for the omissions in Grandma's cookbook. She knew how to proceed and assumed everyone else would.

Cookies, pies, and cakes had the terse direction: Bake! That was all. Gingersnaps were easy to make. Simply pinch off the dough "the size of a marble. Roll. Bake."

"How," Grandma was asked, "do you keep a cookie jar full of these delicious cookies?"

"How do you suppose?" was the answer. "Keep them locked up!" I often wondered why the spicy aroma of the pantry was so intact.

Loaves and loaves of homemade bread were baked weekly. "Nothing to it! Just combine the ingredients and add enough flour to make a stiff dough. Be sure to pinch off enough dough to make a batch of biscuits for dinner, too."

Bread was baked until the "singing" stopped. After five minutes, it was removed from the oven. Freshly baked bread was always covered with a clean, red checked tablecloth as it came from the oven. (These cloths are now precious family keepsakes, used for picnics and outdoor barbecues.)

There were, of course, many tricks of cooking that only Grandma understood. As a special treat after church on Sunday afternoons, she made goodies for the children. Fudge was cooked until it "rolled in water." For caramel corn, the syrup was cooked "long enough."

A straw pulled from the broom was used to test the doneness of a cake. If the inserted straw came out clean, the cake was ready to be removed from the oven. Simple! We were "shushed" out of the kitchen when cakes were in the oven. "Never, and I mean never, run or jump heavily in the kitchen when a cake is in the oven. It will fall if you do," admonished Grandma.

There were other unique customs practiced in her kitchen that she tucked into her recipe book, hand-written in her own inimitable style with special "tails" on the "S"s. Unless you had watched her cook, however, these written hints were not enough to duplicate Grandma's innate skills.

Inheriting outstanding recipes of good cooks may be a special joy, but duplicating them more often than not leaves you completely in the dark. It is a good idea to watch them prepared, if possible. That way, little tricks in preparation "sneak up on you."

I remember watching and following step-by-step the method of preparing outstanding liver dumplings. Mine flopped. They disintegrated. Questioning my "teacher," I was told, "Oh, I forgot to tell you, the water must be vigorously boiling when you drop the dumplings in. And —keep it boiling."

Old cookbooks, hand-written, regional, or those published early as 1894, can be fun to read but today many of the recipes are meaningless without directions.

With food as expensive as it is today and the ingredients variable, it might be wise to confine your interest in reading, not preparing, them—unless you know what you are doing. At any rate, it should be possible to emulate some of Grandma's special dos and don'ts. It is easy to add the salt to the stew fifteen minutes before "taking it up." If that confuses you, take the advice of another veteran cook who always, before dishing up the meal, says, "Let's lift the dinner."

And let's lift a toast to Grandma and her kind! They made eating fun and memorable.

MOTHER'S OLD IRON COOK STOVE
Mrs. Melvin Getlinger

Mother's old iron cook stove was, undoubtedly, the most important piece of equipment in our log house. It not only provided heat for the family cooking, but for canning hundreds of quarts of food for winter use. The old stove heated water for laundry, it heated flatirons for ironing clothes, and it provided heat for the east end of the house. The heat of its scorching coals was even used to soften metal to be pounded into an emergency tool or to solder a leaky milk pail. Finally, it provided the setting for many an evening's entertainment.

Many times Mother would be found preparing food on the friendly old stove for strangers seeking work in the area, visiting happily as she worked. The stove needed cleaning often, and sometimes travelers would offer to carry wood or empty the ashes in gratitude for food and temporary lodging. This was all welcomed by the older children who would otherwise be responsible for giving the stove a thorough cleaning once a week.

The ashpan itself, behind a door of its own, had a pull-out container where ashes accumulated, and those that fell to the sides of the pan were removed with a long-handled fire shovel. If a stranger cleaned the ashes, the children made sure that any ashes that spilled on the floor were swept up and the floor mopped.

Cleaning the black soot from the inside of the pipes leading to the chimney was by far the worst job. Father usually helped with that, taking the four-foot sections outside, stirring, tapping, and scraping them with a metal rod until they were all clean. It was not always an easy job to get the pipes connected again either, and such fussing as there was!

There were several "soot areas" that had to be cleaned too. There was one over the oven, one under the oven, and one between the oven and the water reservoir. Every area was behind a very small door, and we had a long metal toothless rake to pull the soot forward into the dust pan.

The fire could be started either through the firing door in front or through one of the lid holes on top. The door in front had hinges on the bottom and the lids had a special foot-long hook to lift them off.

There was a small rectangular draft door on the left side of the stove. It had four-inch-square isinglass windows that could be slid open as a unit. If a lot of draft was needed, as when starting the fire, the whole door would be opened until the flames began to roar, then it was closed and the sliding isinglass windows would be used. We could almost always tell when the fire needed fuel by the flicker of the fire or the glow of the coals showing through the isingliss windows. Then Mother would speak in German, "Kinder, mach hulche un der feuer." If the children resisted, she would repeat, "Kinder, mach hulche un der feuer und scrie stecle." This meant, "Children, put more wood on the fire and no sass!"

You can bet that during canning season we had to add much "hulche" to the fire. We had no pressure cookers in those days, and a canner of fruit cooked nearly an hour. A canner of vegetables cooked two hours and a canner of meat cooked four hours.

Mother was fortunate to have a sixteen-quart water reservoir bolted to her stove. It was a rectangular metal box on the right side of the stove and had a hinged iron lid. It was also very practical, using every bit of extra heat that the old stove radiated. On wash day the water in this reservoir was a welcome addition to that which was heated on top of the stove in the old copper boiler.

Mother also used to "take in" men's bosom shirts to be laundered, starched, and ironed. On such days three flatirons would be found heating on the old cook stove. Mother "tested" the temperature of the iron by licking one of her fingers, then touching the iron quickly. If it sizzled, she could iron, making the gathers and flounces of the fancy shirts stiff and immaculate. She changed the iron handle to a hotter iron whenever necessary. The men and boys in the neighborhood paid mother about ten cents a shirt, and the next time she went into town, she would buy the children a treat of oranges, or a hair ribbon for the girls, and, of course, a new can of stove polish.

In the cold winter, we would wrap the hot flatirons in heavy cloth and put them in our featherbeds before we snuggled in all warm and cozy.

On very cold winter mornings, all the girls would crowd around the old cook stove, and all the boys around the living room heater, to get dressed for school.

When everyone came home in the evening, there was a big black iron pot of soup or stew waiting for supper. These big black pots could be set directly on the fire for cooking if the stove lid was removed, and yes, they were very sooty on the bottom!

Several days a week, the aroma of baking bread filled the kitchen. Six loaves at a time were baked in the oven, three loaves side by side in two large bread pans. When the children returned home from school, they delighted in slicing thick pieces, spreading them with home-churned butter, and eating them with a glass of milk,

some of the children seated on the old wash bench because there were not enough chairs to go around.

One smell, not so pleasing, that often filled the kitchen in winter was that of wet wool mittens drying under the old cook stove. The family would lay them on the thick metal platform that protected the floor from sparks from the old stove.

During the evening, Mother would be found sitting by the stove spinning, or knitting mittens and socks for the family. On special occasions the children would make popcorn on the old cook stove and sit beside her eating it while she told stories of her pioneer days—about driving oxen and tending sheep, about friendly Indians, begging gypsies, and frightening wild animals.

On New Year's Eve, Father would bring in a bar of lead, and chop off pieces with a hatchet or old knife. The children would melt them in old spoons on top of the old cook stove, then pour the melted liquid into a big pan of cold water to watch it take different shapes. The whole family would gather 'round to see, laughing and joking.

One evening when Father returned home from work, he was carrying a new can of black stove polish; and he, himself, spent the entire evening cleaning and polishing the old iron cook stove until it stood proud and shiny on its short black legs. Its soot was removed, its doors and lids were immaculate, and its reservoir was free of rust and moisture. Then he told us that our old cook stove had been sold. The next day Mother would get a rest from cooking. The next day, being Saturday, Father hooked the team of horses to the wagon and drove into town, taking the old iron cook stove with him.

When he returned that evening, there was a brand new Monarch range on the wagon. It was much like the old stove, but was taller, had six lids instead of four, and had a much larger oven. It had a new feature, too — a warming oven built over it, much like the upper ovens of today's modern ranges. It, too, was proud looking, black and shiny, and would accommodate cooking for a rapidly growing family that would ultimately reach twelve in number.

Mother was grateful for the new stove; but we were all a little sorry to see the old one go. It had served us well for many years, and I like to think that it is a beautiful antique, still standing in its new home, waiting for someone to light the fire, making its isinglass windows glow. And I like to imagine that someone's little children are gathering round its gentle warmth, enjoying a bowl of popcorn, and listening attentively to tales of long ago as whispered by the fading flames of Mother's old iron cook stove.

YE OLDE KRAUT CROCK
Ida Carstensen

So, we had to get up — four o'clock in the morning, still dark, even the birds are quiet and the night clouds just starting to roll away. Our objective — to get to the haymarket (sort of center of town) to pick out some of the farmers' choicest. White Wisconsin potatoes, red beets with large clumps of damp black soil still clinging to their roots, onions beautiful in their russet satin thin skins and bunches of cut flowers still wet with morning dew—some picked the night before by the farmer's frau and kept damp and cool for market in the morning.

However, this morning we are most interested in the largest and firmest heads of cabbage; their destination— our old sauerkraut crock brought up from the root cellar and now standing scrubbed and resplendent in the center of the kitchen. On the old wooden table nearby lays the round three-inch-thick kraut board, discolored from years of salty brine and the huge scrubbed stone (size of a man's head). They will add the crowning touch to all our work—keeping guard till the kraut is ready to be taken.

Now, we have selected many of the most perfect and most solid cabbage heads to be put in the two brand new bushel baskets resting on the old coaster wagon. We buy some dill, shiny red apples and accept a few scraggly blooms offered by our farmer's wife before we start our trek home through the semi-darkness t oget to the business of the day.

All is in readiness — the wooden kitchen table has been cleared and spread with a huge off-white muslin cloth, the cabbage cutter lies nearby, and the huge crock still holds place of honor in the center of the room. First the heads of cabbage must be dunked in the old round washtub (bathtub on Saturday nights in front of the now dark base burner), then wiped dry and quartered or halved before being sent to the cutting board.

Now, a layer of finely cut cabbages, three or four inches deep, then a good handful of pickling salt and perhaps a sprinkling of caraway seed. Everyone knows good kraut must be firmly packed down for best results before another layer is added. What better way than to have a delighted and eager youngster (with feet scrubbed to a glowing pink) stomp it down? How I remember stomping up and down in that old kraut crock! How proud I was of my part in this annual home event, especially in the cold frosty winter months when the compliments would flow over our ham hocks, spareribs or kielbasa and kraut!

Now, the layers are stomped down to perfection, a

few red-cheeked apples are nestled on top and the fat round board pressed in place with the huge white stone crowning all. The white muslin cloth is carefully tied around the top to keep out unwanted visitors and the crock is ready to be carried to the cool cellar — a job for two good men.

Everyone is now ready to relax with a steaming cup of coffee (mine is baby coffee—half and half) and a generous slice of homemade apple strudel.

Me, I'm ready to crawl back in the featherbed and dream about the weeks to come when I can make all those unnecessary pilgrimages to the root cellar, cautiously lift the clean muslin cloth, sneak two fingers down into the salty brine and sample the chewy, tangy, delightful strings of half-pickled kraut or maybe steal one of the now spiced apples, putting all back in place with no one the wiser.

MAKING SAUSAGE
Mary Gmoser

Considerable time and hard work were involved in making sausage sixty years ago. Preparations started days ahead of the event.

The streetcar took us to the end of the line in West Allis, Wisconsin, where Dr. Hrdlicka waited for us with his horse and buggy, to take us to his farm.

On our arrival, the men were already at work. Children were kept out of the area. My curiosity got the best of me, and I watched. What I saw fascinated me. I saw things I could not get out of a book.

Killing the hog required several men. The hog was given something to eat in a trough, and while it was eat-ing, two men would grab its hind legs, flip it over on its side, and pull it over to a spot of hard ground. One man with a pitchfork would stand by and position the fork between the jaws of the hog, with a tine on each side of the jaw, and drive the fork into the ground. It could not move its head, nor kick. Another man would shave a portion of skin over the heart, and insert a sharp knife into it.

A woman caught the blood in a large bowl and kept stirring it with a slotted wooden spoon to prevent it from clotting. It was to be used for blood and tongue sausage later.

The hog felt no pain. It was then lifted and placed on some heavy chains in a trough filled with hot water. Powdered pitch was poured on it. Two men on each side of the trough would pull the chains back and forth while turning the hog. The pitch, in combination with the hot water, caused the bristles to stick together, and be easily removed by hand.

A slit was made in each hind leg to expose the tendons by which the hog would hang. It was removed from the tank by a portable winch, and hauled to a hanging frame made of six-by-six timbers with one-inch wooden pegs for hooks, and shaved all over. It looked clean and pink.

The butchering started. The intestines came first and had to be thoroughly cleaned. They were to be used for sausage casings. While the women were busy with washing the intestines (a very tedious job), the men were cutting the meat. Knives were sharpened frequently by a skilled craftsman.

Some meat was cut for porkchops, some for smoking, like hams, bacon, schpeck and butts, and some for boiling. Odds and ends, snouts, ears, skin and bits of meat were boiled with spices, cooled, deboned, cut, or ground and made into various kinds of delicacies and sausages.

The stomach was used as a casing for schwartle (skin) magen (stomach). The filling consisted of some of the snout, ears, skin, bits of meat and some tongue. It was highly spiced, and seasoned with cayenne pepper. After being boiled again, it was placed between two boards with a large stone or flatirons on top. This permitted the liquid to drain off, thus making a more solid sausage. Then it was smoked.

The smaller intestines served as casings for eternice (a Bohemian liver sausage with herbs and spicy seasonings, which was fried before eating), garlic sausage, and other small sausages, each with its own characteristic flavor.

The larger intestines were used as casings for either head cheese, or a sausage made with spices, herbs, and mustard seed. Pa, being an herbalist, was the seasoner. He always brought his own herbs, seeds, and spices along.

The winter "schpeck," on the back of the hog, was covered with paprika and smoked, to be eaten during the winter. The soft fat under this was rendered in large kettles (outdoors if weather permitted), stored in crocks, and used for frying and baking. The crackles from it were used in various ways, eaten out of hand, in a sandwich, salad, or cooked with beans or other vegetables. Feet were pickled. Nothing was wasted. The fat removed from around the intestines was used to polish and waterproof boots.

All meat used for sausage was parboiled, and either cut, or ground to size, seasoned with herbs and spices (each adding its subtle effect to the whole), stuffed into the casings, boiled again and smoked.

Much meat was smoked to preserve it as there were no refrigerators at that time. Some fresh meat was kept in a deep well with a roof over it. The well water was always icy cold.

Much cleaning, cooking, chopping, grinding and stuffing was done in the summer kitchen which had two large wood and coal stoves, two large sinks and one smaller one. The small one had a hand pump on its wooden top. All sinks were made of zinc.

If the weather permitted, much cooking was done out-of-doors. The outdoor grill had a large copper boiler on it in which the meat was parboiled before it was chopped or ground.

The kettles in the kitchen were either gray mottled, or dark blue with white-speckled enamel.

The hams and other fresh meat that were to be smoked, were soaked for several weeks in water (which had been boiled and then cooled), with salt, garlic, spices, and sometimes, honey and onions. They were smoked for several weeks, with hickory branches providing the smoke.

Sausage making for our family usually took a whole weekend. The aromas coming from the kitchen with their pungent, spicy smells were a joy to the nostrils and made everyone drool.

Such was sausage making in a bygone era, as I remember it.

MAKING LYE SOAP
Cyrilla Muller

The making of lye soap was an annual event. This took place in the spring after the butchering was finished and the warm weather set in. It had to follow full moon to be successful.

I was only a little girl but the affairs are still vivid in my memory.

Father constructed a leach. This was a receptacle of sorts, large enough to hold the wood ashes resulting from the winter's fuel. Wood was burned in the furnace and kitchen stove and was our only source of heat.

The leach was made of boards and was wide at the top and narrow at the base. Probably six feet long. The whole contrivance rested on a trough of sorts and sloped to one end. A large crock jar was placed at the end of the trough to receive the lye.

Well, all winter long the ashes were put into this leach. When the frosty days of winter were over, my father would make three large holes in the top of the ashes. Then water was carried in pails and poured into the holes. After several days the water would seep slowly through the ashes and flow slowly into the trough to the jar. This was how the lye was obtained to make the soap.

A large iron kettle was suspended from an iron bar which rested across the points of two huge boulders in the yard not far from the leach. This location was a perfect place for a fireplace sort of design for cooking the soap. As the jar filled up with lye, it was emptied into pails and carried to the kettle. When the kettle was about half full of lye, Mother would bring all the waste fat drippings, cracklings left after rendering lard and all the old grease from winter's cooking which she had carefully saved for the purpose and put into the lye. Then a fire was started under the kettle. We children picked up the pieces of wood and debris around the yard and barn for the fire.

When the lye was heated the fat began to melt. Then more lye was added until the kettle was full of the mixture. Sometimes water was added. No measurements were made but Mother had a way of knowing when there were sufficient amounts of each ingredient to give the desired effects.

More or less wood was added to the fire to keep the soap cooking but not boiling over. It usually took a day to make a kettle of soap.

Mother tested the soap by dipping out a small amount into a shallow dish. She would stir the sample and notice its consistency as it cooled. When it had just the right appearance, she would decide the job a success and let the fire die out. It would take all night to cool the soap and the next day the family assisted in carrying pails of the stuff into the cellar where it was emptied into ten- and twenty-gallon jars. This amount lasted a whole year until soap-making time again.

The soap was called soft soap. It did not harden, but had a thick, dark, jellylike consistency.

We used the soap for every household use all year. The only thing forbidden its use was milk utensils. We bought little other soap and soap powders.

This was a thorough example of a recycling job, although we had not heard the word. All waste products were consumed and made into a usable product.

Sometimes if there was enough material two kettles of soap were made. If the soap would not thicken, and Mother would notice the moon was wrong, she would wait until after the moon was full and then begin the cooking process again. She declared this always worked.

After the kettle was emptied and there was usually some lye left, she would take the frying pans, baking dishes, and any discolored dishes and put them into the kettle with lye. After a couple hours the pans would be removed and thoroughly cleaned and they would be bright again like new.

The soap-making time was hard work and tiring,

but it was also a happy time. Like all children, we enjoyed the fire and watched the cooking. While the soap was slowly simmering, we often sat on a rock or block of wood and talked and laughed and made jolly of the time.

Often Mother and I would look over some old magazines that she had saved of her young "dress-making" days. There were all dress styles of the times and it was fun to look at the bustles, puffed sleeves and tight waists and long floor length skirts in style when she was young.

I had five brothers who had little use for this pleasure and so they romped and tussled about. But when the time came for emptying the soap kettle, they were invited to partake of the gaiety. This job was not too handsome and they were always cheered when the last pail was cleared and their sport could again resume.

SPRING HOUSECLEANING
Estella Bhryn

Spring housecleaning, like everything else, has changed with the years. A sure sign that spring had really arrived was when one or two heaters were taken down and either carried to a back porch to rust during the summer, or hidden in a back closet. The putting up or taking down of stovepipes was sometimes accompanied with such profane language that younguns were sent outside to play until the pipe was down and the soot had settled. Company, especially a clergyman, was ill-timed.

The woodbox had to be cleaned if it took a week. The best way was to have a bee and invite the neighbors who lost mittens, pencils, washboards, ash shovels, boots, parts of harnesses, hammers, and dishes to be present and claim their property as it was sifted out. The average woodbox yielded enough variety to set a newly married couple up in housekeeping.

Cleaning the back yard was a back-breaking job. All winter dishwater, wash water from clothes washing and baths, along with potato peelings, cabbage leaves and wood ashes were thrown there to enrich the ground, and how simple it was to heave broken dishes and bottles and ham bones into the back yard. Some were gathered up and taken to the country to be dumped along the roadside or in a farmer's pasture; sometimes it was easier to just pass this and that over the neighbor's fence into his yard, hoping that he in turn would pass it on to his next neighbor.

Basements were generally dark, damp holes with dirt floors and a solitary small window for light. Entrance was by raising a trap door, either outside the house or in the kitchen or pantry floor. The darkness as one descended made you wish you had cat's eyes.

Cleaning was simply a matter of carrying up the stairs and out potatoes and carrots that had grown long vines, and cabbage, pumpkin and squash that had rotted to a spongy mess. Often the vines were picked off the potatoes, and the tubers used for seed. Pumpkin and squash were thrown along the fence or in a ditch in hopes that they would reseed themselves.

There were always glass canning jars of spoiled fruit and soggy pickles, a stone crock with the remains of well-fermented sauerkraut, and jugs of sour wine which was always tasted before being thrown out.

With the heavier work done, the lady of the house took over. Curtains were carefully washed and starched by boiling starch and water to the proper consistency, not too thick, not too thin. They were then pinned on curtain stretchers to dry in the sun. There were several hundred, or so it seemed, small pins set close together, and how exasperating it was to get done and find the edges hadn't been perfectly stretched and the curtain hung unevenly. The lady who could stretch several curtains without pricking her fingers until they bled on the sharp pins had nimble fingers indeed.

On a hot sunny day the parlor carpet was taken out on the lawn and aired, or hung on the clothes line. The lady of the house crawled around the four sides of the rug armed with a carpet tack hammer and a small dish. She carefully extracted each tack which held the rug to the floor, and placed the tacks in her mouth until she had a row to spit in the dish. When the last tack was out the rug was taken outside to the clothes line where it was beaten with a wire rug beater. The clouds of dust which rose varied with the savagery of the beating. When the lady's back, and the back of the rug, were about broken, the rug was carried into the house, the tacks nailed in once more, and the beauty of the rug was admired until the next spring when the procedure was repeated.

Heavy mattresses were given the sun treatment by being carried outside and placed on either saw horses or chairs to keep them off the ground. They received a good beating with the rug beater, and perhaps a sprinkling of kerosene around the edges as a "No Trespassing" sign to unwelcome intruders.

When at last the house shone from top to bottom the homemaker wondered why she was tired, why her back ached, and why she just had no get up and go anymore.

THOSE WONDERFUL YEARS OF TAKING TURNS
Frieda M. Lease

How few opportunities there are left in today's style of living for children to take turns in sharing responsibilities around home.

We were, it seems to me now, among the more fortunate. We grew up on a farm back in the early part of the century when there were yet no electric gadgets and other work-saving inventions to interfere with our wonderful training course through "taking turns." The training involved sharing pleasant as well as some not-so-pleasant tasks. Even pulling the home built oak sled, complete with heavy wooden runners, up the hill during coasting seasons held responsibilities not to be taken lightly. We thought highly of the crude vehicle shared by five of us. It was never left out in the weather, but properly housed in the woodshed at the end of playtime. And, as with some of our other cared-for possessions, it outlasted our childhood years.

No one ever forgot whose turn it was back then to lick the frosting pan after a Saturday's baking. Such sweet anticipations were natural when, unlike today, candy bars, ice cream cones and suckers were considered special treats for birthday parties and those once-a-year events as Sunday School picnics and county fairs.

I was seven the summer I inherited the water jug task. My two older sisters who had each served her turn before were promoted to perform more skilled duties like helping with cooking and sewing. In July I learned the meaning of "the harvest season." The higher the temperature registered the more often I must tote the water jug across the hot sandy fields. I was allowed to wear my shoes for this job during the midsummer days because sandburs would otherwise slow my pace and cause the cold well water to become warm. "This will stay cool for an hour. Bring another jugful at four," Pa ordered as he wrapped a grain sack around the jug and set it inside a shock of rye bundles to insulate it against the glaring sun. After two summers of jug carrying I passed the responsibility on to my younger sister.

A routine duty, and by no means a small one, with which we took regular turns was keeping the woodbox filled and gathering enough dry corncobs and kindling wood needed to start morning fires. In winter there were the heavy chunks to be carried in and piled in an orderly fashion near the round oak heater which served as the central heating system to warm both upper and lower levels. Wood-burning stoves used in houses without storm windows and uninsulated walls required heaps of wood and attention. Never again would there be such a satisfied, secure feeling as that brought about by having ample fuel on hand to keep stoves going through those harsh, cold nights. But, like the water jug, the woodbox too lost out to newer ways. And only old-timers can understand what it was like then when winter settled in and snowbanks along the road came up over the top of fence posts. With roads blocked, rural people were isolated for weeks at a stretch.

Bringing the cows in from the pasture was a chore I took turns in and often wished over with, particularly on foggy mornings, when the herd chose to chew their cud lying down in a remote corner, making it hard to locate them.

Cleaning out chicken coops and nests were also among the less desirable jobs. But gathering eggs was a pleasant venture, like playing a game of hide-and-go-seek. In searching for hidden nests we climbed straw stacks, crawled under the corncrib, and roamed through tall weeds. Nests which went undiscovered tattled on our negligence after an allotted time. As when on a morning the mother hen who had stolen her nest would appear in the dooryard, trailed by her brood of seven to ten chicks, and in clucking language beg to be fed.

Now, on looking back to that long ago time, I am more than ever aware of the lessons learned in the wonderful years of taking turns and sharing responsibilities.

IT'S POTATO-SPROUTING TIME, REMEMBER?
Margaret Damp

I cleaned out the vegetable bin this morning, and behind a bag of parsnips was a long white sprout from a gnarled potato. I held it in my hand a minute, and, suddenly, I was fifty years younger. I could hear my father say, "It's time to sprout the potatoes. How about coming down to the store Saturday morning and taking care of them for me?"

Father was a country storekeeper, and "The Emporium" as he laughingly called it, was my second home. The organized confusion of a general merchandise store was commonplace to me; the indescribable odors of vinegar and freshly ground coffee, of pickled herring and sweeping compound and chocolate peaks smelled the way I thought stores were supposed to smell.

"Potato sprouting time." About then my usual Saturday chore of cleaning the living room and polishing all the furniture with O-Cedar polish looked very attractive. But no arguments were allowed. A suggestion from my parents was, in fact, an order.

Any country girl knows it's the nature of potatoes to

send out sprouts in late winter, and she knows these have to be broken off or the potato grows soft and useless. It isn't a hard job. The tender sprouts can be rubbed off with a thumb or snapped off with the fingers and will fall into an old basket like fat white worms. A revolting thought.

The store basement was not planned to be attractive, only dry and reasonably warm with ample storage space. Small windows barely above the ground let in minimal light and no view except a quadrangle of sky. A naked light bulb dangled on its green cord from the ceiling near the furnace, its power no more than forty watts.

Father would get me settled on an old chair with the back broken off, arranging several bushels of potatoes at one side. Then he went upstairs to "wait on the trade." I could hear his footsteps back and forth above me, and the sound of voices, though the words were unintelligible. Any entertainment was my responsibility for this was long before transistor radios or piped-in stereo music.

Pick up a potato, rub off the sprout, take another. My thumb grew tender, then sore, and I switched to the other hand. I looked at the shelves stacked with wooden boxes of prunes and dried peaches, wooden pails of jelly or peanut butter. There were cartons of shoes for all ages, and a box marked "corsets"—mentioned in a whisper, if at all. I read all the labels as I worked. When a small mouse poked his nose around a corner I was pleased to see him. He was someone to talk to.

I sang rousing songs: "Hurrah for Wood County," "Pull for the Shore, Sailor," "Marching Through Georgia," and "The Spanish Cavalier," wondering why the silly man kept crying about "excelsior."

I counted a hundred sprouts before looking to see if the basket was empty. It wasn't. When Father could get away from his work, he would come down to visit so I would know he hadn't forgotten me. He would sit down on a nail keg and busily rub off sprouts with his strong hands, making grown-up conversation about saving the potatoes so we wouldn't have a loss on them.

"People depend on our store to provide them with things they need, and we have to keep their confidence," he told me. "You are doing your share to make this possible," he smiled and nodded at me.

Sometimes he talked about the camping trip next summer—how we would take our tent and pack the food box on the running board of our Willys-Overland, and maybe spend a week at Hill's Lake near Wild Rose. Spurred by his companionship, I worked faster and at last it was noon.

What did father pay me for my work? I don't remember, but it wasn't much by today's standards. He used to give me a penny a sack when I mended gunnysacks. I had to cut squares from a worn-out sack and sew them on a hole in a pretty good sack, using a big darning needle and store string. They were rough scratchy bags with lint that got in my nose. I hated the job, but the work needed to be done.

I forgot about the money, but I remember the praise. Father would lay his hand on my shoulder and tell the customers, "I had some help this morning. Margaret has been sitting down in the basement sprouting potatoes and mending gunnysacks. She is a good steady worker."

Would I sprout potatoes for him again? Yes, any Saturday morning about this time of the year.

YESTERDAY'S BONUSES
Mrs. Mildred S. Hanson

When I went shopping recently with the discount coupons I had clipped from periodicals, I was reminded of my childhood days. Then, we did not have coupons with so many cents off the purchase price, but perhaps we had other "bonuses."

I recall how eager I was to accompany my father on Saturday evenings to our grocery store. When he paid the weekly bill, the grocer would always give us a bag of delicious penny candies. I enjoyed the "jawbreakers" the most as it was fascinating to see what flavor and color the next layer would be until I came to the heart, which was a nut.

The grocer also gave us an extra soup bone or two when we bought our weekly beef roast, and the package always contained liver and other meat scraps for our dog and cat. My father never forgot to buy red and white mints. They were saved for Sunday morning at church to keep me from wiggling too much during the long sermon.

These thoughts also brought to mind other bygone customs. Although we lived in a rather large city, the tradesmen who came to our door regularly were always treated with respect. The milkman belonged to our church, and we trusted his clean products. He brought milk in a large can from which he poured our daily supply into our own pitcher. He churned his own butter, and he placed it in green crockery jars. Moisture beads were still visible on top, and the butter had a distinct salty but fresh flavor. It served to enhance the nutlike crunchy texture of the crust slice of Mother's fresh baked bread. Occasionally, he also brought us free buttermilk which contained a blob or two of unchurned butter. We not only enjoyed drinking this as a beverage, but Mother used it in baking fluffy pancakes and rich chocolate cake.

The other day when my milkman apologized because he had only blueberry-flavored yogurt, I remembered the curds and whey dish I enjoyed so much as a child. It did not need any blueberry or other flavoring and was far superior to yogurt. It was a junket with a sweet velvety coating of cream on top that Mother made with a "starter." We kept a small portion from each supply to begin the next "fele-bunk," as it is called in Swedish. We often ate it with a piece of hard tack or rye-krisp with a liberal spread of butter.

Every Friday morning we would look for the fish man. In summer, he would bring us fresh caught Lake Superior trout or salmon which he had packed in wooden boxes lined with chopped ice. What a treat this was, and so effortless on our part. A few weeks before Christmas, we always bought large dried codfish. In order to make this pliable, my mother and I would soak the fish in a solution of lye and water for several days until it became softer. The lye was then rinsed thoroughly from the fish in several soaking waters.

On Christmas Eve my mother cooked the "lute-fisk," which is Swedish for lye-fish, in water for just a few minutes until it was white and flaky. The best part was the sauce she made. It was a mustard gravy, consisting of a white sauce flavored with enough mustard for piquancy. Plain white boiled potatoes, a cooked vegetable, lingonberry sauce, which resembles cranberries, and a rice pudding baked in milk, studded with plump raisins and flavored with cinnamon and sugar, completed the traditional holiday supper.

The cinnamon and other spices my mother used in

cooking and baking were never purchased at the grocery store. These she bought from the salesman who carried a superior brand of baking products as well as home remedies. The latter consisted of cough syrup, ointments for burns and chest rubs. As there were no detergents those days, she relied on the fels-naphtha type soap he sold. This we shaved fine for laundering, washing dishes and scrubbing floors. The soap chips were dissolved in a high washtub of hot water which was placed on the stove. In it went all the white clothes, and they were boiled clean and sparkling, then rinsed thoroughly. The salesman also sold ammonia and vinegar for cleaning windows. For every large purchase, the customer would get a bonus gift of the family's choice, with a certain price limit.

The delectable odors emanating from our kitchen when Mother baked her delicious cinnamon rolls and cardamom buns always brought neighborhood children around our back porch screen door. They knew they would get a sample. As I had the dubious privilege of cutting open the numerous cardamom pods and splitting the seeds into tiny pieces, I sometimes bribed a playmate to help me, and he or she would earn an extra roll.

My mother usually served the bread with fresh ice cold lemonade. The ice was purchased from our once-a-week iceman who brought the weight of ice specified by the card placed in the window. He always wore a long black leather apron and carried the heavy cakes of ice with huge tongs. While he was delivering the ice to various householders, the children would chip off pieces from the cakes of ice in his wagon and pop them into their mouths. Of this, the iceman was well aware, although we did not know it, as nothing was ever said to us by him.

The other "bonus" we enjoyed as children was the money we earned by selling scrap iron and bottles to the "junk man." He came with his tired old horse pulling the wagon filled with all his previous collections en route. We always enjoyed the "haggling" with this bewhiskered old man, but I wonder who derived the most enjoyment from these seemingly heated debates about the worth of our "products." When our items would amount to nine cents, somehow we always received a dime, or if we collected more junk, we received a quarter instead of just twenty-three or twenty-four cents. We speak today of recycling old bottles and cans as something new, but this old collector of junk, and others like him, were ecology minded fifty years ago. They would sell what they gathered or bought to a firm that converted them to re-usable glass and iron.

Although I certainly am not advocating our reverting back to the so-called "good old days," I feel we have lost many pleasurable bonuses since that time. Pre-packaged foods may be convenient and certainly more sanitary, and I confess to using them as well as other convenience foods. Still, there is something lost in their preparation, a freshness and a flavor that cannot be recaptured entirely by cooking or baking. I would not want to buy my milk in a pitcher, nor would I return to some of the practices of food preparation of those days. I am only grateful that I have experienced some of the simple pleasures of by-gone days when bonuses did not consist of coupons or money. They came from the generosity of the grocer, the honesty of the tradesmen who brought their products to our doorstep, and the integrity of our fellow man.

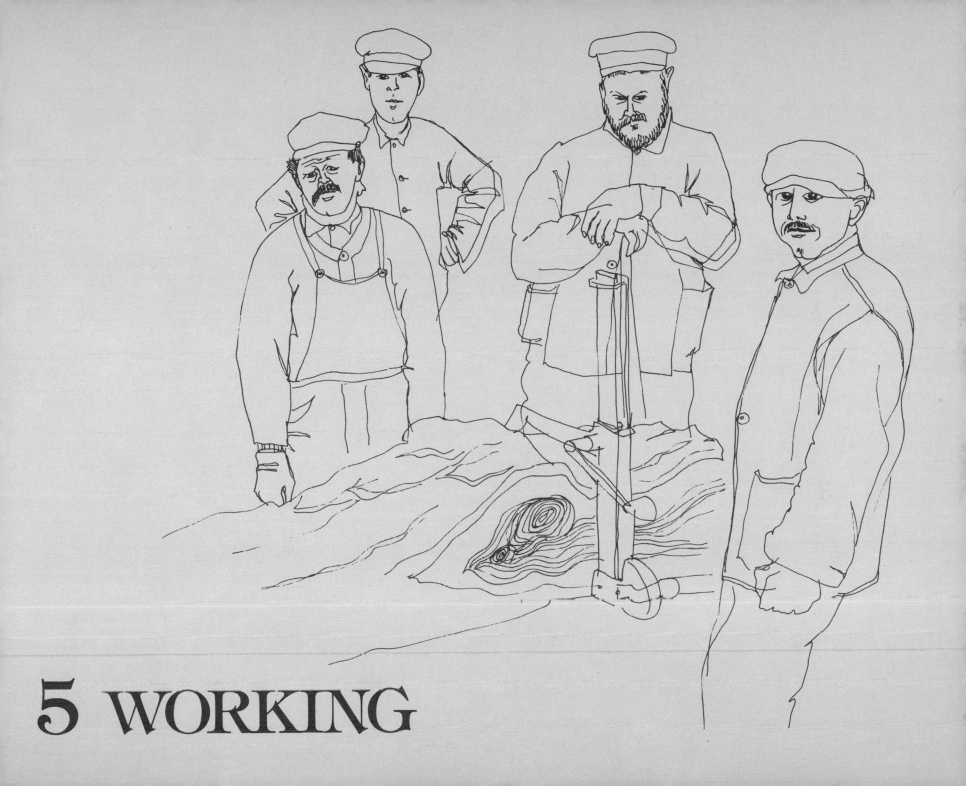

5 WORKING

THE DRESSMAKERS
Catherine Otten

When I was a child, Aggie and Maggie came to our house to sew for a whole week. They were not only dressmakers, but also Mama's dearest friends. Our family always looked forward to their annual visit, for a holiday atmosphere prevailed during the time they "lived in" with us. Meals were always special too, with fancy desserts every day.

The dressmakers sewed everything. They made dresses, coats, caps, hats, underwear, night clothes, curtains, dish towels and anything else that needed a needle and thread treatment. The old treadle Singer sewing machine was kept steadily humming from early morning until suppertime. Those two maiden ladies were busily sewing when we children got out of our beds in the morning, and were still hard at it when we came home from school.

"You will have to slip this on for a fitting," was heard by anyone of our family at any time while the dressmakers were at our house. No matter what we were doing, we stopped and went into the sewing room to be fitted. Our sex did not matter to Aggie or Maggie. If one of us girls was not on hand to try on a dress or petticoat when fitting was necessary, one of my brothers had to stand in for us. I remember hiding away when the call for "fitting" came, so that I could watch the struggle and discomfort when the dressmakers caught one of them and hung a dainty, soft ruffled garment on him and pinned him securely into it. The boys always lost out! Aggie and Maggie paid no attention to their vigorous protests! Fitting on a model, any model, was important and the job had to be done before the victim was released.

Dressmaking was an intricate job those days. Hems and seams were large and thick with plenty of material for letting out. Even the pretty white cotton petticoats had to be fitted. Embroidered ruffles trimmed the bottoms of these overslips, and eyelet beribboned embroidery finished off the top. Pretty and dainty as these slips were, they must not show under the dresses. The only time they and their matching panties made a public appearance was on the washline after being soaked, boiled, washed, starched and hung out to dry. The washlines were a beautiful sight to see, and the smell of those freshly washed clothes blowing in the wind gave out a fragrance unmatched today by any commercial perfume.

Nights were always fun while the dressmakers were at our house. Aggie and Maggie could be lots of fun once they took off their aprons and tapelines, and took the pins out of their mouths. Games that we could all play together, popping corn, making fudge, pulling taffy or telling stories was in order those evenings.

However, at least one of those evenings did not include us young ones. That was "the girls' night out." Mama, Aggie and Maggie would spend hours after an early supper that evening getting ready for their fling. When they were finally dressed, they looked and smelled like actresses, but "like nice actresses" we hurried to tell them. We always thought that Mama looked the best! Instead of her usual housedress and apron, she was elegant in a smart suit or in her best coat. Her thick, dark, shining hair, smelling of tar soap, which was the popular shampoo those days, was neatly tucked in and around and under a gorgeous plumed or feathered hat. They all carried fancy beaded or crocheted bags, one more beautiful than the other. The bags usually contained a fancy hanky, a powder puff, a fancy coin purse, and a pair of opera glasses. As I remember, the anticipation on their glowing faces was the most beautiful part of their outfits.

The "fling" usually consisted of a show at the Davidson, Pabst, or the Schubert theatres, followed by a late supper at Charley Toy's, the Princess or Tillema's. One of the girls' favorite actors was Harry Minturn who played some of the leading roles for the Harry Minturn Stock Company at the Schubert Theatre. He became the idol of many a female, old and young. The Davidson was the leading theatre for touring dramas, while the Pabst was the center for all of the operas and concerts that came to Milwaukee. These were all expensive luxuries for these hard working maidens but they had carefully saved up for their annual extravagance, and these expenses were chalked up to "cultural and social treats."

After hugging and kissing each one of us kids, the "girls" gathered up their long skirts, and hiked two blocks to catch a streetcar or a jitney bus on National Avenue. Either one of these means of transportation took them downtown for a nickel. Their final extravagance of the evening was to take a taxicab home, which they also charged up to "social experience."

The morning after "the fling" usually was pretty special too. There were always treats for us kids. Sometimes it was a box of saltwater taffy or a bag of caramel corn, or a box of chocolates. Sometimes it was little glass novelties filled with tiny candies. For years I saved a little glass telephone, a little boat, a gun and a train—all made of glass, all pleasant memories of "the girls' night out."

Occasionally, at the end of the sewing week, the dressmakers' young men came to call, and Mama and Papa would join them for an evening at the Schlitz Palm Garden. The same delightful anticipation and prepara-tion went on during the day for this event. The girls went about in their pretty dust caps all day to hide the kid curlers that lay like corkscrews on their freshly sham-pooed heads. We kids were full of anticipation too as we dreamed of the wonderful surprises that we would find as our reward for their romantic night on the town. We were never disappointed. Those mornings after were even more fruitful since the male companions tried to outdo each other to show their character in making little children happy.

The sewing week came to an end all too soon. The sewing room was tidied up. The sewing machine was closed and put away in its corner. The newly made garments were carefully hung away. Aggie and Maggie packed their suitcases and went on their way back to their regular jobs. Maggie was a housekeeper for a well-to-do family in town. Aggie went on to another sewing job in someone else's home. Mama went back to her regular routine of being a housewife, mother and storekeeper.

Today, it is hard to believe that this delightful week was "the girls' vacation." These many years later, it all still seems filled with wonder. What a happy harvest of wearing apparel and pleasant memories of those weeks we reaped when the dressmakers, Aggie and Maggie, came to our house to sew.

AUNT JOLEE'S FEATHER-STRIPPING BEE
Alma M. Fabisch

The afternoon sun shone pale through the haze. It was the time of year when winter was loathe to recede, yet spring did not yet have strength enough to take over.

The countryside was bleak and dirty, waiting for the rains to wash its face.

Maggie left her companions at the crossroads after school. She took a less familiar path on the dirt road to the west. The teams and wagons had made deep ruts on warmer days, and so she picked her way along the edge, stopping occasionally to poke a booted toe through thin ice, or run along a dirty icy bank that had been a deep snow drift a few weeks earlier.

Maggie hummed as she went, keeping time by tapping the dinner bucket that had once been a lard pail against the buckles of the schoolbag slung over one shoulder. One stubby braid of her blond hair had come undone. She stopped to check her pocket to feel the ribbon that had held it that morning.

Mamma had said to her after breakfast, "Come directly to Aunt Jolee's, I'll be helping at the feather-stripping bee." Maggie did not know what a "feather-stripping bee" was like, but she really didn't care. Anything at Aunt Jolee's was fun.

In the springtime, if she was lucky, she could sometimes find a box of yellow ducklings behind the kitchen range on a cold wet day. Uncle Beck always let her hold one of the tiny bits of fluff, and as she held them to her ear in cupped hands, they said "wheat, wheat, wheat" in a contented way. Sometimes there was a gangly pale gosling or two, already showing spots of grey. Maggie liked to watch them, but they were not her favorites.

On summer days the half-grown birds seemed always to be asking for food. Maggie knew where to find the wet mash to sprinkle into their V-shaped wooden troughs. She liked to fill the deep round water pans, and watch them swim around, dunking their heads, then saying, "quack, quack."

In fall the birds roamed through the grove and pasture, foraging some of their food. In late afternoon she watched them come home, single file, like schoolchildren marching to class. Uncle Beck always had the feeders full, and the gate open into their low boarded pens. They were less friendly then, and often flapped their wings and made scolding sounds.

She was now nearing the farmyard when Laddie the family collie gave a welcoming bark. Uncle Beck looked up from the basket of corn he was filling at the crib and called, "Hurry Megs, I need your help." Maggie quickly put her things on the nearby wagon seat, and followed Uncle Beck on his round of chores. They gathered the eggs from the hen house, fed corn to the hogs, and scattered hay and ground grain to the cattle.

Maggie could hear a dozen women seemingly all talking at once, even before they opened the kitchen door. Small children were running about, their clothes and hair white with feather down. The women sat at a long table in the dining room, piles of feathers before them. It was like an assembly line, and as the feathers were passed along the women grasped those with hard quills by their tips and pulled off the down, discarding the quills in boxes at their feet. Aunt Jolee was gathering the finished piles and putting them into cloth bags. She smiled and said, "Here's your Mamma, Megs — and I'll bet you're hungry." Maggie found her mother and stood watching the women work. Aunt Jolee had removed nearly everything from the room, so it seemed barren. Maggie wondered whether she would have to miss her supper.

Soon the men began coming. Some sat at the kitchen table for a game of cards; the others just sat around to talk of the weather, crops, and so on. Someone shouted, "That's all Jolee." The men tied the bags and carried them to the shed while Uncle Beck emptied the boxes of quills. Everyone helped to tidy the rooms, and before Maggie remembered she was hungry, stacks of dishes, sandwiches, potato salad, baked beans, pickles, plates of cake, and all sorts of good food were brought from the pantry.

Tired children, and no doubt tired parents, soon retrieved their wraps from the big spare bed. Nearly all had lanterns as they stepped out into the cold and starry night. Some had a horse and buggy, or small milk wagon, but Maggie and her parents walked. It was not far across the fields, and Papa carried the lantern to light the way. He carried Maggie too, piggyback style, the last part of the trip and she sleepily asked, "How soon will Aunt Jolee get her ducklings again?"

KETTLE OF GOLDEN BUBBLES
Kathleen Knutson

When flapjacks steam under their sweet blanket of maple syrup, years float backwards and I am a kid again.

As the spring sun melted the snowbanks the sap in the maple trees began to rise. The small notches cut in one of the tree trunks oozed liquid.

In the evening Pa and Grandad came to the house with an armful of sumac stems. The whole family took part in making the sap spiles, or spouts, from the branches.

Over a flat block of wood, Pa chopped the straight branches every six inches, then split them in half lengthwise. Grandad slanted one tip with his pocket knife while Mamma and I scraped out the soft, brown centers, mak-

ing half-pipes that looked like little boats with one end. This lasted until late in the evening.

Next morning the clang of pails and the excited talking of men brought me out of bed with a start. I hurried into my clothes.

Pa was the first to finish breakfast and put his warmest lumberjack clothes on, disappearing outside. Mamma started packing food into a big market basket. This meant that the whole day would be spent in the woods preparing for tomorrow's syrup fire.

Outside I could hear the click of old Nobby's hooves, the grate of sleigh runners on the gravel stones and the impatient snort of the big white horse as Pa brought him to a stop.

I put on my warmest jacket. Although the March sun was warm, the wind was cold and cutting. Grandad, now robed in a long raccoon coat, cap and mittens, took my hand in his and we walked to the cutter.

Riding in the old-fashioned, shiny, black cutter with its red plush upholstery, and tucked in with a buffalo hide robe brought giggles of delight.

Nelly and Nobby were a team of snow-white horses. Nobby was hitched to the stoneboat loaded high with a big cast iron kettle, milk cans, spiles and two-quart tree buckets. This procession entered the woods.

Where the maple trees grew thickest, Grandad stopped old Nobby, tying him to a small sapling.

"Is this where the syrup fire is going to be?" I asked Grandad.

He nodded. "All these maple trees," he explained looking about him, "are what we call our sugar bush."

"Why call it that?" I asked.

"Well, I guess it's because of the sugar we get from the bushy maple trees."

Nelly and Pa now joined us with the load of tin and iron utensils. Pa took a drill from the load and was already boring holes in the huge tree trunks and fitting spiles into them.

Carrying the tree buckets that were about the size of a two-quart honey pail, I followed behind him, hanging them on the spouts and thrilled to the musical "ting" as the first drops of sap hit the empty bucket's bottom. Soon the woods echoed the rhythmic "ting, ting, ting" as more buckets were hung in place.

When Pa and I returned to the boiling place, Grandad had the kettle ready to hang on the rod over a scooped-out place in the ground. Together they pulled fallen limbs as near as they could to the kettle, cutting them in easy-to-handle sizes.

The big gold watch that Grandad pulled from his pocket told us that it was eating time. Pa kindled a bonfire of small branches and hung the coffee pail over it. Grandad brought the heavy market basket of food from the cutter. A fallen log was cleared for a comfortable place to sit. Feeding sacks were adjusted to the heads of the two horses. Then we all sat down to a tasty meal, spiced by the smell of burning tamarack boughs and lulled by the warm crackling fire.

After lunch, I walked from tree to tree to see how fast the sap was running. Thus the afternoon lapsed into dusk and we journeyed home.

I rose before dawn the next morning. The day began much the same as the one before.

In the woods I inspected the buckets. Each was full to the brim. Pa drove Nelly with the stoneboat laden with milk cans through the woods, emptying the buckets into cans.

After Pa had poured the sap into the kettle, the fire was started, blazing golden red around it. Soon it began to bubble. As Grandad stirred, the bubbling liquid sent up steam that floated skyward. Now a sweet aroma filled the air as the boiling, bursting bubbles let off little gusts of steam that mingled with the perfume of the burning tamarack.

For nearly six hours Grandad and I stirred the contents in the kettle, which by now was reduced to much less than half. As the fire burned low, the sap was stirred and ladled so it would not scorch.

Pa called to Grandad from the outer circle of trees. "Finished cooking the sap?"

"It's ready to apron off. We can take it now," Grandad answered.

They fastened a clean flour sack over the milk can and Grandad and Pa poured pails of auburn, sweet syrup into it.

At the house that night the milk cans were carried in. Next morning a clean clothes boiler, now full of maple syrup, sat on the kitchen range.

I loved this last stage of the boiling down process. For this "sugaring off" Mamma gave me a cup of cold water. Every now and then I was allowed to dip out a teaspoon of syrup and drop it into the cold water. When it became thick on the bottom of the cup it was done.

That night around the dining room table with several neighboring families, we had a "waxing off" party. Each person was given a saucer of clean snow and a cup of syrup. As the warm syrup was poured on the cold snow it became yummy maple wax. I can't think of any other candy as sweet and exciting as this.

THRESHING TIME, 1910
Alexa Young

For a child of six, the anticipation of it all was almost too much to be borne, because everything connected with the annual threshing spelled pure excitement. The coming and going of the big, horse-drawn wagons entering the yard, filled with bundles of golden grain, and returning empty to the fields; the hearty exchange of pleasantries, or banter, between the drivers, who, in spite of the work, and the heat, seemed to be in a festive mood; the sumptuous meals Mother always prepared for them—these all contributed to the feeling, as the big day approached, that there must be a gas-filled toy balloon inside me.

It always began with the unannounced contest, between my brother and me, as to which of us would first see the steam engine come into view, on top of the high hill adjacent to our farm. That belching, puffing black monster was an awesome thing, and the fact that it was not able to descend by the steep, stony, winding road, but instead, would cut through Mr. Kasten's hillside pasture, seemed, somehow, to add to the drama of its arrival.

Threshing was a co-operative undertaking, each farmer sending at least one wagon, and one or two men to each farm in the neighborhood.

After the engine and separator were finally in place near the big barn, the whistle would be blown, and the first drivers would begin to feed bundles into the machine. At this time, one would, naturally, wish to go near, to see the actual process of threshing. I can still recall the day my father, his hand firmly holding mine, led me to the area of activity, and (although I'm sure that he was a busy man) took the time to explain to me what was going on inside the big separator. At the time, I was most impressed by the small device on the grain spout which registered the number of sacks of threshed grain. To think that a mere gadget was able to count as high as I, who had finished a whole year of school! Before he headed me back to the farmhouse, he showed me, from a safe distance, the very long, heavy, twisted power belt, which joined engine and separator and which flapped dangerously. Dad explained this very real hazard, and warned me never to come to the threshing area, unless my brother or sister had hold of my hand.

My elder brother was the stacker. He and Dad believed that a smooth, neatly proportioned straw stack was a thing of beauty, and that the man who was able to build one had reason to be proud of his skill. So, while a few farmers were content to have a free-blown pile of straw, my brother spent all day walking about on the soft surface of the stack, directing the flexible blower here and there, and touching up the outer edges with his fork. It was a dusty, prickly, unpleasant job, and by evening he was exhausted. I could easily understand why, because, in winter, when my own short legs had to be lifted high in order to plow through the deep, soft Wisconsin snow, they became very tired too.

Within a few days, he would tidy up the ground at the base of the stack, and then a little girl could play her annual, personal game of "I spy." It was the short, cut ends of binder-twine I was after, for they would be visible here and there and were easily pulled out of the stack. The finding was the fun part, but, knowing how saving my Swiss and German parents were, I always hung them on a hook in the farm workshop.

It was at about this time, too, that my middle brother would lean a ladder against the stack, and we would climb up to the top and slide down the slippery sides. This was jolly fun and could be repeated until some grown person caught us.

Near noon, the engine whistle was sounded again and the men gradually moved toward the house, where they first refreshed themselves with beer drawn from the keg set up under one of our ancient burr oak trees. Soft drinks were available for children and Methodists. Soap, water and towels, too, were available nearby.

The meals were served on the long kitchen table. The room was not too crowded because the big Monarch wood range had long since been moved out to the summer kitchen. The table was well stocked with meat, potatoes, gravy, two hot vegetables, stacks of homemade bread, real butter, an assortment of Mother's pickles, relishes, and preserves, and, of course, an unlimited supply of coffee, cooked in the huge granite pot. At noon the dessert was pies, and at suppertime, cakes and cookies. Our farm was larger than most, so Mother had to prepare to feed threshers for at least two-and-one-half days. Roasts were served at noon, and fried potatoes, home-cured meats, sausage, and cheese for supper. But the high point for us children was the final supper, for then we would always have "bought" wieners, an item rarely purchased, since we made our own sausage.

Immediately after supper, all of the men went home, except two: the engineer and the fireman. They would spend the night in one of our spare bedrooms because it was necessary for them to get up so very early. It seems it took a very long time after a fire had been built in the engine to get up a proper head of steam. At age six, strangers sleeping in our house gave me an uneasy feeling; understandable, since as recently as the year before I would always hide behind our little smokehouse if a stranger drove in while I was playing out-of-doors.

Naturally, everyone hoped for good weather during threshing time, and each farmer felt relieved when his grain was safely in the bins. But only one of our neighbors ever voiced his feelings. When his threshing was finished, he is said to have remarked, for all to hear, "Well, good! Mine's done. Now it can rain!" It was so typical of my parents' understanding of human nature, that my father seemed merely amused when he related it to Mother, who said, "Oh, he couldn't have meant that. He simply didn't think before he spoke."

THRESHING ON THE FARM
Mary McCrorey

One of the most enjoyable events of my childhood was threshing. I loved to hear the machine coming with the engine's chug! chug! and see the black smoke puffing into the air while the long shrills of whistles announced its soon arrival and warned father to be ready to thresh.

The whole farm was a whirl. The barnyard was excited. The roosters crowed, the gobblers gobbled, the hens cackled and the guineas with their clatter nearly drowned out all the noise the others made. In the pasture the horses snorted and ran round and round. Only in the pig lot was everything calm and content. There was good straw bedding, plenty of feed and water. What more could a hog want?

Meanwhile I was sizing up help, wondering on which young man's wagon I wanted to display my skill of economizing space and loading more bundles than anyone else.

Agreed. All set. We started out. If there were to be any awards, the ground pitchers wanted us to earn them.

He threw those bundles up so fast we were nearly exhausted by the time the load was ready for the machine. On the way I became a "bouncing betty." The driver hit all the bumps and ditches to make me so. He kept looking back to see if we were both still there—and we were — holding hands. We both needed support and knew it. Our load threshed out more grain than any other. Only reward was praise, and we did a lot of crowing over that.

Loading the next load was equally as interesting, maybe a little more romantic. A message was waiting for me to report to the house. There Mother said, "You are now half-past fourteen, old enough to help with dinner and too young to chase boys. You may help set the table and keep flies off food while the threshers eat."

I didn't like my assignment but did see a possibility: one thresher who always called me "Mollie" — I showed my dislike for him when I filled his hat with fireflies when he visited with my father on our front stoop, but he ignored my gesture. I thought now I just might get a chance to swat a fly on his bald head. I got the chance but felt sorry for the fly and didn't swat.

Screens were homemade frames of wood with mosquito netting tacked where wire now is used. There was a strip of paper fringe sewed on a calico strip and tacked across the top of screen. When the door opened the fringe flopped and scared the flies away on the outside. On the inside three or four people waved the towels to push those on the inside to the outside. I was given a willow branch with a bunch of leaves on the end to fan the flies away from the food so the men could eat in peace. We turned the plates upside down over the knives and forks as likewise the tumblers so as to start the threshers off without a speck.

Counting the machine crew, help in field, water boys, neighbor women and children plus a couple stragglers, Mother served thirty dinners.

When the machine was gone, we children cleaned up the wheat the sacker had spilled on the ground lest a stray animal gorge itself, bloat up and die.

In the meantime we were looking forward to threshing time next year.

THRESHING DAY ON THE FARM
Mrs. Tillman Dahl

In recalling my childhood, I believe the conditions under which we lived could be considered the best possible. With my seven sisters and brothers I was brought up on a farm with a lovely wooded area where we played and explored to our heart's content. Also we were blessed with a wonderful set of grandparents, living in another house on our farm, whom we loved to visit, especially since they would usually have some little treat for us. With so many siblings, money was scarce so we had few toys, but we were quite imaginative in the games we played and we enjoyed each other's company. In common with most children, I'm sure we took many of our blessings for granted.

One occasion, however, that we did appreciate and looked forward to in our younger years was threshing day. It ranked in our minds almost with Christmas and Independence Day in importance. In those days, the neighboring farmers would all band together and go from farm to farm helping each other with the task of bringing the oats, barley and wheat from the fields to be threshed out in a machine that would be taken from farm to farm in turn. The huge threshing machine was drawn and powered by an equally enormous steam engine. When the operator of the machine would complete the work at each farm, he would blow several ear-splitting blasts on the steam whistle to let the next farmer know he would soon be there. When our turn came, we children would wait as close to the driveway as we dared for the half-fearful thrill of seeing the two monsters pass slowly by.

In the meantime, the women of the family would busy themselves with preparing food for the twenty or more men. There was, I believe, a small amount of friendly rivalry among the neighbors as each one tried to compete with or outdo the others. So the meals were sumptuous, usually consisting of several varieties of meats, relishes, vegetables, breads and desserts. Since we were a large family and of necessity were fed plainly and even frugally, we waited each year for this feast with much anticipation.

Our dining room was huge and all the tables available were pushed together to make one long enough to accommodate all the men at the same time. I recall how mortified my mother was when two tables somehow separated and one unfortunate fellow received a plateful of food in his lap.

The youngsters who were old enough to help were pressed into service bringing water from the well some distance away. To do this, we had to pass between the machine and the teams of impatient horses with wagons waiting their turn at the machine. So it was an adventure, half-pleasurable and half-frightening each time, and of course, that being our only source of water, we made numerous trips.

As we grew older, the glory of the day began to fade as we realized the enormous amount of work required of both the men and women. Besides bringing the sheaves of grain to the machine and pitching it in, the threshed-out grain had to be hauled to the granary and emptied into bins. Also, one man would be responsible for creating a presentable and weather resistant stack from the straw.

In 1928 I married my own farmer and then I was the one who had to take charge of the food preparation. By that time, steam engines had been replaced by tractors and the machines were smaller so we didn't have as large a crew to feed as in the older days. My sister-in-law and I helped each other with the cooking and somehow we managed. But the excitement had left the occasion forever and we were always happy when it was done.

Later, combines came into use and threshing day became a thing of the past. But I still cherish the memories of those long-ago days.

THE EXPERIENCES OF A COMMON LUMBERMAN
Irving Goessl

My parents moved up from Manitowoc County in 1884 because the farmland there was so overgrown with Canada thistle. In Clark County such a pest was unknown. Dad bought eighty acres of virgin timber in this area for six hundred dollars. The Poplar River had its source very near to this farm. Four miles from our property men had built a large dam on the river and when the gates of that dam were opened in the spring and the logs were let out, the log drivers would run the logs on the high waters all the way down to LaCrosse. The men would walk along the river banks and guide the logs to their destination.

Dad sold hemlock logs, landing them right on our own property at the river banks. In those days he received two and a half dollars per thousand for the logs which had been scaled by a scaler who went along the river before it broke up. Each owner would have his name on the rollway of the logs and would then be paid by what the scaler found there at the time. Barney Brady was in charge of the men who floated the logs and he used to let some of us boys sit on the banks and watch the workers. It was a sight that I'll never forget. We didn't see any of the men break rollways because this took place farther down the river from where we were allowed to sit, but it was enough of a sight to see the entire river filled with floating logs.

There was a sawmill at Curtiss, five miles from our eighty acres, and the owner would have paid us three dollars a thousand for the logs, but Dad would have had to haul the logs into town. This would have been expensive so he just hauled them about one hundred rods from where he cut them to the river bank where they would be floated down to LaCrosse with the rest of the logs on the banks. One advantage of the sawmill was that it would take logs other than hemlock. Here one could sell basswood but they would scale only the white wood around the sides; and the heart, which was redwood—about a six by six—would be tossed out and burned. One could go to the mill and ask for the redwood to be cut into lumber. All one had to pay was the price of the saw bill, which came to about three dollars a thousand. Other hardwood such as birch and maple had no sale at all. Pine was in the greatest demand at the time. Afterwards the hemlock was used because it could be floated down the river.

The hardwoods wouldn't float, and if they were taken to the sawmill to be cut into lumber there would be no sale for them because everyone in the area had his own lumber.

During these years of the 1880s we lived in a log house that my dad had built completely by hand for us. Dad began clearing brush and stumps away and digging a hole for the cellar just by hand with a shovel. He hewed the logs and built the house using neither a hammer nor a square. Every window in this first house of ours would open. To assure this, Dad was careful to construct the windows with great precision. He used a saucer of water to level the sills and a string with a little stone tied to it that he held up to get the sides of the windows straight. He had just a common wooden hatchet to drive the nails. The logs were plastered with sand and lime and that house stood from 1884 until 1906.

Dad was not really a lumberman but was considered a farmer at the time, although his main occupation was lumbering since he had bought timberland. After he had a little clearing, he bought a yoke of oxen and one cow. In the wintertime he would work out in a logging camp about three miles from our homestead. The lumber camp where Dad lived in the winter consisted of two large buildings built somewhat like a barn. One building was the cooking shanty and the other the sleeping shanty. They didn't need much else because from sunrise to sunset they were out working and were too tired to think about any forms of entertainment. They were just glad to get to their own beds.

The usual logger's wage in the 1880s was sixteen dollars per month. However, if the men would stay until the camp broke up in the spring, they would have their wages increased to twenty dollars per month for the entire winter. Dad stuck it out until everything broke up so he got the top wages of a lumberman at the time.

Life was not luxurious but a man did an honest day's work and I believe we were much happier without the tensions of modern-day society.

NO ORDINARY CAMPFIRE
Samuel H. Thut

This campfire was on the bank of Rib River below the Dells, at a small clearing in a beautiful stand of virgin hardwood—during the last week of March 1921. This campfire and the others of them for the twenty-one days of this log drive were perhaps the only comfort this crew of rivermen enjoyed. The food was excellent but the other accommodations were as simple as that of the native American Indian.

A person of this age of affluence and with an ignorance of the past, upon seeing this would believe it to be a primeval rite, only there was no dance or worship: this was a crew of log drivers drying their underwear while holding up their shirts and trousers after a sunup to sundown day of wet, cold, hard work. Contrary to some versions, going to bed with wet clothes or even damp ones was unthinkable at that season of the year.

In northern Wisconsin the last week in March and the first two in April the weather can be anything but pleasant. During the night the temperature can go below zero with very little warming during the day. However, with the ice out and the river running full from melting snow the logs had to be driven or guided downstream to the boom that held them at the sawmill.

These men were to loggers the highest order of lumberjacks. They loved adventure, hardship and danger. Their shoes were "corked" with sharp hardened steel spikes in order to work on slippery logs, ice, or moss-covered and slippery rocks. Their clothes were pure wool and that included their underwear which was either red or gray flannel or woolen knit.

It was this underwear and their socks that most needed to be dried. The old saying—if you wore woolen clothes it did not make any difference how wet and cold you were, you would always be warm and dry—applied to a man only while he was working or active.

After supper, served picnic style, dished up by the cook and cookie from the wanigan, the campfire was the next most important event. There was no warm camp bunkhouse to go into, only a tent with no heat, with pads to sleep on and enough blankets to keep out the cold. It was the discomforts of the log drive that separated the men from the boys. The campfire or the sunny side of the river were the only ways to escape discomfort.

Not the Boy Scout or Indian type of campfire but a campfire big enough to dry the clothes of thirty men was needed. The two men that moved the wanigan each day after the move down river would cut several hard maple or birch trees into four-foot lengths, split them and cross-pile the split wood and larger limbs into a pile five or six feet high. In the bottom several tiers of finer dry limbs or dry "rampike" wood was built in for kindling or a starter. When the crew was all into the campground this pile was lit and by the time supper was over it was a roaring, well-controlled fire. Now the drying ritual started. Each man who was wet took off his shirt and pants and held them up to the fire to dry, turning himself in the process to dry the underwear he was wearing. The distance he stayed from the fire was governed by the amount of heat he could stand. As the fire got hotter the circle became larger. It was surprising how fast the underwear would dry. Heat from the body and the intense heat from the fire would make steam rise in the cool or cold evening air.

Through all this these men maintained their dignity and never took off their undergarments. Modern day "streaking" would come fifty years hence. These men had identity; their thrills came from their skills and endurance.

Skeptics might say did they ever take a bath? Well, they never took one before they went to work. Their baths were a fringe benefit no other occupation enjoys and it was as easy as falling off a log. This writer enjoyed sixteen of them in twenty-one days. Now these baths were not the type in which you linger long or luxuriate. It was back to the bank and hustle to keep warm. After all, the lumber company was paying top wages for the work of driving their logs to the mill and was unconcerned about your pleasure or body odor.

MY JOB IN A SAWMILL
Jerry F. Condon, Sr.

A thirteen-hour shift in a sawmill isn't any way to riches. Take it from me! I know.

It wasn't as hard as pulling a crosscut, from daylight till dark, wading in knee-deep snow, carrying a crosscut saw, a pair of wedges, a pair of axes, a little bottle of coal oil, to keep the saw from sticking in the frozen tree, plus a measuring pole eight feet long.

My eighteen-year-old back muscles still ache, just thinking about it now. My partner and I didn't know of a better way to make a living in those days. But we were willing to learn.

We got a job in the sawmill in Stratford. It seemed to us to be a very good idea. The mill cook was the very best in town. The "night life" in Stratford presented a glittering array of entertainment—compared to life in a lumber camp.

You could dance with real girls, instead of a lumberjack with a handkerchief around his arm to mark him as a girl. Our camp fiddler only had a few tunes that he could play, without "fouling" up.

We considered ourselves very fortunate indeed, with a high-paying job, thirty dollars a month. And to "live right in town." How lucky can you get.

We went to work at 7:00 a.m. and by noon we had an hour lunch break. The head sawyer, old Frank Lassieg, came to work via a horse and rig, and he took his meal right in town, at his home. The old horse that he drove was piloted by Frank's daughter, who surrendered the lines to Frank when he crawled in to drive home. Then she would drive home again, till evening. He was a tremendously big man, and when he drove the buggy settled down on the springs till it appeared it must be about to tip over. His daughter would slide over to let him drive the horse and it would tip-tilt up the road, crab fashion.

We would carry our lunch in a dinner pail, complete with jar of coffee which would be a trifle cold at noon. We hadn't ever heard of thermos bottles. Maybe we enjoyed our cold beef sandwiches so much, we were sure we were "living in the lap of luxury." No kidding.

I was picked to turn cants, and ride the carriage. I was an expert with a canthook, could move fast enough to fill the bill. A sawmill carriage is driven by a cable, carrying the log past the big saw at considerable speed, and as the log came back, past the saw, the head sawyer chose which way it should be canted to obtain the maximum amount of lumber, and thickness thereof measured in one- and two-inch planks, or sawed railroad ties.

One had to be alert to the head sawyer's signal, dog the spur of the carriage into the log, and be fast enough on your feet so you remained upright while the carriage came zipping back past you for the next cut.

My first morning on the job was coming along just fine. I was anticipating Frank's signal; before he made it, I'd have the cant, turned down, dogged, and back past the saw, with effortless ease, while the scream of the saw, and clacking of the big drive belt, was in cadence with the pulse of the sawmill.

I was dreaming of the time when I could become a head sawyer, and draw forty-five dollars a month, when a birl on the log we were sawing hooked the skid, causing the set works to leap into the air, come to a screeching halt, pitching me, headfirst, into the sawdust pit, where I'd have broken my neck if the pit wasn't there. My cant hook went whizzing against the wall of the mill, ending up with a crash. Old Frank hurdled the set works and came up to the sawdust pit, puffing and blowing like a porpoise. He leaned down into dark sawdust hole, just as I was picking myself up. I blew sawdust out of my mouth, picked up my hat, and signaled Frank to give me a hand up.

"Don't tell me you ain't hurt," he wheezed. When I assured him I wasn't hurt, his only remark was, "Begod boy, you're all joints." Later that afternoon, we stopped to oil the set works, and old Frank assured me that I had the job "cinched."

My erstwhile sawing partner also said that he thought a sawmill was really a "top" job. "Just think," he said,

"We won't have to rig and file our crosscut after dark anymore. We never had life so easy. We have it made. There's several million feet of logs piled along those rollways. And there's a million houses that need building in this country."

I worked several years in the mill. Old Frank and I became very good friends. We cut the last stand of virgin pine in Marathon County. It was located along the Eau Pleine River, south of Stratford, Wisconsin.

Many years have gone by since I worked in a sawmill. Many changes have taken place since those bygone days. I've considered myself privileged to have seen changes in life and our times to a degree that no other age could ever imagine.

MY FATHER WAS THE ENGINEER
May Augustyn

Now, after so many years, the snort of diesel engines reminds me of No. 219 which my father so proudly throttled for the old Wisconsin Central Railroad in the early 1900s. Dad was fond of the 219, and often called her the "Iron Lady." She was a sturdy little engine, full of bottled hissing power when her fires were high. She had a huge black stack out of which mushroomed dense black smoke when she puffed. Her gigantic headlight looked like a full moon popping over the horizon on a summer night.

The low mournful "woo-woo-woo-woooo" of her whistle rolled over the Wisconsin farmlands and Kettle Moraine hills, sending residents of sleepy towns hurrying to the dark-roofed depot to see who got off and on the train, how many mailbags were dumped off, and if the station agent got more than one truckload of express for the moneyed gentry.

When the tubby engineer got the "highball," the signal to start, from the conductor, the Iron Lady puffed and puffed laboriously, and if her big wheels spun a bit Dad let down sand for more traction. Then she thundered off down the rails winding faster, and ever faster, across the valley and hills like a huge snake smoking a pipe.

The rail men nicknamed their fellow workers, and often these names came from the traits or tricks that the men showed. These tagged them with the rest of the fellows. "Johnny High Pockets" pulled his overalls up until the pockets were almost under his chin. The men laughed but Johnny didn't care—he wore his clothes as he wanted to.

"Mickey Doodle" was a good-natured, freckle-faced Irishman, liked by all the men. He sang and laughed into their affections.

"Knock-'em-down Jenkins" was quite another sort. He clapped people so hard on the back that he almost knocked them on their faces. Everyone learned to get out of Jenkins' way unless they wanted their spines twisted.

"Rain Barrel" was a short tubby fellow, and though the men teased him about his shape they all liked him. The teasing did not bother Rain Barrel as he went happily about his work.

One worker was never without his pipe. The men were sure he took it to bed with him, so he was nicknamed "Johnny Pipe."

"Holy Flag" boomed out on the roundhouse air. Something happened or you would not hear Holy Flag yell like that, chuckled the men. Regardless of the happening, "Holy Flag" was this man's favorite expression and explosive.

The railroad men soon learned which men to trust and like, and which ones were tricky where their own interests were concerned. One man was dubbed "Smooth Dobyns." These smooth ones were not as smart as they thought they were, for the rest of the men soon learned to gang up on them and not let them get away with their underhanded tricks.

We lived on the east side of Waukesha. Just over Gredler's Hill to the north of us was the roundhouse. The 219 stayed there when she was off duty. We children were unusually excited on a day when Dad would say to us, "Now if you children are good, I'll take you with me when I slick up the 219."

We were too small to climb aboard the 219 when we got to the roundhouse. Dad or some of the men working there boosted us up into the engine cab and onto the high leather seats. We felt we were on top of the world as we perched on the slippery seats while Dad examined the 219 to see what needed to be done.

The great bunches of waste that the men used to wipe the engines looked like ravelings of many colored threads, and were a pleasure for small hands to play with.

We peeked through the narrow front windows of the engine cab and watched the bell which Dad clanged for our pleasure. Sometimes Dad let us try to pull the bell cord, which was usually greasy from the gloves the engine men wore. We didn't have much luck ringing the bell as we were not strong enough, but it was fun to try. The sudden loud peal of the bell in the small cab space was enough to pitch us off of our seats unless we hung on tight. "Oh gee," was our reaction to the shrill sound.

The steam dome was up front near the whistle and bell. The whistle was familiar to us because Dad gave two "toots" when he reached the Arcadian Avenue crossing to let Mother know he was on his way home.

The headlight was so big we gazed at it with awe. It was even more frightening when lighted, and looked like a huge beast which might devour us any minute. It was one of those things kids love to shiver about, and we shivered in our tower on the cab seat.

Low on the front of the 219 was the cowcatcher. Dad explained to us the reason for its name: "Years ago cattle wandered onto the tracks. Some were killed, but others escaped this fate and were pushed aside or into the ditch along the tracks. When cows were killed there was trouble with the farmer, but he got no money from the railroad company. It was his business to see that the cattle were kept off the railroad right-of-way." I remember Dad telling Mother when he came home from one run, "We killed a cow today and the farmer raised hell. I don't see why they don't keep their cows fenced in."

The firebox was a dark, awesome place when Dad opened the door to show us where the firemen put the coal which kept the engine going. It took big scoops of coal to fill that cavern. I often heard Dad say in winter, "The poor fireman shoveled tons of coal because of the bitter cold and the wind bucked us all the way. He was hardly able to straighten up."

He had to keep the steam up or the train would bog down and stalling in winter was no fun for either the passengers or the train crew. It would cost the railroad company money, and the men their jobs.

It was fun to watch the engine chug up to the water tank near the track. The man in attendance pulled a long chain and a spoutlike pipe came down; the water poured through it into the engine tank where it was stored. It was forced into the boiler later as needed. When the engine had had enough to drink the man pulled the chain up, and the spout rose into space and back into place, ready for the next thirsty engine that came along. The red water tank was encircled with strong iron bands, and was a huge wooden vat mounted on four high legs.

Mother dressed us in pink, blue, and white ruffled dresses, which were not too clean when we returned from a visit to the Iron Lady. Then, too, our small sister sometimes had an accident when she was away from home and no inside conveniences were available. But in spite of these minor tragedies we had a wonderful time on our visits to the roundhouse.

Now our visits to the 219 are only cherished haunting memories, a part of Memory's Magic Web which spins the yarn for Yarns of Yesteryear, of memorable days gone forever.

FIFTY YEARS-PLUS AS A RURAL MAIL CARRIER
Clarence Rhode

I started carrying mail to the farmers on a regular route in the vicinity of Neshkoro in 1918.

When I first started there were no snowplows, therefore no roads were passable for cars in the wintertime. Cars were put on blocks for about four months.

I had horses to take me around the route—buggies and a cutter which had runners for traveling on the snow, which at times was four or five feet deep. Then I'd leave the roads and travel across the fields to get the mail to most families. Sometimes if I knew someone was expecting medicine I walked up to that party's house.

Another carrier and I built a snowmobile out of a

Ford car to use in winter. Quite different from snow-mobiles today.

To keep warm when traveling in the cold weather, I heated some bricks and stones on a stove at my rooming house. These kept my feet warm for hours in forty below zero weather.

After I traveled through the snow and made a track for them, the farmers would go to town to do their shopping.

Occasionally I used snowshoes, especially when I knew there was mail important to someone.

Mail delivery on Christmas Day was compulsory—no slogan then which said "Mail early"; so if people received a package on Christmas Day we were there to deliver it.

I had wonderful people on my route. I rejoiced with them when they received mail from their children who were away from home. I sorrowed when they received bad news.

Many little extra jobs were required of me. One note read, "If it looks like rain, please take the clothes from the line." Or, "Please take the bread out of the oven. It must be done when you come by." Or, "Will you stop in and help me turn the mattress? I am cleaning house."

One day one of my patrons walked away from his home at night and was too feeble to find his way home, so I found him and took him home.

When I started, the route was twenty-five miles long with a hundred and fifty families — when I retired in 1969 it was sixty-two miles with two hundred families.

Every year I was honored with a safety driver's pin because of no accident on the route. I drove over one million miles.

A FARMER'S PERSPECTIVE
Walter R. Wright

I was once asked to write a paper on the relationship of man's religious faith to his vocation, or how one supplemented the other. There were four of us in this group —a banker, a mortician, a college teacher and a farmer— certainly a variety of perspectives. I thought it should be easy for a farmer, as no vocation permits, or requires, man to work in closer harmony with the Creator than that of the farmer. The farmer walks daily with sunrise and sunset; no man knows better, from personal experience, what happens to seeds that fall on stony ground, or among thistles; no man knows better the comfort and richness that falls with the warm spring rain on thirsty fields. He even accepts, though somewhat reluctantly, the fact that the rain falls equally on the just and on the unjust. He accepts philosophically the awesome majesty of the storm that destroys his crop, or the water laid a foot deep over his entire field of corn, as I have experienced it. No man knows better, or works more closely, with the natural laws that govern birth and life and death. No man is more conscious of the beauty of autumn, as the earth prepares itself for the annual death of winter, and the resurrection of spring. No man waits more eagerly for the first green mist of spring, and the first wedge of honking geese slanting down toward the pond. Of all the months, I think April is the favorite of the farmer; September and October carry the vivid beauty of autumn and the richness of harvest, but April is always full of the continuing promise and hope of spring. The farmer plants, not only seeds, but dreams, as well. I never experience an April without recalling Jane Merchant's lines:

We know that April always comes again;
We know that April never comes to all.

From my youth, I have rich memories of rising on misty May mornings to hear the drumming of prairie chickens in the marsh to the south; or, on quiet August evenings, hearing the quail clearly insist that his name is "Bob White," from the wheat stubble across the road; or, on hot summer nights, hear the whippoorwill's insistent call from the woods adjoining our farm. These sounds are all gone now — in our area — but the memories are rich and unforgettable.

One of my richest delights has been walking through the August cornfields, with the tall, erect, male tassels high above my head, arrogant and profligate, sifting their rich pollen down upon the fragile, delicate silks just emerging from their green sheaths. And to observe, in the damp, smooth earth between the corn rows, the autograph of coon and mink and pheasant and, sometimes, the sheep-like imprint of deer.

I had an experience once that illustrates the power of the miracle of autumn. This is a true story and it occurred some years ago when I was working as fieldman for the Holstein Breeders. It was my job to meet farmers from other states who came to Wisconsin's Dairyland to build, or replenish, or improve their herds. I would take them to breeders' farms in this five-county area and help them to select and buy the kind of cattle that suited their needs. This time, the buyer was a man from Pennsylvania, who had bought here regularly for several years. He usually bought two or three semi loads at a trip. This time, he was looking for a load that would include three or four head of exceptional quality, which he could enter in a show and sale near his home. We had been traveling for several days in this immediate area without finding just what he wanted. He knew cattle, and he knew what it would take to top that show. That kind of cattle was hard to find and harder to buy. On this day, I was taking him to look at some fine herds I knew of around Oxford and Friendship. The one herd I especially wanted to show him was owned by a man with whom I had dealt before, and had found him to be honest and reliable and forthright. He had one fault that bothered me a little. He seemed unable to complete a single sentence without sprinkling it liberally with profanity. I do not believe he even realized he was doing it.

This was one of those bright, sunny, mid-October days, still with the warm sun of summer, but with Indian-summer cobwebs floating in the air, and the "haze on the far horizon." The hills and fence rows were screaming with color. It was almost overwhelming. This man's pasture was out below the bluffs that outline the course of the Wisconsin River, above Friendship. While Pennsylvania and I were extremely conscious of the beauty surrounding us, we did not bother to comment on it. We were sitting on our heels, in the pasture, talking pedigrees and records and prices. During a pause in the conversation, there was an exclamation from the farmer. We turned toward him and—in deference to my boyhood training—I shall have to paraphrase, most inadequately, what the man actually said, but he was looking off across the field, and he said, "Look at that blankety-blank bluff; ain't it purty as hell!" We were somewhat shocked, but we agreed that it was, and went back to cattle talk. On the way home, we discussed this incident. (By the way, this buyer happened to be a Sunday School teacher in his Dutch Reformed Church, back home.) We both agreed that there was awe and reverence in his tone, if not in his words. We agreed that, if God heard it — and we were sure He did—He would know that it came from the heart and not from the mouth. But there *we* were—almost suffocated by outrageous beauty, but forbearing to mention it, while this man had an irresistible paean of praise torn from him. And paean of praise it was! Of course, David said it better when he wrote, "The heavens declare the glory of God and the firmament sheweth his handiwork!" But, David was a king, *and* a poet, *and* a musician.

And right here I learned a lesson, which is the moral of this story and the reason for telling it, a lesson I have not forgotten, nor ever will: I, in my own conceit, had judged this man. I had judged him to be incapable of an appreciation of beauty, or those things we lump together and refer to as "culture." I had considered him coarse and insensitive. I was ashamed of myself. Why will people who consider themselves Christian never learn not to pass judgment on their fellow mortals, judgments often based on misunderstanding, or insufficient evidence, or plain prejudice? Why will they continue to ignore one of the most direct and explicit admonitions, and one of the briefest, in the Sermon on the Mount: "Judge not, lest *ye* be judged!"

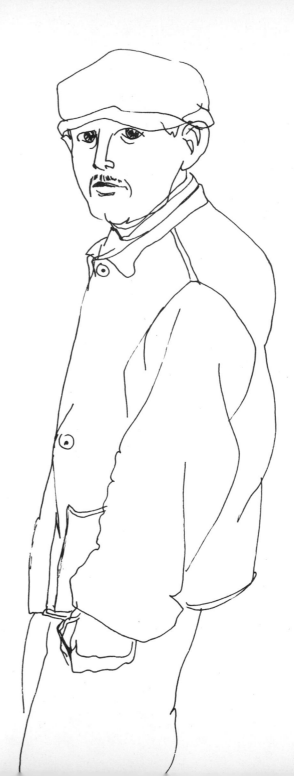

6 HARD TIMES

WORLD WAR I, A CHILD'S MEMORY
Ruth Burmester

July 13th, 1918

Appointment at the dentist's — dreadful day! Filling that six-year-old molar the dentist is, and I cannot breathe well with the rubber dam clamped across my mouth. My heart sinks as I see a new file being put in the drill.

Dr. Thompson has white hair and long white moustaches. He makes me think of the picture of Dreyfus in the bound copies of *The Review of Reviews* at home. Halfway between elbow and shoulders are arm bands that hold the sleeves of his immaculate white shirt up out of the way of his work. If the pain makes me cry, he stops and kisses me (why do grown-ups always kiss?) and as I blink through my tears, he says, "There, there, now, Miss Ruth! Just a little more drilling; it won't be long. Just relax your mouth now, that's the stuff. You know we have to get those germs out of there, those old 'Germans,' then it won't hurt anymore."

So I steel myself for further pain. He had called the germs "Germans." Well, then, kill them. Kill them, quick! At home the grown-ups are all talking about America and the war against the Germans. War! War! The papers are full of it. Germany! Austria! France! England! Belgium! Our new hired man, "Finn," was a Belgian. He had lived in Liege, had served five years in the Belgian Army. He wanted to know all the news in the papers but he could not read English. So my brother James read them to him. After the United States entered the war, April 1917, Seraphin Van Coulter waited even more anxiously for the news in the daily mail. His mother and other relatives still lived in Belgium.

James was released early in the spring from high school. It had kept six days a week during the winter, so that farm lads could help with spring work. Everyone was urged to raise more food. Plant a Victory Garden! was the cry. Buy Liberty Bonds! Children, each week a ten-cent War Saving Stamp, fill your book! When Papa went to town for groceries he could not bring Mama her usual fifty-pound sack of sugar. No, five pounds to a family it was, and the dark, lumpy beet-sugar, poor stuff for canning, Mama said. With a fifty-pound sack of white flour, he must take substitutes, too: ten pounds of rice, rye, or potato flour. The Food Administrator, Herbert Hoover's name was spoken of blackly; he was cursed for the economies he visited on households.

In country school we felt the spirit of hate towards the Germans. Teacher and older pupils were intense with it. Atrocious things had been done to people in France— their ears, their hands cut off by the Huns. We made quilt blocks in school, sewed them together, went one afternoon to a nearby lady's house and tied a comforter. The older girls knit sweaters, socks, vests for the soldiers. Shells of hickory and butternuts were saved and taken to school; they would be sent away to be used in making gas masks for the soldiers.

Our Uncle Ray was a soldier. He had sent Mama postals and letters. She was his only sister. The messages came from Camp Fremont, California, where he was stationed with the 320th Field Signal Battalion. He wrote: "The Signal Men occupy the lookout posts at night and carry a curved knife that is used to cut the enemy's throat from the rear. The Germans hold the Signal Men in the same esteem as smallpox."

In the spring of 1918 word came: "This Division is ready for foreign service and will no doubt embark for duty abroad before June." He would, he said, prefer to remain in this country, say, as chauffeur for an officer with a 90-HP Automobile, but it looked as though he would get a ticket to France. He meant it to be "round-trip" with a stopover "in Paris, of course." And as he did not intend to "go into a cemetery feet first," she might expect to see a handsome man when he came back from France "and had time to comb his hair." And other wisecracks.

"Address not permanent" was written across the last letter from California, in his vigorous handwriting: "Direct mail as usual. We leave soon, but mail will follow."

Back to the dentist's office, that thirteenth of July— "Miss Ruth," Dr. Thompson was saying, "I guess you'll have to come back. There's another cavity, in this upper tooth here." He flicked at it with a slender pick. "We'll have to give you another appointment. How about August seventh, will that be soon enough?"

"Soon enough," I echo, feeling enormously relieved that the date is nearly a month off.

Time passed. The men folks rested, noon hours, through haying time, cultivating, and harvesting, under the shade of the trees by the front porch and James read aloud from the *Chicago Tribune*; they studied maps, talking of the war, of the Kaiser. Letters from men in service began to appear in the local papers. Our neighbor's son, Clyde Bennett, had enlisted, aged eighteen, was one of the first to go across, 32nd Division. He wrote: "I would like a picture of little Helen dressed the same as when she held that service flag for me, a picture that isn't too big to carry in my blouse pocket, for that's the only place I have to carry it; I want it to show not only her

face but all of her so that I can see how tall she really is." The Boches had got Jimmy Dempsey.

Mama took us, as was her custom, down to Devil's Lake on the train for the Country Life Picnic near the end of summer. When brother Gene was four, he had amused us all at his first sight of the lake water by saying, "Ooooh, Mama, look! It rained here yesterday!"

Many farm families were at the picnic, some of them Mama's relatives: Mary Watt and Lutie Pruyn, two older brothers and their wives, the Huntington sisters. There were great baskets of food (women contrived wonders even with substitutes): pies, cakes, sandwiches, fruit and vegetable salads, the first summer apples and plums. An hour after eating Mama would let us go swimming (in old clothes she had brought in a hamper). On the sandy beach, in the shallow water, we would have great fun. The railroad tracks were close to the picnic grounds, curved around the bluff at the foot of great granite boulders, along the east side of the lake.

As we were about finished eating, there came a train up from the south, a train with troops on board, bound for Camp Douglas. It stopped to let off a few excursionists. While they were descending the steps, some of the soldiers, from the opened windows of the train, waved, hailing the picnickers.

Mama, at the sight of them, straightened. Her mind flew to Ray. In the Signal Corps. And far from home. Perhaps right now on the battlefield of Europe. She thought, too, of her pa, in his recent grave on Walnut Hill. And of Ma, in hers, dug so soon beside him.

She swooped up a chocolate cake from the table, and off she sped. To that train with soldiers on it. Shouts awaited her coming, eager hands reached forth when she arrived, loud were the exclamations of thanks! Fat Cousin Helen, catching on quickly, followed Mama, a berry pie, a pan of caramel bars in her hands. Other ladies hastened in their wake, sandwiches hastily thrown in a towel, baskets of Whitney crabs, plums, treats for the soldier boys. Greetings and felicitations flew back and forth between the young fellows in uniforms and the mothers, sisters, relatives, of somebody-in-camp, somebody-with-the-A.E.F.

Then the engineer leaned far out his cab, saluted with his hand and made a fancy ooo-ooohing! whistle sound out over the lake waters, the conductor swung on board, the train got under way, wheel shafts pushing faster, faster. Along the serpentlike length of the coaches, as it disappeared around the curve, were waving arms of soldiers. Mama stood, her body like a statue, back to us, one hand raised in a slow oscillating motion of farewell, the other hand clutching an empty cake plate.

September brought school again for us and news of fliers fighting in France. Though they had boasted they "would be in Paris by Christmas" the Germans were being forced back in the Great Allied Offensive. The local papers showed longer enlistment columns, service flags hung from windows of nearly every home in the neighborhood. One showed a gold star: John Kropp had been killed in action. Steven Miles was burned, his eyes injured by the explosion of a mustard gas shell that killed two and wounded two others besides himself. Alvin Wheeler was severely wounded in action. "We heard the big guns start up about midnight," Clarence Bohn wrote. "They kept it up all night and all the next day. The sky was red for miles on all sides of us." Emanual Reimer told of all that could be seen: trenches, dugouts, barbwire entanglements, trees with only stumps left, shell holes one beside the other, some as big as the basement of a

house. "We went through the artillery line," he said. "And there I saw sights I did not care to see and cannot relate to you now. If Sherman could see the horrors of this war, I wonder what he would say war is now. For he never saw an aeroplane, bombs, gas shells, and the terrorizing tanks."

From Chateau Thierry, Belleau Woods, the Argonne Forest, the grim news kept coming: Andy Ray had got shell-shocked. (He was to go about our town for the rest of his life, shaking with a permanent palsy.) Tony Tasser lost a leg. Aunt Josie's son came home, the sleeve of his uniform turned up at the right elbow. Mrs. Bennett's telegram came near the end of October: "Regret to inform you your son, Clyde, killed in action at Soissons."

Early in the morning of November eleventh, as we went to school down the dusty road, swinging our dinner pails, we heard from the town, four miles off, the fire whistle blowing, blowing, the church bells ringing, ringing.

"What is it for?" we asked the teacher.

"Why, the Armistice has been signed. The war is over!" she said.

Then we shouted and ran and sang "America" and "The Star Spangled Banner" and for an hour the teacher did not hold school.

The war was over! Talk about the dinner table at home, now, was of what would be done to the "war criminals." The Kaiser. He must be punished. Little Gene slipped to Mama's side, thinking of another man who had caused much grief. "What," he asked of her, "are they going to do with Hoover?"

It was an a wash day, late in the afternoon, early part of March 1919, when Mama was bent over her tubs, that a khaki-clad figure stepped over the benches toward her. "Why, Ray! How did you get here?" Then her arms were around him and she was crying. Crying with thankfulness, relief. It was so good to see him. To see him come walking on his own two feet, feel his own two arms about her. Back from the hell he'd been through, nine days and nights on the Hindenberg Line, and out of a hundred and twenty men that went in with him, but he and eight others had come out alive. She cried and she hugged.

He held her tight. He did not cry.

"He doesn't talk about the war at all," my teen-aged brothers came complaining to Mama after a couple days had passed. "No," she said, "he doesn't." It was dusk, her hand found a match in the safe at the corner of the kitchen as the boys turned away. "He wants to forget it." She went to the window, thinking of his limp. Her eyes found the evening star on the far horizon, the new moon glowing above the hill. She thought of the letter to Clyde Bennett's mother written from a nephew then in France, soon after Armistice Day: "From almost every window in Paris the Stars and Stripes are flying and it is carried above every other flag in the crowds that parade the streets. The people gather round us, throw flowers over us, the girls try to kiss us, and the old people beg us to come and have dinner with them. They are all happy about the great victory won, but as I write this I can see one dear mother whose happiness is not so great. She had a boy in the Army, enlisted same time I did, was just my age, we were always together, though not in the same company. What he had was mine, what I had his. We came to France together, entered the lines together . . . I was sent that night with a message and as I passed Company A, I said, 'Is Bennett still with you?' Somebody spoke up 'Yes,' and I knew he was all right for the time

being. A few days later I was gassed, had to go to the hospital, and when I returned . . . they said he was killed at Soissons . . . That that night while the battle was still going on not far off, and the moon coming over the hill, they buried him with the rest of his comrades who had fallen that day . . ."

Moon coming over the hill. She turned with a sob and lifting her arms, lighted the bracket lamp. "Forget it," she breathed. "If he can."

There's a postal photo of Uncle Ray in Mama's album. It was taken when he had got back to this country, Camp Lee, Virginia. A fine figure of a man, posture ramrod straight. His uniform fits as though custommade, though it bears unmistakably a lived-in look: jacket buttoned snugly across the chest, breeches of proper drape about the knee, leggings wrapped in exactness about the well-formed legs, gloves firmly held in hand, shoes trim. His overseas cap is set at correct angle, his chin drawn tightly back, his visage stern. "Yours received," is on the back, "glad you are well, also Grandma B." "Dec. 1st I received the rank of sergeant, earned, not given." At the bottom: "Kaiser Bill's 'granite front' was churned to chalk."

No. He did not cry on that day he was reunited with his sister. It was much later. I remember how we all sensed Mama's release of tension when she heard of it. It was after he had got his discharge at Camp Fremont and had got back to the old home at Baraboo and after quite a passage of time (I have a feeling he put off going there) on a day when he went out to the cemetery with his older brother to where their parents lay in the quiet of Walnut Hill. It was a balmy summer day, the great elms spread their limbs out in benediction over all, threw shadows onto the smooth green turf of the near hillside.

Butterflies poised on flowering shrubs, birds called in the treetops. How far from this! he thought, how far. This peaceful graveyard. From the bursting shells, the mortal agony of the battlefield, the No-Man's Land where he had been. There, on Walnut Hill, alone with his brother, he sank to his knees and wept.

WAR EFFORT
Katherine T. Haefliger

In the summer of '43 young Bill waved to us, got on the bus with other army enlisted, and Hitler's tanks had knocked our world apart. The old routines seemed useless. I found a job as a timekeeper at the Ordnance plant twenty miles away. It was adventure to be with people I did not know, exhilarating to earn money, and the bus rides were delightful. Waiting for the first bus in early morning, the air was fresh and still. Birds and a passing dog looked at me with astonishment, for it is their world, that first hour of the day.

People on the bus were talkative. "The news was good last night. The radio says they invaded Japan, or maybe it was England. Or what is that other country? Oh my, what's the world coming to — all the sin in the world!"

"Oh people are pretty good."

"Well, some people, Honey."

They remarked as a pretty girl got on. She called, "You just wait till I get my permanent! I'll be so fixed up I won't speak to none of youse. Yeah, it's just too bad you ain't pretty." Laughter seized us all together.

Black-eyed Susans and dusty weeds lined the road.

"Gee, it's breezy when you get out on the road! God, it's sure blowin'!"

At the clockhouse I could hardly pull open the door. Two guards had half the little building, the timekeeper the other side. "She don't talk to us," they remarked. They kept their radio going, "O Eliza, Eliza Jane," and "Lay that pistol down, Mama." My feet moved to the music and it was hard to concentrate on counting cards and hours.

Going home from the four-to-midnight shift the bus would squeak and bump out into the dark, the only light our headlights. We would sing for a while. Always "Oh the moon shines tonight on pretty Redwing," and last "The Old Rugged Cross." It seemed an answer. Two guards were talking, "By God, we had chicken pie today. Last time it was all pie. Heh!" He slapped his knee. The other said, "I dunno why they exercise us on horses. We don't have nothin' to do with horses."

"What I think isn't fair—that darn intelligent test. Ninety-six questions! By God, that's too many questions! They see how fast your mind works -k-k-k," he clicked his teeth.

I transferred to the unloading room to inspect incoming components of grenades and bazookas. Aran unloaded and cut open the boxes. The talk was like a Bach fugue—strong bass over there, other voices in runs and turns.

"Poor old Aran! He wants to sing 'Deep in the heart of Texas,' but he don't know the tune or the time or the words."

"Next time I git married," said little Mary Lou with the dusky-rimmed blue eyes, "I'll know what to look for in a man. I got gypped last time. Boy, he promised me everything!"

"Oh no, you didn't get gypped, Mary Lou. Marriage ain't all gittin'! The older I git the harder I work, but I wouldn't give up my kids and my husband for nothing."

I asked a woman from Tennessee, "Has the TVA helped the farmers?"

"I don't know. I chopped cotton sunup to sundown."

"You could move to Illinois."

"Illinois ain't no good for cotton."

In a rest period we sat on the ground in the wide doorway. As far as one could see was only the blessed earth and blue sky. We listened to a meadowlark. At end of day we swept up the box debris. A new worker declared, "I don't sweep!"

"We ALL sweep!" shouted another.

When the bell sounded we crowded into showers, dressed in our own clothes again, and waited for the clockhouse channel to open.

Some transferred to the cartridge bay. There we sat on high stools at a long table and taped the boxes. One woman talked long, "Funny how I met him. I was working in a coffee shop. He come in there, been out on a drunk and couldn't cut his ham. I cut it for him. He had egg all over him. Next day he come back to apologize. I had a date with him. I was the dumbest cluck that ever lived. But a waitress is the only job you can tell people off. I've had lots of fun at it. I like young fellows. We talk and tease each other. Old fellows — all they think about is government."

On the night shift one woman used to fall asleep, then wake with a jump and say, "How much you got done? If that's all you got done I'll have to help you."

Conversation was continuous. "Brother, I'm for Roosevelt. Because all the things he's done has proved out right. Those big questions we don't know nothing about."

Another admonished the woman next to her, "Myrtle, don't tell them you are sick. Act interested in the work you do instead of what you can't do."

"Well I guess you never had ulcers."

"That Riley — he expects too much of people. He thinks they should be good-lookin' just for him."

When spring came, the rides were lovely, the air sweet, the sky clear, the windows wide open. Redbuds and peach trees were in bloom. Getting on the morning homeward bus, a man called, "How you fixed for seats this bus?"

"Oh there's five or six seats and nine or ten laps!" I sat down with one leg in the aisle beside a woman spread out and falling asleep.

Colonel M, an old school friend of my husband, came to inspect the plant, and he came to visit us one evening. "Well, old Mac! Come on in! We'll have a Scotch and talk it over!"

"Well Bill! How are ye?"

Their talk progressed smoothly as a string quartet, the tones crowding each other up and down, the Scotch burr like resin on a bow. His 'hrrh" and his laugh shook and rattled in his throat, his questions clear staccato. They talked of business and engineering.

I transferred to the tetryl bay. Little cups of powder were set into grenade components. These I covered with tiny disks and shoved the trays of eight along for the next job. The room was bright and cheerful, the procedure like a dance. In mind I sang to keep a rhythm, gradually increasing speed. Beginning with "O God, our help in ages past," I increased to "The Farmer in the Dell." At rest periods we stretched out on the floor or the work shelf, and talk was lighthearted. At lunch we were restrained by the presence of "white-suits" at a separate table. Their power made a difference. One bay leader reported one day, "They were loafing." But we were all joyful when production rose.

One day managers and engineers strode through, considering the introduction of an automatic conveyor. There would be no individual rates of speed. We were tense and frustrated. Working at the conveyor we became parts of a machine that controlled us. Our free spirit was gone, as the heart is missed in computerized music. Keeping the attention on a moving belt was monotonous. We lost our pride in beating our record. Production in the free bay was one-fourth greater. On Samson's treadmill I felt we would pull the plant down in our frustration. In a five-minute rest period I stepped out the wide doorway and picked up a little rock. It made them laugh.

A grenade without a safety pin went down the conveyor one day, and someone at the end called, "Somebody take dis heah—too hot foh me!"

Boarding the morning bus a baritone sounded, "We in a hurry to get out a heh this mahnin'. This bus the slowest speed I know of!" I sat beside a woman who asked me if I'd been sick, and said, "The boys in the army don't take no layoffs."

The guards talked of their travels. "The Bad Lands —they look like chocolate ice cream all crumbly."

"See any slums?"

"Plenty. They live in little shacks in little towns. But of all the worst cities I ever seen—this is it. You go downtown and nobody says 'Hello.' So unfriendly—all minding their own business."

Home was calling me back by the autumn of '44. The wild grapevine that in summer shades the back porch had blown away and left it in a sunny glow from the maple tree. Blackbirds were creaking like rusty pumps and jerking about in fallen leaves.

My adventure ended at Christmastime in Black December. Coming home, the snow was covering the earth. Our cherry tree was plastered. I shoveled off the porch, the snow a foot deep over the newspapers.

GREEN MONUMENTS
Henrietta L. Ryall

Have you ever been puzzled on a country road with no house in sight to find a sturdy hedge of lilacs just across the fence? Many years ago we were moved to stop and investigate.

It was spring. Rolling down the road, our black Model T Ford roadster zigzagged, following the ruts in the sandy road, taking my husband and me on one of his regular farm visits. A farmer at his mailbox waved a friendly greeting, and we heard him call to his wife, "There's that new County Agricultural Agent. Just out of college, and he gets two thousand a year. Wonder if he knows how to milk a cow?"

We had collected a handful of asparagus that grew along the fence rows. Then we saw one of those clumps of so-called "wild" lilacs occasionally found near the road, strangely distant from any house. We stopped for some of the flowers to carry home. In 1920, we felt free to help ourselves to most wild flowers.

"There's been a well here, see that old pipe sticking up over there?" cried my husband, going in for a closer look. Scattered about were broken bits of flowered pottery that looked like pieces of Grandma's old teapot, a broken brick, the wheel from a doll carriage. A weedy hedge proved to be asparagus, and nearby was time-honored, aromatic caraway. Surely these were the remains of someone's transient dream of a farm, and of a home of his own.

Stopping at a farm down the road (the mailbox said "Holger Hansen"), we learned the story of the lilacs. Because its poor soil could be sold cheaply, parts of central Wisconsin tempted local land salesmen to buy tax delinquent land and sell it to inexperienced prospects. Some of these innocents were city people who had childlike dreams of a carefree life of independence on a farm of their own; others were newly arrived immigrants from Europe. Later friendships revealed a wry sense of humor in these fine people, who lived in the area were were visiting that day.

"We are the best people in the world, with the world's worst land," one farmer told us.

One winter day brought Axel Miller from the city to look at a farm. Anxious to find better conditions for his young family, he purchased a farm.

"The buildings ain't much, but you can fix them up. The land is level and weed free," the land salesman pointed out. And indeed, few weeds marred the snowy fields that day when Axel Miller was farm hunting. Coupled with the background of jackpine, the weed-free fields would have told an experienced farmer, "Watch out!" But it looked fine to Axel Miller.

"Axel had big plans," said Mr. Hansen, continuing his story about the Millers. "We needed a teacher in the district school, and we were glad to hire Axel's wife, Anna. She was well trained, and we paid her thirty dollars a month. She taught two years, and then she got in the family way again." (In those days, pregnant was not a word to use lightly in mixed company.)

"It didn't show much, so we let her finish the year," concluded our new friend, with a slight smile.

The years that followed were not unkind to the Millers. With sufficient rainfall, the sandy soil raised a quick crop and provided a living and tax money. True, their savings had gone into the farm. Continued crops of rye, corn and potatoes were fast depleting the soil, a debt that must soon be paid. Some of the neighbors had found jobs in the paper mills to the north. Axel Miller still depended on his land.

A growing hedge of lilacs screened out the dust from the dirt road that passed the house. Anna had supplied many pails of water to the lilac roots. The shallow well had small capacity, and there were many demands on it, and on Anna's time and strength, but lilac time repaid Anna, filling the house with fragrance. The lilacs "earned their keep" as Anna expressed it.

A garden supplied much of the Millers' food. Anna pumped pails and pails to water the green rows. Summers were fine, but winter brought tax time, and how to pay the taxes?

"Axel, Esther says Holger got a job at Port Charles. Maybe you should see if you can get taken on," Anna suggested one day. "The pulpwood will never pay the taxes this year."

Axel had a stand of jackpine that was salable for paper pulp, and added to their small income, but fifteen years were required to replace the trees cut for each year's harvest, and Axel's small wood plot was exhausted.

When Axel applied the next day, the mill had stopped hiring. Then came the winter of despair. The summer had been dry, and crops of rye and corn had been scorched and scanty. Food became a problem. The children's school lunch sometimes consisted only of boiled potatoes.

War had broken out in Europe. In the cities there were plenty of good jobs supplying food, armaments and other materials for the allied nations. Axel left for the distant city to find work. In time, his family, with their meager belongings, joined him. They never returned, and the farm was sold for delinquent taxes.

There was no demand for delinquent tax land during the war. The modest buildings fell into disrepair. Other needy farmers cannibalized them, taking windows and doors, planks and chimney bricks. Soon there was nothing left but the perfume and beauty of the lilacs to remind passersby of the hardship and heartbreak of the Millers' futile dream.

On the back roads of that rather barren land, one still sees, after many years, hardy green lilac bushes, monuments to the industry and love of beauty of the Annas and the Esthers of past generations.

THE FOREST FIRE
Laura Carlsen

It was in the spring of 1897. We had just moved to a homestead in northern Wisconsin in what is now the Town of Crystal, Washburn County, where my father hoped to make a new start after losing our home and his dairy business in Duluth, as a result of the Panic of 1892.

We had no other means of transportation at the time, so on this particular day in April my father had set out on foot for the railroad station at Spooner, eight miles away, to meet a brother and brother-in-law, who were also in hopes of homesteading in this area between the tracts of cutover timber land which the big logging companies had recently denuded of the fine stands of white pine timber.

The slashings, pine stumps, and carpet of dry pine needles left an extremely dangerous fire hazard and, with the clearing fires of the homesteaders which frequently got out of control, forest fires were frequent.

On this day, after my father had left and my brother and I were ready to start for school (over three miles distant), my mother noticed a fine spiral of smoke about a half-mile away, where a fire had burned the day before.

Mother realized that the fire, which had apparently died out the night before, had smoldered in a stump or rotten log and needed only a gust of wind to start a new fire.

So Mother equipped my brother with a heavy wet sack and instructed him how to put out the fire. Then he was to cut across the woods and go on to school, which he did, and I had to walk to school alone.

I had just passed my eighth birthday, had never walked alone in the woods before, so whenever a rabbit scampered through the dry leaves I was terrified. But I bravely trudged on all the way to school. It was a bright morning but, as the day wore on, a pall of smoke obliterated the sun. There was "a fire somewhere" our teacher observed.

Shortly after we left for school that morning, a north wind sprang up and fanned other smoldering fires till a full-fledged forest fire came sweeping toward our humble log cabin. Mother was terrified, but had experience with prairie fires in western Minnesota as a girl. She went into action alone. No telephones of course, nor close neighbors.

She went to the spring and saturated her clothing and hair. Then, with wet sacks and pails of water, she fought the fire for over two hours. She had it under control from the north. She was exhausted and paused for a rest, then noticed that the wind direction had changed, swung to southwest, and was blowing harder. Another fire was coming from the south!

Already exhausted, but desperate, she knew that we would lose everything if she could not bring that fire under control! Her only hope now was to set "back fires," a dangerous proceeding, but the only way. She must set fires close to the cabin, then put them out as she went along, till she had covered an area that the oncoming fire could not jump or find grass enough to burn right up to the cabin. Not only was the heat intense, but the smoke was thick and choking.

It was now late afternoon and my brother and I were on our way home from school, but when we were about a mile from home the smoke became so thick we were choking, so we started to run, hoping to get out of that dense smoke. It grew worse!

My brother, who was thirteen and had better understanding than I, began to have fears that our home was gone, but, not wanting to alarm me, remarked, trying to be casual, "Better save our breath, I'm afraid it's thicker further on."

And just before this, my father and his brothers returning home had the same thought. My father said, "Boys, I'm afraid we will have no place to sleep tonight!" But, as they made the last turn in the road into our clearing, through the thick smoke—there stood the cabin! And Mother, completely exhausted, hair and eyebrows singed, was there to meet us as my brother and I arrived at about the same time. "The spirit of the pioneers"—in a courageous woman—had saved our humble home!

7 HEALTH

TONSILLECTOMY IN 1892
Ottilie Mueller

I was born in November 1884, and greatly troubled with tonsilitis during early childhood. My temperature would be much higher than normal until white specks formed on my swollen tonsils. I would be very sick and weak for a while after the fever had left.

It seemed there was no help known to prevent the frequent recurrence of a sore throat, which always ran its full course in spite of gargling and folk medicine. Mother used to swab my tonsils with pulverized alum. The flavor and puckering in my throat was not very pleasant. But what I really dreaded was the bandage of a piece of real fat bacon sprinkled with pepper and long enough to reach across the front of my throat from ear to ear to cover the tonsil area from the outside. This bacon, with peppered side next to the skin, was tied around the neck and kept there until the skin had blisters. Then it was replaced with a soft cloth and a layer of cotton batting for several days.

At that time Wausau was still known as Wisconsin's hinterland or as the native Americans called it, the Far-Away Place. But somehow rumors had circulated that tonsils could be removed with surgery.

My parents, fearing I would not live long enough to grow up, decided to find out about this method. Mother took me to see the only surgeon in town—Dr. Sauerherring. He was smoking a big cigar when we entered his office. Mother told him about my sore throat and he put down the cigar; then, without washing his hands he said, "Open your mouth."

With one hand he held down my tongue with a to-bacco-tasting finger, then without another word reached for a gleaming instrument with the other hand.

When the instrument was close to my face, I heard Mother shout, "Wait! Wait! This I must first talk over with my husband."

The instrument was slammed down on the table. The doctor looked so angry it scared me. Then he said, "If people won't do as I say they need not come here."

Outside in the fresh air again Mother said, "Before we go home we'll see what Dr. Kanouse recommends." (Dr. Kanouse was a Civil War veteran and had lost one lung.) He asked a few questions, looked in my throat and said, "Well, Mrs. Abraham, don't worry so much anymore. This little girl is in her ninth year already so have patience and keep on as you have been doing. Sometime between her twelfth and fourteenth birthday she will have outgrown this trouble."

His prediction turned out to be right.

During my eighties when I had several general checkups I was told, "There is a lot of scar tissue around your tonsils. They must have troubled you years ago. It is good that they are there yet."

Now I am a nonagenarian and surprised to know that removing bad tonsils was not absolutely new in the nineteenth century. In Fielding Garrison's *History of Medicine*, he refers to descriptions of tonsillectomies sometime between 625 and 690 A.D.

DIPHTHERIA SEVENTY-FIVE YEARS AGO
Henry C. Spear

Before the turn of the century I was a boy growing up in Grand Haven, Michigan. An epidemic of diphtheria struck our community, and one of my older sisters and one of my younger sisters came down with the disease. The population of the town was six thousand. Hundreds of families were quarantined. The schools and churches were closed. Big red cards were tacked on the homes near the front door. A man sat on a chair in front of each house that was quarantined and saw that no person went in or out. Most of the houses in those days had fences around the property. The front and sides had white picket fences, and the back had a high board fence.

Neighbors and friends who did not have the disease prepared food dishes and took them to the homes of the sick. They had to give it to the man sitting on the chair and let him take it into the home. People did not like this as sometimes we did not know what family did the good deed. One woman was determined to get up to our back door and hand her dish into the house in person. She came through the yard behind our home and tried to climb the fence with her dish. She made it over halfway and then she slipped and her long dress kept her hanging above the ground. I was usually playing in the back yard with my little wagon and my other two sisters. I ran and told the watchman in front of the home what had happened. He ran into the back yard and got the woman down, gave her a bawling out, took the dish from her and carried it into the house. She walked to the front of the house and around the block to get back home.

At that time medical knowledge in regard to diphtheria was not what it is today. Most of the patients were confined for many months and every victim who did not die was left with some defect that did not clear up until long afterwards. One of my sisters lost her voice. She had a bell to ring to call for help. My other sister lost her hearing. The boy across the street from us was our fastest runner, and he had to learn to walk all over again.

To prevent us from getting the disease they kept a sheet that had been soaked in some disinfectant up over the bedroom doors. I remember very well the antidote that we kids got every day. It was spoonfuls of warm water that had been flavored with whiskey. I remember how mad my mother got when I said, "Oh, that's good. Give me some more."

One day my older sister was pushing me in my wagon in the back yard when we struck a hole. My face went forward and the wooden stick handle went into my mouth and knocked out some of my teeth and cut my lip. I ran into the house crying and my mother gave me a whipping for waking up my sick sisters. She washed the blood off my mouth and stuck some "court plaster" on the cuts. I remember that for several weeks I chewed my food on just one side of my mouth.

THEN, NOW, AND INTO THE FUTURE
Elaine A. Gardner

"Creature" they called her, "the crazy one — more like an animal than a human being!"

The kitchen is a vivid memory, but the focal point is the big wood-burning stove and the girl who crouched behind it. She may have had a given name, but I had never heard it. She really didn't need one. No one ever spoke directly to her. I wonder how old she was; a guess now would be as inaccurate as my five-year-old mind could have guessed then.

She had a pretty face, I remember. And a braid of dark brown hair with teasing wisps escaping from the center part to touch her cheek and curl above the eyebrow. Her dress was usually plaid, bright, frilled and feminine in the fashion of the day. Only the heavy toed black leather shoes laced high above the calf spoiled the effect of tender grooming.

The girl's body was misshapen and her legs were completely useless. Her place was behind the kitchen stove bedded on a patchwork quilt much in the manner of the family dog. No doubt the stove provided warmth, but more probably it served as a shelter against the world she was a part of but had no share in.

The day I first saw her there were seven of us sitting in the kitchen: my parents, an aunt, my older sister, a cousin just two years older than I, the girl's mother, and myself. I was drawn to the girl with something more than curiosity. I wanted to know her, to have her like me, and to be friends. I thought she might want the same from me. We caught ourselves looking at each other, sneaking glances, feeling confused, and, in her case, frightened, when our eyes met. I remember her eyes wild with bewilderment and fear but not dimwitted or dull.

I inched toward the stove careful not to attract the attention of the others. When I was close enough I reached out my hand. I wanted her to touch me. Instead, this unaccustomed gesture sent her scurrying from the far side of the stove. Belly to floor, elbow to hand, paddle-fashion, she skittered into the open, covering the distance between us and a shanty storage area at the other side of the room with agile speed that could have been accomplished only from having done the same thing many times

before. I can almost hear the sound again, cries, half-shriek, half-growl emitting from deep inside her, penetrating the darkness of the closet where she took refuge. Her surprising reaction rooted me to the floor. The upheaval I had caused among the adults added to my terror. I must have been literally dragged from the kitchen. I remember being boosted onto the seat of our Ford sedan which was parked conveniently near the side door and my sister being shoved in after me with the command to "Stay there and take care of her!" while my cousin ducked timidly between the grown-ups who were turning a confused and irregular departure into a near calamity.

On the way home my behavior was under attack, but so were "those people" for allowing "something like that" around "normal" people, the implication being that "the creature" was something to be shameful of and her proper place a darkened room behind locked doors. The world was not yet ready for her and her kind. Is it today? Yesterday must be remembered best as a beginning of better tomorrows.

BATHTUBS IN MY LIFE
Goldye Mohr

The first bathtub in my life was a double-duty fixture. On Monday it held the family wash through all those cycles my mother deemed necessary to get clothes properly clean: soaking, boiling in a copper kettle, back to the tub for a vigorous scrubbing on a corrugated washboard, then on through three rinse waters. Only a slipshod housewife was content with two rinses.

Tuesday through Friday the tub rested on its hook in the shed; on Saturday night it was brought into the kitchen to become the family bathtub. Cold water came from a pump at the iron sink; hot water came from the teakettle on the kitchen stove. Bath water was always too hot at the beginning, too cold at the end, so dawdling was no temptation. Nor did sitting in a round washtub with your knees under your chin encourage a long, relaxing soak.

When the last child had been dunked and scrubbed, only one job remained—mop up the spilled water, scrub the kitchen floor, and hang the bathtub out in the shed for a rest over the weekend. No wonder a bath once a week was considered perfectly acceptable in polite society even though bath powders, deodorants, bubblebath and perfumed bath oils were not available. In fact, many folks had a vague notion that only wicked beauties in Turkish harems anointed themselves with perfumed oil instead of using plenty of soap and water like good Christians. Soap was plentiful and potent, store-boughten if you were lucky, home-crafted soap made with lye if you weren't.

I was in the second grade before I ever saw a real bathtub. This was not surprising since there were only two in the whole town. One belonged to our local congressman who had been down to Washington and learned a few things about high living.

The other belonged to my friend Irma, and how lucky I was to know Irma! She not only owned a bathtub, she had a delightful easygoing mother who was never hampered by notions of good housekeeping. I had a real fondness for both the lady and her bathtub. The tub was long and made of tin by the local tinsmith. One end was sloping, the other end had two real faucets and a hole for draining the water. Stripped down to a modest bathing dress of white muslin panties with ruffles and an undershirt, two little girls with wet bottoms could slide shriek-ing down the sloping end of the tub into the water. It was a full afternoon's entertainment. I remember, too, the refreshments Irma's mother gave us afterward — thick slabs of homemade bread spread with butter and topped with sugar and cinnamon.

Eventually the town got a waterworks and a sewage system, if a pipe leading down to the river can be called a sewage system. Nobody worried about water pollution in the early 1900s. Running water always purifies itself every two-hundred feet, they said. They said it, and they believed it, and every summer they went swimming in the river to prove it.

The years went by and everybody began to get bathrooms and bathtubs. Some old-timers still had a feeling it wasn't quite nice to have a bathroom right in the house where you cooked and ate, so they compromised the situation by boarding up one end of the back porch and putting the bathroom out there—a chilly solution to the problem.

Others bought a Hoosier kitchen cabinet for the kitchen, and put the bathroom in the pantry. If you were lucky enough to have a small, extra bedroom upstairs, you had an ideal setup. A little bedroom made a big, barn-like, hard-to-heat bathroom, roomy enough for three bathtubs. Tile floors and walls were still in the future but a printed linoleum was an available luxury.

The bathtub was something anyone would be proud to show the neighbors. Squatting solidly on four short legs, it was painted white on the outside and gleaming porcelain on the inside. Best of all, water ran in and drained out through pipes. The space under the tub served no useful purpose; it was a dirt-catcher, a dark inaccessible hiding place for lost collar buttons, hairpins, and even an occasional mouse or a scuttling water beetle.

The next bathtub in my life did away with this under-the-tub nuisance. It was "built-in," gleaming porcelain on the outside as well as on the inside. Ah, the elegance of it! A built-in bathtub was what divided the modern from the old-fashioned; it was the ultimate status symbol.

But not for long! Those designers of things to help you not only keep up with the Joneses but a step ahead soon came up with something else—tinted bathtubs. Pink, yellow, blue, green, even black fixtures bloomed out all over. Overhead showers and fancy shower curtains were added, even shower stalls with glass doors. Pull-up bars were tacked on to help those too old, too infirm, or too fat to hoist themselves out of the tub. Faucets, too, were changed. Not content with two spigots hot or cold, somebody designed a single knob that pushed in and pulled out, turned right and left, so you never knew whether you were going to get hot or cold water, a full gusher or an exasperating trickle.

I have seen in my day some pretty fancy bathtubs: marble ones with gold fixtures, sunken baths, elegant saunas that swirl the water around and make you feel as though you were bathing in the washing machine. It was even a bathtub that enabled me to fulfill a lifelong ambition to become a dancer. This particular bathtub had angled mirrors set ingeniously around it. When you stood up and lifted a leg you were a whole line of perfectly synchronized (rather plump) chorus girls. Only an illusion, of course, but satisfying—the nearest I shall ever come to being a Rockette.

After nearly a century-long struggle to keep clean, the final chapter is about to be written. I am contemplating going into a Retirement Center. Yesterday I saw a model of the bathroom in my new high-rise apartment. No tub at all!

The glass enclosed shower compartment has a plastic bench to sit upon. The shower is a long flexible tube that can be moved up and down, fore and aft, round about. There are no faucets to turn, no knobs to push in and pull out. Hot and cold water comes pre-mixed; you dial it like making a telephone call. To get the right mixture, I suppose all bathers must be able to read without their glasses or wear them while bathing.

The ultimate touch — a thing I have never had and hope I'll never need — the latest thing for the protection of the elderly, more or less independent citizen, handy to the hand, easy to use, connected to some guardian angel at a far-away desk, is: A PANIC BUTTON!

8 BOTH OF US

VOICES THROUGH THE STATIC
Alonzo Pond

"Hello Central, Give Me Heaven" was the title of a song we used to sing—was it over sixty years ago?

In Janesville, Wisconsin, I never knew a telephone Central in the flesh but her voice personalities were real friends. I honestly believe, if I had said, "Hello Central, give me heaven," no matter who was at the board, she would have connected me with Margie, my high school girlfriend.

There were two phone systems in Janesville; the "old" Bell and the "new" Independent. Bell Company instruments were black walnut; the new system used golden oak. All business firms had both, side by side on the office wall. Anyone could tell which was which system just by looking at the instruments.

My family had the new system. My girl's family subscribed to the old. For several months there was reciprocity. A caller could "cross over" by telling Central the system and number of the party to contact.

Central knew all of us teenage callers and got as big a kick from our romances as we got from hearing from voices of our sweethearts. Central also knew which couples were special friends or "enemies." Once I answered our ring to hear Margie's voice. Central interrupted in a conspiratorial whisper.

"Want to listen?" she said. "Fred and Betty are quarreling."

Margie and I had a "box seat" for our friends' tense effort to resolve their disagreement. We scarcely breathed in our eagerness to hear the battle. Suddenly we were cut off from the drama. Later Central called back.

"Sorry I had to cut you off," she said, "but my supervisor came in. I didn't get caught, though."

A month or so later I asked for a crossover to talk to Margie. "Sorry," said Central. "They have taken out the crossover service."

"Gee! What'll I do?" I said. "I've just *got* to talk to her. It's pouring rain or I'd ride my bike over there. It's really important."

"Wait. I'll see what I can do," said that sweet voice.

A few seconds later Margie and I were in contact. After I hung up I called Central back.

"Thanks, kid," I said. "How did you do it?"

"Called Evansville and got the Bell line through Evansville's long distance switchboard." Margie and I lived in the same town about sixteen blocks apart but our voices went to Evansville, eighteen miles away and back. I'm certain we were more thrilled at the magic genius of that Central than my granddaughter is at a voice from the moon. Think of it! All the way to Evansville and back to talk across town!

Years after my teenage romance I still considered the voice of Central as a dependable friend. It was Christmas vacation. I was home from Beloit College. My sweetheart that year was a schoolteacher in Beloit. She, too, had gone home for the holidays.

Just after Christmas I got an invitation to a dance, scheduled for the day before Anne would be back. I had her R.F.D. address out of Stevens Point but no phone number. I didn't know whether her family had a phone. Neither did I know her parents' initials. Nevertheless I called Central.

"I've got to get in touch with my girlfriend," I said. "It's a problem because I don't know a phone number nor her family's initials."

"Well, I can try," answered that ever-helpful voice. "Give me as much information as you can."

"Her name is Anne Erickson. Her folks live in the country near Stevens Point. She teaches third grade at Beloit and went home for the holidays."

There were plug-in noises, then I heard a distant voice: "This is Stevens Point."

Janesville Central explained my request.

"Oh, I know Anne," said Stevens Point through the steady static. "Just a minute."

Those iron telephone wires hummed louder and louder over the snows of that northwoods countryside. Then the voice came back.

"She's not home. Her mother says she's visiting her grandmother at Rosholt. That's on another system but maybe I can make a crossover." Then, a few minutes later: "Here she is, Janesville. Go ahead."

The static drowned my "Hello, Anne. This is Alonzo."

Janesville broke in. "We'll try to get a better connection."

By that time I couldn't even hear Stevens Point, let alone the voice of Anne twenty miles beyond.

"Can you hear the Point, Central?" I asked. "Will you relay my message and ask the Point to pass it on to Anne? I can't hear a word through the noise."

Janesville told the Point that Anne's boyfriend wanted her to go to a dance and that Anne should cut short her vacation to be at her room in Beloit a day early. I could hear Janesville clearly and a word now and then from Stevens Point but the static hum that night was terrible. The two Centrals had to repeat their words several times but eventually Janesville's voice came clearly to my ears with a gay lilt.

"Your answer is 'Yes.' The Point has fixed you up with a date," said our switchboard angel. "Don't be late. And I hope you and Anne have a good time."

"I wasn't sure you'd be here," I said when I called for Anne at her room two nights later. "Those telephone girls sure worked hard to put through my call."

"The line was so noisy, I could hardly hear the girl at the Point," Anne said. "I made out that I was to go to a dance and come back a day early but I wasn't sure who I was to go with. It seemed logical that it would be you. No one else I know would be crazy enough to send an invitation through a relay of two girls at different exchanges over three separate telephone systems a hundred miles apart."

We enjoyed the dance and supper afterward but I still remember those nameless friendly phone girls who battled the complex circuits and noisy wires to make a dance date for me!

SIGNS OF SPRING
Dorothy Pond

The little German Band was the first sign of spring in Sun Prairie about 1900. On the first warm Saturday in March or early April the eight o'clock train from Madison was sure to bring a few stocky brewery workers with round, red cheeks. Four or five of them backed down the steps of the smoking car tugging a big bass horn, a long, shiny trombone, a cornet or some other portable band instrument.

They really looked springlike as they walked jauntily up the four blocks from the station. Their dark blue band tunics, trimmed in gold braid, were buttoned tightly across their ample stomachs. The bright sunlight glinted from the patent leather visors of their uniform caps.

Sometimes Papa, standing in his grocery store window, would see them coming before they reached the corner of Batz's store and telephone home.

"Tell Dorothy the little German Band is here."

I'd grab my red jacket and have it half on as I ran out the kitchen door. Even before I reached the corner I could see the men forming a circle and the sun shining on their bright instruments. The first notes of "Ach, du lieber Augustine" brought a crowd. Storekeepers with broad smiles on their faces stood in their doorway listening. "Du, du lichs mir im Herzen" was followed by other German songs. The sprightly music and the warm sunshine intoxicated the crowd and they gave generously when the hat was passed.

There were seven saloons on our Main Street. After the concert at Batz's corner was over the band marched up the street stopping before each saloon to play a few pieces. A bartender came out and invited them in to "wet their whistles." The progress up the street became slower and slower.

In the afternoon the band walked through the residential section. The neighborhood children gathered on porches to listen. Mother gave us a nickel or a dime which we clutched in our fists. When the concert ended we shyly approached the men and dropped the coin into an outstretched palm. They smiled and said "Danke shon." We scuttled back to the porch hoping they would give an encore before moving on up the street.

Once in a while an organ grinder with his funny little monkey on a chain came from Little Italy in Madison. The swarthy, mustached Italian turned the crank while his music box played "Juanita" and "O Sole Mio."

The monkey, dressed in a little military coat and cap, danced and pirouetted. When the tune ended the monkey took off his cap and held it out for pennies. I was always a little afraid of him and sometimes dropped my coins on the walk. Then he got down on all four feet and picked them up and handed them to his master.

Spring brought out other itinerant people, too. The most welcome one was the scissors grinder. If I were playing out in the yard and heard the tinkle of a bell I hurried into the house calling "Mamma, the scissors man is coming."

My mother hurried to gather up her shears. A tall figure with a small grindstone on his back came striding down the street. His coat and vest were flying open and his battered felt hat was always set at a jaunty angle. How many times, lately, I've wished for the scissors man. These newfangled gadgets don't sharpen shears as well as those skilled artisans with their grindstones did.

This reminds me of the village dressmaker. In February Mamma always called Lizzie and said, "Can you give me three days the last of March?" If one were affluent one reserved a whole week.

On the appointed day Lizzie came. She was always dressed in a starched white waist and a black skirt. We had cleared the big dining table right after breakfast and I helped my mother bring out patterns, pieces of yard goods, thread, needles and pins. My father had lugged the sewing machine from the back bedroom into the dining room the night before.

For three days Lizzie cut, fitted and sewed. How I hated to stand still to be fitted and especially to have the skirt hung. Lizzie was meticulous about evenly hung skirts. No one could ever say that clothes that Lizzie made hiked up in front or sagged in back.

Easter hats were so important in those days. Six weeks before Easter the traveling milliner came to town. One of the dry goods stores opened two rooms upstairs and the talented lady moved in with boxes and boxes of untrimmed hats and flowers, laces and ribbons. With her help one chose a basic style frame, and she deftly tucked a bunch of flowers, a ribbon bow or a bit of lace on the brim and, like magic, it became an Easter bonnet. I remember most vividly one that I had: a wide-brimmed red straw with a black velvet band around the crown, the long streamers hanging down the back. Wanda tucked a bunch of green grapes on each side and I was in the seventh heaven of delight. Those milliners were real artists.

I remember too, the umbrella mender. Umbrellas were important in those days because people walked. The umbrella mender was never quite as sprightly as the scissors grinder. He was always an older man. His satchel held extra ribs, fancy handles and tips. Nowadays we have to throw away a broken umbrella. With closed cars we don't need them much anyway.

The gypsies — I don't know where they spent the winter but spring brought gypsy caravans to our town. When their gaily painted wagons drove by, doors that were never closed otherwise were locked. Children were called in from play and told to stay inside. Clerks in stores became extra vigilant. It was said that one store owner who was slow and deliberate moved like lightning when the gypsies came to town.

Back in the good old days spring was a rebirth for a small town.

THE BIG BLAST
Eleanor Morgan

A few miles from my hometown, Kenosha, was a small village named Pleasant Prairie. Against the protests of farmers for miles around, a powder mill was built in the year 1899. A year before, a man purchased acres of land for the purpose of raising cattle, he stated. The people in that area felt they had been hoodwinked when he built the powder mill instead.

It was a dangerous place to work and twenty-two men were killed there during the next dozen years. Many others were maimed or burned. Those days the law required and enforced few precautions, and there were no benefits for the victims and families when accidents or death resulted.

At the time of the explosion in 1911, the DuPont Company owned the plant. On the fateful evening of March ninth, the explosions started in the glaze room from a spark landing in the unfinished powder. Then the whole mill exploded, and the shock was felt more than five hundred miles away.

Kenoshans felt the tremors, windows were shattered, and I remember a banging at our front door as if giants were trying to enter. My Uncle Tom was sleeping in the morris chair in the sitting room. The whole house shook and he was thrown out of the chair. It happened just a few minutes after eight; we were not yet in bed, and there was much confusion in our household as we had no idea what had happened. My dad guessed that it was the powder mill. Perhaps he felt it was bound to have an explosion sooner or later. We went to the west window, and in the southwest we could see flares of light as many small explosions followed the big one. Several of our windows had broken and the shattering noise added to our fright. My mother was hysterical, and I remember her sitting on the steps leading upstairs, her teeth chattering, and my dad trying to calm her.

The next morning, my Uncle Tom walked with a friend to the village of Pleasant Prairie to view the remains. The explosion had ripped through the village like a tornado. The earth shook similar to an earthquake and had left the village in ruins. Miraculously, only one man was killed, and some escaped with minor injuries. Not a house was left intact. A large boarding house collapsed. Women were walking the streets with babes in their arms, begging people to take them in. Doctors had been sent out and brought many of the injured to Kenosha.

The blasts had left large holes which later filled with water. Sometime later, a child drowned in one of these ponds and then they got busy filling up holes which had filled with water. Carloads of dirt were used but some of the holes were so deep they gave up the fill-in project for a time. The DuPont Company made good its promises and rebuilt stores and homes in Pleasant Prairie. They also settled with the owners of damaged property in Kenosha. Machinery was moved during the blasts in the American Brass and Badger Brass factories. Many leaded windows were knocked out of churches.

The plant was rebuilt in 1913 against the protests of the people. It flourished until 1930 when it closed its doors, much to the relief of the village.

Years later, I talked to one of the men who worked there at the time it happened, and he jokingly said, "At the first blast I started running, and when the second blast was heard, I was in Kenosha."

EARLY DAYS IN WISCONSIN
Alvin H. Morgan

I was born in the late 1890s in the village of Union Grove, Wisconsin. I will try to describe the ways of life in that small town of eight hundred in the 1900s.

I started school in the chart class. It was much like the kindergarten of today. The grade school consisted of three rooms, one teacher in each room. The high school was upstairs. There was an assembly room and two classrooms. The high school was accredited. There were never more than forty pupils at one time. There was no extra curriculum. Most pupils went only through the eighth grade. Very few finished high school; most dropped out before graduating. There would only be four or five in the senior year.

We had to supply our own entertainment. The games we played were Run Sheep Run, Pom Pom Pull Away, Fox and Geese, Blind Man's Bluff, Duck on the Rock, baseball and basketball. There was not any Boy Scouts or any organization for children.

A small creek ran past the outskirts of the village. The large boys dammed up the creek for a swimming pool. No one used a swimming suit. It was there I learned to swim dog fashion. We plastered ourselves with mud, and then lay in the sun till it hardened. Our clothes hung on the thorn apple bushes. Quite often when we came out, we found some prankster had tied our clothes in knots.

There were three small factories: a tile factory, a creamery, and a grist mill. A flax mill was run by a tarred rope belt from the grist mill. There was no electrical power; power was supplied by steam engines. We loved to watch these monsters as they ran the machinery.

There were eight passenger trains that ran through

the village each day, also many freight trains. We were at the depot to see as many as we could. Our aim in life was to be a brakeman or engineer. The older boys would catch on the rear of the trains and ride out of town and then jump off. In the wintertime, the smaller boys would hitch onto bobsleds and ride out into the country with the hopes of catching one coming into town. Some farmers would lash out with a whip; then we soon got off.

In the winter we had the most fun. A steep hill, known as Boxes Hill, was on the outskirts of town. Most kids had sleds of some kind. We also had a large bobsled that a half-dozen could ride on. In cold weather, we iced the hill and went down on skates. Only the brave ones tried this. Our skis were barrel staves.

The people were all patriotic. On Memorial Day, the schoolchildren marched to the cemetery to give honor to the dead. Some of the Civil War veterans walked, and some rode in buggies. A large flag was strung across Main Street.

An icehouse was built beside a large pond. Ice was cut and stored for use in the summer. There was no gas or electricity then. The street lights were large kerosene lanterns set atop posts. They were lit every evening. One store had gaslights which were supplied by carbide. A lamplighter trimmed the wicks, filled them with kerosene, and lit them each night. When they were not cutting ice, we skated on the pond. We would take one of the lanterns off the post, carry it to the pond and set it in the middle of the pond for light. There was no police force in town. There was no need. The older people took care of that. The only things we ever stole were grapes, apples, and watermelons. We were very careful not to get caught. If we did, it meant a good swift kick in the rear end or a good cuffing. One night the gang was going to steal grapes. For some reason, my father would not let me go downtown that night. The grapes were across the tracks from my home. About ten o'clock, I heard two shotgun blasts. That ended stealing grapes at that place.

When I got into high school, a baseball and basketball team was organized. Our first court was a vacant carriage house. Later, a hall was built. We had no coach. The school did provide suits and equipment. We elected a manager who provided the games for us. There were not the number of high schools that there are today. We had to play larger schools than ours, such as Burlington, Elkhorn, Racine and Racine College, a prep school. We lost more games than we won.

In the summer, we walked to Eagle Lake to fish. It was a three-mile hike. My father had a boat there tied up to some willow trees. The oars were hidden in the tall grass. This was the only precaution we had to take then. In the winter, we made a little money trapping. We also hunted rabbits that were sold for twenty-five cents to the local meat market. Shotgun shells were fifty cents a box. We were very careful not to waste any.

On a summer afternoon, you could hear the old men playing horseshoes. In the alley, we would listen to their tales of yesteryears. They told of the village trying to get an artesian well. They drilled all winter and got down several hundred feet, but no water ever flowed. The time of the big snow when the cut east of the village was filled level with snow, they were isolated for days. A snowplow at last was sent out with several cars behind it. They came full speed in the drift. The engine was buried and stuck. There were frantic efforts of the workmen to shovel down to the engine before the fireman and engineer suffocated. There was a man that had an early model car, I can't remember the make, but it had a disc clutch. When he had had a few drinks, he would back the car to the village limits, then turn around and back it all the way home.

It was growing up and doing our own thing that helped us in later life.

HANGING BOBS
Mary J. Phillips

Did you ever "hang bobs?" Maybe that sounds a little rough or bloodthirsty. But if you were a boy or girl living in a small town in Wisconsin about fifty or more years ago, you can recall the fun we had hanging bobs.

Wood was the main fuel used to heat most buildings. In wintertime, farmers went into their woodlots, cut the trees, sawed them into cord wood and brought the wood to town on bob sleighs drawn by horses.

Roads were not plowed out as they are now, so after the first good snow the fun started. Girls and boys waited anxiously to run after the sleighs, stand on the runners, hang on to the uprights of the wood rack, and ride as far as the farmer was going, or until another sleigh happened to come along going in the opposite direction.

Most farmers wore long, shaggy fur coats, high boots, fur caps and big mittens. They stood at the front of the load, driving the horses. Usually they were good guys and let us ride, but once in a while one would yell, "Get off before you get your foot under the runner." There was one driver in particular who waved his big whip around, threatening us. We recognized him from afar by his long hair and beard. Most of us kept out of his way. But some of the more daring kids liked to tease him, and gave him a hard time, jumping on and off his rack.

Once in a while some farmer who recognized us would let us ride all the way to the farm with him. Then we all hiked back. I recall one day when we rode over two miles, not realizing how far we were going. It was a long cold walk back to town. Maybe kids were tougher those days.

There was no traffic problem as most cars were off the roads in wintertime. With bad roads most of the time, we either went by train, horse and sleigh or cutter. My dad kept the car in driving condition until after Thanksgiving Day. On that day we went to a family party at my aunt's house, about a mile from town. After that, he put the battery and tires in the basement to wait for spring.

Most people agreed that hanging bobs was all right for boys, but girls should be more ladylike. However, we rode along in our homemade coats and caps, long black stockings, laced-up shoes and black rubbers. Don't forget the long-legged underwear. Snow pants were unthought of then. Some of us had black leggings buttoned up the side with shiny black buttons. Most of us had mittens made by some relative, usually a grandmother.

Things were simple then. Maybe we were easily entertained. Anyway—those were the days!

MEMORIES OF MY BOYHOOD ON THE FARM
P. C. Phillips

I was thinking last night of my daughter's and son's childhood. I was wondering if we had done all we could to make their childhood happy, and if we had always guided them right.

Then I thought about my own childhood and of how much different it had been from theirs, not because my wife and I had tried to raise them differently, but because of the technological and social changes that had taken place since we were children.

I will start back as far as I can remember and tell of the things most vivid in my memory.

One of my first memories is of gypsies coming to our door, begging. If my father was not around the house, my mother would get us children into the house and lock the doors. We would huddle around her skirts as she talked to them through the screen door. Bands of them went by each summer trading horses and picking up what they could, "on the sly." Usually some of the neighbors would miss some chickens or a pig. Some of our neighbors prided themselves on being good Yankee horse traders, but I never heard of one of them getting the better of a trade with gypsies. My mother would never turn a tramp away without a handout and we had the average of one a week. At least some of them were more dangerous than gypsies, but Mother was not afraid of them.

I probably should have explained that we lived on a farm along the main road from Mineral Point to Dodgeville, Wisconsin. That is why we had a superfluity of unwelcome callers.

Another memory is of being snatched out of the path of the first car I remember seeing. My father and some neighbors were working on the road in front of our house. In those days, about 1907, there was a poll tax that had to be paid. The men in the area would work this out by doing road work. All roads were dirt. I remember ruts being hub deep in the spring. The soil was red clay and it stuck to the horses' hooves and wagon wheels in big gobs. Children made marbles by rolling clay into balls

in our hands, and drying them in the sun. The car which almost ran over me was taking a man to jail in Dodgeville because he had robbed the Mineral Point bank the night before.

On Saturday afternoons, my parents took the team and surrey and drove to Mineral Point to do shopping and visiting. This was Farmer's Day in town. They took a case or two of eggs, depending on how well the hens were laying, and traded them for groceries. We youngsters very seldom got to go except on a Saturday before Christmas, to do our Christmas shopping. One Saturday when we were a few years older, we were left home and told to replant about a quart of corn that the gophers had dug up. After that we could go fishing in a creek about two miles away. As soon as the folks left, we buried the corn in a hole and took off for the creek. They never did find out about that.

On the last day of school each year, we had a picnic. We went to Blotz Mill so we could fish. I guess I was born with a fish pole in my hand as it still is my favorite sport. We had only a string, a hook, a sinker and bottle cork. A willow stick from along the creek completed the equipment. Our means of transportation was a hay rack. One of the older boys drove the team as this was a busy time of year for our fathers.

The happiest days of my life were spent with my dog Jerry who was part bulldog and part terrier. He had the characteristics of both. He was afraid of nothing, hated cats and all the cat family, especially skunks. This was very evident three or four times a year when he came home smelling like one. He and I dug a skunk out of a hole one time. When we reached him, Jerry grabbed a hind leg and I grabbed the tail. We both went home smelling like a skunk that day.

A favorite pastime was drowning out gophers. I would pack pails of water a half mile or more, pour it down the gopher hole until the gopher came out, and Jerry would grab it. Once each year, Dad would let us take the team and milk wagon (the wagon we hauled milk to the factory in) and we would fill four or five thirty-gallon milk cans with water and drown out gophers all around the edge of our corn fields. Dad gave us one cent each for gopher tails. Gophers and ground squirrels dug up corn seed so we would have to replant.

A week or two before the threshing machine came around, we boys picked up the old fence posts to use as fuel for the old steam engine. We also hauled water in thirty-gallon milk cans while the threshing was being done.

These are some of the things I remember about my childhood, that my own children were denied, because of technology of our much advanced age. Was this good or bad? I sometimes wonder. Or are my nostalgic memories just looking backward to the so-called Good Old Days?

9 CHARACTERS

ONCE THESE CAME DOWN THE CITY STREETS
Dorothy V. Walters

What did umbrellas, shoelaces, waffles, rags, scissors, watermelons, ice, popcorn, and goats have in common sixty years ago?

In my Milwaukee childhood each represented what might be called a street trade. Each had its salesman who walked or drove a horse slowly through neighborhoods offering wares or services.

Instead of wearing raincoats in those days, most people, especially women, carried umbrellas. These were covered with closely woven black cotton or silk cloth. When the covering became torn, worn, or faded, the umbrella was not thrown out by thrifty people. It was set aside for the "umbrella mender" to take for recovering when he made his rounds.

A week or so after he had exchanged a receipt for the umbrella, it was returned "as good as ever," and the cost was much less than a new umbrella.

Two or three times a year an elderly notions peddler visited our neighborhood. He was noted for a friendly attitude as much as for the large wen on his nose. Always dressed in black, including a hat, he carried a small black suitcase. This was packed with shoelaces, shoe polish, narrow white ribbon, tubes of glue, safety pins, and other sundries.

Housewives respected his efforts to support himself and usually bought something from his stock.

A rhythmic "ding-dong" coming down the street signaled the approach of the scissors grinder. He pushed a grindstone mounted in a frame between two wheels. The little bell was suspended from the frame so that it rang when the frame was pushed. Besides curbstone sharpening of scissors, the grinder also put sharp edges on knives. He provided a service housewives needed before electric knife sharpeners.

Does your family have an old snapshot album? In it you may find a picture of a tot seated in a little goat-drawn wagon. He or she will be proudly holding reins attached to the goat, which was hitched to the wagon. House to house photographers with these props came through a neighborhood about once a summer in my childhood.

When I was growing up, ice did not come in cubes from the electric refrigerator. It was delivered in large chunks or cakes by a brawny iceman. He knew how many pounds my mother wanted for our top-loading icebox by looking at a card placed in the front window of our home. The numbers "25, 50, 75, 100" were printed in bold type —two to a side—on the card.

The children of the neighborhood tagged after the slowly moving, heavy, horse-drawn wagon which dripped water from the melting ice. We knew the iceman was coming by several noises: the jingling of the scales on the back of the wagon, the clattering tongs with which the man moved and carried the ice cakes, the sawing sound made when he cut a piece of ice to the required weight. While the iceman made his deliveries and collected the tickets which customers purchased in books in advance of his coming, the neighborhood kids took the opportunity to reach into the wagon—even to climb into it—to grab the chill shavings to suck.

Unlike the other vendors, the iceman was not self-employed. He worked for a company such as Wisconsin Ice and Coal. The ice which he distributed was cut during the coldest part of the winter from a lake or river and stored in the company's huge wooden icehouse, insulated from warmer weather by sawdust.

"Wahdemelone . . . *straw*berries, potatoes," bellowed the Italian produce man as he slowly drove his horse through the alleys. His wagon had a top on it to protect his fruits and vegetables from wilting in the summer sun. At his call housewives came to buy more varieties of produce than the neighborhood grocery store might carry.

"Recycling" was not in our vocabularies, but we knew something about it. Besides the produce peddler, the ragpicker or ragman also carried on his business in the alleys. He bought not only discarded newspapers and magazines, but also rags and sometimes bottles. He paid a few cents per hundred pounds for the papers and rags, and he contributed a service in clearing out accumulations of these things. His rattling old wagon was pulled by a slowly walking nag. To me the man's call always sounded like "Raygs—uh, raygs."

A shrill, persistent steam whistle heard in late afternoon or early evening told us that the popcorn or waffle wagon was coming. Both were horse-drawn. A flame (probably generated by kerosene) popped the fragrant corn or cooked the waffles. Butter was poured from a coffee pot over the hot, crunchy corn. Waffles (oh, how good they tasted!) were dusted with powdered sugar and could be eaten in one's hands without too much stickiness.

As you may have noticed, several of the businesses which I have described could be conducted only in late spring, summer, or early autumn. Either seasonally or all year round they provided income to the vendor; and to the customers, services or a pleasurable interruption to the daily routine.

EARLY BLACK RESIDENTS
Clara Skott

Two ex-slaves lived in Middleton, Wisconsin for many years. One of them accompanied one of the eleven Wisconsin regiments returning from Sherman's March to the Sea in 1864. His name was John T. Nelson, the T standing for Tandy. Georgia masters had warned their slaves to beware of the Northern soldiers coming along. But John, unafraid at the suggestion of Wisconsin men, hopped on one of his master's mules and accompanied them. Arriving in Middleton, he became a handyman around the village, so much so that he was known as John Handy. Little seems to be known of him, other than that he lived in a shack not far from the present viaduct west of Middleton.

He is buried in the Middleton Junction cemetery. His modest headstone has the neatly lettered inscription, "John T. Nelson. Died Feb. 22, 1906, aged 90 years." If he were forty-eight years old when he arrived in Wisconsin, these figures would be true. However, this is open to question, for records were not usually kept of vital statistics for slaves.

Our other Negro in Middleton during the latter half of the nineteenth century was named Solomon, born a slave in Virginia. When his mother Lucy was sold at a slave auction, she cried so much for her ten-year-old son that her new master, Abraham Bush, bought him, too. Moving to Kentucky, Mr. Bush took them both along, as he did again later on, to Missouri. His final move was to Wisconsin, to a farm north of Middleton, now on Highway 12.

Their coming here was before the Civil War. Since they were now in a free state, Solomon added the name

Freeman to his given name. Though technically free, both Solomon and his mother continued to work for the Bush family. Their friendly cooperation lasted throughout their lifetimes. They taught Solomon to read. When Lucy died, no record was left of her burial place.

The Bush family increased in numbers, and eventually moved on west, having the proverbial "itchy feet" for far horizons. Solomon built himself a three-room house, on the site of the present parochial school in Middleton. There he raised his own garden. He worked part-time for the Green Grain and Feed Mill, which is now a part of the Middleton Farmers Co-op Company.

Solomon was a deeply religious man and a member of the Baptist church, which held services in the Union Church, "The Little White Church on the Hill." This church had been built in 1870 by the Baptists and Methodists working together. When their supply minister could not come, Solomon was sometimes called upon to preach an extemporaneous sermon. It was based on his much reading of the Bible, and his prayers were spoken of as "the best prayers that ever came out of any man's mouth." He lived his religion, and was long remembered for his kind deeds.

(That church building is still standing, more than a century old. It has not been used for religious services since 1956, when the Community Church, after using it for twenty years, moved to its present much larger quarters.)

In Solomon's later years, he would often be a part of a group of men who would congregate in the village blacksmith shop to while away the hours by telling yarns of bygone days. It's a pity there weren't tape recorders then!

Both of these highly regarded men were given funerals from that Union Church. Solomon lies beside his master in the Middleton Junction cemetery in an unmarked grave. The Middleton Historical Society, now in its second year, wants to locate and mark that grave. Abraham's son John came back from California to mourn his old friend and to take care of the funeral details.

The *Middleton Times-Herald* in 1900 printed a fine eulogy of this townsman, from which this quote is taken: "Perhaps from his unmarked grave Solomon Freeman can still teach us that in our common humanity and brotherhood under God is the real solution of one of the greatest problems of our times." As near as records show, and human memories can recall, Middleton citizens by those early experiences may well have set up an interracial pattern that might profitably have been copied throughout our country.

THE KOHLMEYERS OF LOGANVILLE
William C. Thies

On the west side of town lived Fred W. Kohlmeyer who, being born in Germany in 1869 came to the Loganville area with his parents Johann Heinrich Kohlmeyer and his wife Margareta.

He attended public and parochial school, then worked as a laborer, but even as a young man he was mechanically inclined.

When he was married he lived in a home northeast of town. In the late 1890s he went on a trip to the Alaska Klondike gold fields and soon returned, but the name Klondike remained with him.

Then in 1898 with brother William as a partner he purchased a threshing outfit and threshed in the area.

At this time he was living in a home across the street from where in the year 1903 he built the large new house. At this time they were employing fifteen men.

Two sons were born to Fred and his wife. One was accidentally killed by gunshot, and Ed, born in 1892, went into the business when Fred's brother started farming.

At this time they were operating a sawmill. Lumber was in good demand because of a building boom in town. Their grist mill powered by a steam engine was also a good business. A well-drilling outfit also owned by them and powered by a small steam engine, later powered by a gasolene engine, was operated by Charlie Krueger. Many new wells were being drilled at home sites and on farms because the old dug-out wells did not supply sufficient water.

At this time roads were being improved so a rock crusher powered by a large gasolene engine kept another crew busy.

In 1911 they built a pickup truck, just the front seat, no top, with a small box in the back to carry supplies to the working crews. It had right-hand drive and no electric starter or lights.

One day Mr. Kohlmeyer picked me up while I was walking home from school. This was my first automobile ride and what a thrill it was! Twenty-five miles an hour was quite a speed on just dirt roads.

At this time all freight and supplies were hauled by team, but now with roads being improved the demand came for trucks. So cars were being converted into trucks by putting truck axles on them. Some of the first ones built by the Kohlmeyers were from Winton and Maxwell cars. Both were sold to Fred Ninnaman, who operated the dray line. The wheels on the back axle had solid rubber tires but this proved too much strain on the car's transmission.

So in 1915 Kohlmeyer designed and built his first heavy truck with right-hand drive, square cab, side curtains and a brake lever on the right side of the cab. This was also sold to F. Ninnaman.

Then Mr. Kohlmeyer designed and built his first car. Many of the parts had to be designed, then patterns were made and taken to Madison for casting. The first models had right-hand drive. Later a change was made to left-hand drive with no door on the driver's side of the seat. Some models had extra folding seats between the front and back seats.

They also designed and built a heavier truck with larger air tires on the back axle and overdrive shift for more speed. This was sold to the Ninnaman Dray Line. A fire truck for the village was equipped by the Leicher Brothers. This had a double ignition: a magneto or distributor. One was built for the Reedsburg Township.

The cars and trucks all had a beautiful designed "Klondike" chrome-plated emblem on the radiator. All the assembling and painting was done in their own well-equipped shops.

Their first heavy steam engine was originally a "Buffalo Pitts" double-cylinder engine. This was redesigned by Mr. Kohlmeyer by adding compound cylinders for more power and greater efficiency. He applied for a patent, but because he had no money to back it, he lost out. Soon his idea was used by many others.

Their large "a very Yellow Fellow" threshing machine was also completely redesigned. Every main shaft was mounted in self-aligning ball bearings. These were also of their own design. Mr. Kohlmeyer claimed that the machine could be turned with one finger in a pulley; this he said was a great saving of power.

I remember well helping with threshing in the area. After dinner or lunch if we would try to stay in the shade a little longer after one "toot" of the whistle, the machine would start and Mr. Kohlmeyer would come with a few words of warning. I always can remember his gold teeth flashing. That meant go!

The machine was equipped with steering on both the front and rear axles. In 1917 they purchased a heavy "Minneapolis" gas tractor with a thirty-sixty rating. This was immediately rebuilt. The cylinder head was ground down for more compression to give more power and gas efficiency. A cab was built with side windows, electric lights and a power winch with a hundred feet of cable for emergency pulls. They added a double clutch too: one for traction and the other for belt work.

At this time they built a camper mounted on a rebuilt car-truck chassis for a trip to Yellowstone National Park. This did not prove satisfactory, so the next year they built a larger one on a Klondike chassis. It had electric lights, running water, a shower bath, a complete kitchen, and sleeping room for five people. This then took both Kohlmeyer families to California. It was on this trip that a son was born to Mr. and Mrs. Ed Kohlmeyer. The trip was made without trouble.

Soon it became apparent that they could not compete against the large auto and truck makers, so when Mr. Fred Kohlmeyer retired, the Klondike era vanished. Ed continued for a while doing shop work and selling farm tractors and machinery.

Then the shop was sold, and Ed and his family moved to Chicago where they operated a machine shop which is still being operated by Ed's sons after his death. In Lo-ganville today the name Klondike still lingers in the memory of those who knew Fred Kohlmeyer as a mechanical genius of that time.

"WALK SOFTLY AND CARRY A BIG STICK"
Mrs. M. M. Dunn

October 14, 1912, was a beautiful day and my afternoon and evening off from duties, so I went shopping in the afternoon and purchased a winter coat and hat at the Rosenberg's Shop at Third Street and North Avenue.

In the evening I walked down Third Street to go and see "The Man From Home," a stock company playing at the Alhambra Theater at Fourth and Grand Avenue (now North Fourth) and West Wisconsin Avenue.

When I got to the Gilpatrick Hotel on Third Street between Wells and Cedar (now West Kilbourn Avenue) a large crowd had assembled so I stepped into the south side of the alley and discovered that Teddy (Theodore) Roosevelt was about to emerge and go to the auditorium to make a speech.

As Mr. Roosevelt stepped from the entrance to the car waiting at the curb he was greeted with loud applause. As he stood up in the car to greet the people gathered there and turned to wave to us in the alley, John Shrank, standing about twenty feet behind me, fired a shot that hit Mr. Roosevelt in the left shoulder just above his heart.

He took his handkerchief and put his right hand over the wound, and directed the driver to proceed to the auditorium.

Officers Paul Engel, John Wheeler and Richard Zingler ran through the alley and I told Officer Engel that

Shrank ran to the end of the alley and turned and ran north toward the auditorium. The officers caught him and Mr. Roosevelt went on and made his speech and nearly fainted at the end of his speech.

A train had been dispatched from Chicago and was waiting to take Mr. Roosevelt to the hospital there. The bullet was not removed because of the dangerous location and Mr. Roosevelt went home to convalesce. Later he was elected President of the United States.

Mr. Roosevelt lived until January 6, 1919 when he died in his sleep.

MOTHER
Lenore Beck

This will be mostly about life in Wisconsin, before my time, as told by my mother.

For several years my mother lived in a log trading post on Waubee Lake in Oconto County. They sold cloth, flour, guns, ammunition and other things to the Indians. They bought from them deer meat, called venison, hides and berries, and also ran a hunting camp for hunters from the cities.

One wealthy man from Chicago decided to rough it and camp by himself. It didn't turn out so well and he sent a member of his party to my mother and asked if he could borrow her cook stove, as his chef did not know how to cook over an open fire.

A tribe of Chippewa Indians lived across the lake. The chief's name was Waubeskibinas, hence the name Waubee Lake. His son was Modac and his daughter was Kenewaubequaw which means "morning flower," or "morning glory."

One morning Mother was washing clothes on an old-fashioned washboard in the yard when the squaws across the lake began to scream, "Squita, squita!" A couple of them came running around the lake. They dashed up to Mother's house. Each grabbed a couple of pails and raced to the lake, filled the pails with water and ran back up to the house. They had seen that the roof of the cabin was on fire, so they came to help, and just in time, too. "Squita" means fire, and incidentally, "squitawaboo" means "firewater" or whiskey.

Occasionally the Indians would get a keg of squitawaboo and they would all get drunk: squaws, braves and little children with whiskey in tin cups. That is, all but one brave who stayed sober and guarded the guns, knives and ammunition just in case of trouble. Then the next time it would be his turn to celebrate.

Mother had her own canoe. She set traps around the lake and caught mink, otter and muskrat and learned to skin her game, and cure the hides. She also learned to speak the Chippewa language.

One morning Modac came over and said, "Me no sleep last night. Holla, holla, holla all night."

Mother asked, "Were you sick?"

And he said, "No, me no sick. One teet (tooth), he sick." He had had a toothache all night.

One day one of the Indian guides was in the woods and stepped over a log, right into a nest of bear cubs. Of course, they squealed and the mother bear came running. She took a swipe at the man's head with her paw, pulling his scalp down over his face. He tried to lie perfectly still, but the blood began to smart and pain his eyes unbearably. He tried, very carefully and slowly, to move a hand up to his eyes. The mother bear saw it, grabbed his wrist and chewed it through and through. The guide managed to endure the pain and lie quietly until the bear had coaxed her cubs out of hearing. When he decided it was safe to move, he crawled on his hands and knees back to camp. Luckily, he recovered.

The trading post hauled their supplies by horses and wagons, from Crivitz, about fifty miles away. Supplies included stick candy, of which the Indians were very fond. For some reason, one day Modac struck his grandmother, and when she cried, Mother gave her "cheesaboquitous" or "sugar sticks."

The nearest neighbor was five miles away, and once Mother rode there on horseback to get a "setting" of eggs, a dozen or so, as she had a hen who wanted to "set." That is, the hen wouldn't get off her nest, but wanted eggs put under her. She would set on these for three weeks, only coming off once a day to eat. At the end of three weeks, the eggs had fluffy little chickens inside of them who broke the shells with their bills, and came out into the world.

Mother put newspapers on the log walls for cleanliness. One day a couple of squaws were looking at the pictures on the newspapers. Suddenly they began to exclaim, "Ea yah! Ea yah! Winnebago! Winnebago!" There was a picture of Winnebago Indians, who were unfriendly, and the squaws identified them by the way their moccasins were made. So they shook their fists at the pictures. They would stand and look at the pictures so quietly that sometimes Mother forgot they were there.

I am sure Mother enjoyed this period of her life in the wilds of Wisconsin, and I have enjoyed telling about it, Cowanishashin Papoose (no good child).

ABE'S BEAR HIDE
Dorinda Clark

Hardy men and the black bear were heroes or villains, as you will, of many a favorite tale told and retold in the bunkhouses of Wisconsin's early woodsmen. Folklore of the Baraboo area accounts for the escapades of one burly frontiersman named Abe Wood, a terror to both man and bear.

Abe was tall and powerfully built, with huge hands and feet. A soiled, dome-shaped hat was usually pulled down over shaggy, reddish hair and his sharp blue eyes squinted under bushy brows. But it was his dictatorial disposition and unpredictable rages, often sparked by the slightest provocation, that earned Abe his reputation.

Yet, conversely, he possessed a certain rude sense of justice and generosity. Undoubtedly, these qualities had helped him get along famously with the Indians. After building a small log cabin near the river, he had married a little Indian maiden. Her fancy needlework may have contributed somewhat to Abe's strange appearance.

Trained to thriftiness by the frontier wives, she carefully mended Abe's clothing, often adding colorful patches over worn trouser knees. When these became threadbare, she simply cut off the trouser legs above the patches, and reversed them. With patches behind his knees also, it was often difficult, at first sight, to determine if Abe was coming or going. But he was completely oblivious of the amused glances of the people.

Always on hand and vociferously argumentative at every political and social meeting in the area, he was not easily ignored or opposed. It was at one of these social events, celebrating Independence Day, that Abe became perturbed.

It seemed someone had neglected to provide a place for Abe and his wife at the feast. He accused the master of ceremonies, a Mr. Cornfield, and engaged him in a heated argument. As Abe grew more irate, Mr. Cornfield, a fast runner, took off and evaded him by running behind a cabin.

Thinking Mr. Cornfield had entered the cabin, Abe blustered in. Not finding his enemy, he flew into one of his blind rages. Jumping up onto a table set with dishes and crockery, he proceeded to kick things right and left, smashing every piece. After venting his rage on the furnishings, he left.

Abe Wood knew and roamed the countryside widely. His skill as a riverman and his amazing strength was often put to use rafting logs down the river. He knew its every curve and sandbar.

One spring day, after running into a logjam at Prairie du Sac, Abe decided to take time out and relax a bit. He made a beeline from the river to the nearest tavern and was leisurely drinking his glass of rum, when suddenly a man burst into the barroom screaming "Bear! Bear!" Always alert for action, Abe followed him outside.

A short distance away a farmer named Tagor was valiantly trying to hold a huge bear at bay with a pitchfork. The bear was trying to climb over a fence into Tagor's pasture land. Each time the bear reared up, the farmer would thrust the pitchfork into its face, forcing the bear to drop again to all fours. This would have been quite a daring feat for a man twice Tagor's size, but the little hundred-pound fellow didn't stop to consider this.

Abe rushed to the rescue. He shot the bear, then drawing his knife, proceeded to remove its furry coat. It was a beauty. When he held it up in admiration, Tagor eyed it covetously. But as no one disputed its ownership, Abe rolled up the pelt, threw it over his shoulder and returned to the tavern.

But for Mr. Tagor that wasn't the end. He returned to his cabin seething inside. What right had Abe Wood to run off with that beautiful pelt? "Didn't I stop that bear and hold it so Abe could kill it?" He sat for a while brooding. Then he jumped to his feet and slammed out of the cabin.

Another, and heretofore undiscovered, even unsuspected, facet of Abe Wood's personality was about to be revealed.

In the tavern, excited men surrounded the bar discussing the latest adventure. The tavern door flew open and in stalked Tagor. Defiantly he crossed to the corner where the rolled-up pelt lay. He dragged it to the middle of the floor, unrolled it, then planted himself squarely on the middle of the pelt.

Wood had sighted this motion from the corner of his eye and slowly turned around, his face flushed and threatening. A deadly hush crept over the barroom. The men gazed from Tagor to Abe, their steins poised midway to their lips. Bodies tensed in anticipation of Abe's next move.

Abe paused for a moment and stared unbelieving. Tagor squatted tailor-fashion, arms folded, in the very middle of the pelt. Raising his chin and his voice, without looking at Abe, he challenged: "If any man thinks he has a better right to this hide than I have, let him take it."

Abe hesitated a moment longer, still unable to believe what he saw and heard. Then, bending over, he gave his thigh a resounding slap and exploded into a roar of laughter that rocked the tavern on its foundation.

Little Mr. Tagor had won the pelt.

A CHILDHOOD FRIEND
Mildred M. Rosenthal

Someone has said: "For all the good the past has had remains to make our own time glad." I would like to recall a childhood impression of a truly good man who ministered to a little flock of Methodists in the Township of Forest, Fond du Lac County, Wisconsin, before World War I.

The Reverend Klenski was quite an old man when he came to the little country church which I attended with my family. He had been transferred from a much larger church due to his advanced age and was happy for the opportunity the little congregation offered in closer ties and personal friendships.

Reverend Klenski's wife had passed on some years earlier, so it was necessary for him to keep house and attend to his own personal needs. My mothed washed and ironed his white shirts and checked regularly to see that he had plenty of food and proper clothing.

This revered man was a gentleman of old world courtesy; he was truly a gentle man, mellow and gracious, with a humble dignity I have seldom seen duplicated. He was of slim stature with a slight stoop and walked with a measured tread acquired in the German military service when he was a youth. Occasionally he talked of "the old country," and it was both fascinating and saddening to hear him tell of this faraway land that had been his home.

The nostalgic description of his "fatherland," his migration to America, his early training for the ministry he related to us with such charm, sincerity and humor that he endeared himself to our family circle. When his little black mare jogged down the lane just before dinner, we were never annoyed. It just meant setting another place at the table, and in exchange for his food he provided a wealth of inspirational conversation, anecdotes and descriptions of his early life in Germany: how the people lived and how they praised the freedom he would enjoy in his adopted land, and the compensation it offered. He opened up vistas of a new world; Europe became more than a place on the map to us, it was the homeland of this warm-hearted, kindly man.

"Saturday school" was not a dull, repetitious memorizing of Bible verse, but a truly painstaking tutoring of Bible catechism. Learning to write German in the most beautiful old world script he used was a real challenge. Conversing in the best grammatical style sometimes led to a great deal of laughter, which he never discouraged, but somehow managed to keep even the most obstreperous farm lad from becoming rude or rascally. This revered old man was more teacher than preacher; his thin but forceful voice often broke with the effort he put forth to impress the congregation with the "fire and brimstone" punishment that awaited sinners.

The reverend was a thrifty man, nothing was ever wasted; he had a wonderful garden, even flowers, every summer; the strawberries he raised were the topic of the neighborhood. The minister's house was small and in poor repair, but the manner in which he arranged his meager furnishings made the few beautiful pieces he owned the centers of attraction and comfort. He was noted for the good coffee he brewed and occasionally he made a coffee-cake for the Ladies' Aid from an old German recipe, which the ladies tried in vain to imitate.

One day the Reverend Klenski brought me a little book cut out in the shape of a donkey's head; the "donkey language" in verse form contributed to a gleeful, childhood bond of friendship between us, which I still cherish in memory even as I still cherish the little book.

After about ten fruitful years of faithfully caring for his congregation and others who sought him out in their troubles, the old man became ill and was forced to retire in a distant city. It was a sad goodbye but he made me smile through my tears. I never saw him again.

I shall never forget this man who lived the love he felt for everyone; his oft quoted: "Let your light so shine before men that they may see your good works and glorify your Father which is in heaven" remains a constant memorial "clothed in bright and shining vestments" to gladden the hearts of all who knew him.

GRANDPA'S PRIDE
Mrs. Otto Kangas

There were a number of reasons why the immigrants came from Europe to America, such as freedom from religious persecution, devastating wars, and poverty; but in the case of my grandpa, Friedrich Drews, it was a matter of pride.

He was born in 1841 on a small farm near the village of Ottendorf, District of Naugard, Pomerania, which at that time was a part of Germany, and which is now a part of Poland.

Friedrich, with four sisters, grew up on the Drews farm, married Albertine Buchholz, and had two children, Bertha and Albert.

At that time Ottendorf was a small village, which originally was a settlement or colony taken from the estate of Klein-Leistikow. The colonist did not have the best farmland, and half of the acreage was under water,

so a large family had a hard life there. However, one family was able to live on the Drews farm, and each daughter took a dowry when she left.

Friedrich worked as a shepherd on an estate. He was short of stature, and his pride was deeply injured when the landowner told him that such a small shepherd whose straw bundles dragged in the dirt was of no use to him. These shepherds had to get their own straw and bundle it, and were called the "shepherdbund." When Friedrich returned home, he told his wife that he would not remain another hour as a shepherd for this fellow. Since many families were emigrating to America, he sold what little equity he had, and in 1874 with his wife and two children, emigrated to Wisconsin.

He applied for his naturalization papers that same year, and in 1879 became a citizen of the U.S.

At first he had to work at the Barker-Stewart sawmill in Wausau for a number of years to earn enough money to buy his homestead in the town of Easton, Marathon County, Wisconsin, in 1880, and to build a log house to live in. He wrote letters to his sister, Bertha, in Ottendorf, Pomerania, complaining that he had to work on the farms for pay during the day, and clear out the woodland at night to get arable land. He started farming with one cow and one pig, and a bear killed the pig and ate it. At first he used a team of oxen to work the farm, until he could afford to buy two horses. Finally, he was able to acquire a herd of seven cows, and some calves.

After some time, Friedrich sent letters and photos back to Ottendorf, showing the homestead and a steam-powered threshing machine. He wrote to his sister, Bertha, that he would not exchange his lot with the greatest farmer in Klein-Leistikow.

Friedrich raised nine children on his homestead,

four daughters, and five sons, and was able to give each of his five sons a farm when they married, one of whom was my father, Fred Drews.

Friedrich Drews died in 1928 at the age of eighty-six on the homestead, a proud American. In his case, pride was not his downfall, but his success.

GOD GAVE GRANDMA GERTRUDE GUTS
Mrs. Albertus Lemmenes

Actually, she was not my grandma. The truth is that Gertrude begat Catherine, Catherine begat Jennie, Jennie begat Albertus and Albertus begat me: therefore, Gertrude was my great-great-grandma. No doubt she has had over a hundred descendants (I just can't count them), but I wonder how many of them realize what a great heritage she left us. Other grandparents bequeathed us brains and beauty, spunk and sparkle, even fame and fortune, but from Gertrude we inherited a bit of her huge God-given portion of good old-fashioned "guts." Perhaps I should use a more sophisticated word such as perseverance, pluck, fortitude, or endurance, but mix them all up and you've got guts. Was God putting Gertrude to the test as he did Job in the Old Testament? She passed each test, renewed her faith, and bounced back ready to be tested again.

Gertrude was born in Holland to a wealthy distinguished family named Von Zwaaluwenberg. Her Dutch name was Gerritje. Her first encounter with catastrophe was being disowned by her family. Her parents employed a red-headed gardener named Henry Rozeboem. Class distinction, so prevalent in those days, was blown asunder when Henry and Gerritje fell in love and were married—what a blow to the dignity of the wealthy family to marry into the poor Rozeboem family! They immediately disowned her and she received no inheritance from the huge estate. (About thirty years ago a small fill-in item in a newspaper stated that the well-known Von Zwaaluwenberg estate in Holland had filed bankruptcy papers.) Gerritje endured the taunts of her cousins who threw pennies at her in derision. Her husband Henry became a miller and a baker. The two jobs often went together in Holland; they thereby eliminated the middleman. The bake shop was connected to the house (the two-hundred-year-old structure can still be seen at Nunspeet). One day Henry fell down the winding staircase of his Dutch windmill with a sack of flour on his back and broke his neck. This meant much extra work for Gerritje as she had to care for him. Proud flesh developed and doctors kept leeches on his neck to eat the proud flesh and to stop the infection. He lived six years after this. He was bloated and Gerritje found it hard to make clothes big enough for him. Besides, she had to help more now at the bake shop. She had had no formal education, even though she was brought up by a wealthy family — education wasn't thought necessary for girls. It was difficult for Gerritje to make change as she sold the baked goods. She couldn't add or subtract but used matches and sticks to figure with. This process was slow and irritated her and she was anxious for the day when one of her children who was learning arithmetic would take over.

Having six children meant many trials for Gerritje. When one of the babies was born there was floodwater covering the entire first floor of the house up to the dormer window on the second floor. The doctor who helped in the delivery rowed a boat to the dormer window. Imagine the slow wait for the water to recede, and what a mess to clean! Later a child of theirs was drowned in a canal near the home. When Henry died at the age of fifty, Gerritje wondered what to do with herself and five children. Although her family in Holland had disowned her, she had a brother in America who befriended her. He told her to come to Wisconsin with her family and he would have a log cabin ready for them. After she came to this country, she was known as Gertrude. She met with trials here, too, as she tried to make a living for herself and children. She worked hard in the fields to earn money for the family. One fall she worked long and hard to earn five dollars by husking corn by hand, only to have the money stolen from her.

We are proud to have Gertrude's picture on the parlor wall. Her stern countenance is expressive of her hard rugged life, but, look again, and you see a smile there, too.

So gung-ho, Gertrude, so gallant, so gritty, so gutsy! I think of you as you lie in peace in the little Presbyterian cemetery near Fairwater, Wisconsin. You have rested there nearly a hundred years. Your Dutch Bible became worn out as it gave you faith and hope with each new day. Your love of God was as strong as His love for you. Thank you for the great heritage you left to five generations and many more yet to come. Great-Great-Grandma, you were great!

MA
Mrs. J. L. Tibbetts

We all called her Ma, including Pa, until we were quite grown-up and had met people from outside our neighborhood, school and church. Here every mother was either Ma or Mama, which was reserved mostly for pre-schoolers. Ma was the strongest person I have known in my entire life — not physically, but morally, spiritually, and religiously, including strength of convictions and willpower. Physically she was not weak by any means. On the other hand, she was not at all masculine, but really quite feminine. She was rather tall, but a little stooped and round-shouldered from hard work and had a small, round, protruding belly—no doubt the aftermath of bearing twelve children.

The strength of her moral convictions was well illustrated on numerous occasions, one of which originated at the age of thirteen, soon after the family's arrival from Germany. Ma had made friends with neighboring American girls, with whom she sometimes stayed as babysitter and helper while the parents were away at a not too distant lumber camp which the father ran and the mother served as cook while the regular cook was on a drunk or recovering from one. On Saturday night the girls shampooed their hair and wound it on small scrap metal strips they had picked up at a tinsmith's shop. This was a new and exciting experience for Ma and being eager to become Americanized, she followed suit. The next day, being Sunday, the hired man took a load of hay to the logging camp, and the girls, dressed in their Sunday best, and with curly, curly hairdos rode along to camp on the load of hay. When they arrived at camp, to Ma's chagrin who should be there but my grandma and grandpa. Grandpa gave Ma a few menacing looks but said nothing that could be overheard by others present, but at the opportune moment he grabbed Ma by the hair and said, "You put your hair up, and if I ever again see you with it hanging loose, I'll cut it off close to your head," at the same time scanning the walls as if looking for a scissor to make good his threat immediately. Trembling with fright, Ma promised never to curl her hair again, a promise she didn't break in the ensuing eighty-four years of her life.

Ma and Pa were married at the ages of sixteen and twenty-two respectively. Ma's family were staunch Lutherans, and Pa's family, who migrated from eastern Germany to Wisconsin by way of a twelve-year stop in Ontario, Canada, were Evangelicals. Pa's family was very poor and this plus the difference in religion made him a most unwelcome suitor in the Barfknecht household. But Ma's willpower prevailed, she not only married Pa but also embraced his religion, in which she "found her Saviour" as she often related.

Church attendance was a must for our family, whenever and as often as there was a service. Our farm was three miles from the church and in summer we all piled into our top buggy with side lanterns and fringe around the top and pulled by Sally and Jack, a black mare and a buckskin. In the winter we went in a bobsled, made cozy with a layer of straw in the bottom of the box, covered with blankets, a few heated bricks at our feet and more blankets for covers. Ma and Pa rode on the spring seat— the rest of us in the sleigh box behind. Ma and Pa both had fur coats bought from a mail-order catalog. Ma's three-quarter-length coat was described as Siberian dog and was mostly black hairs which were brown near the hide and had a few white hairs mixed in here and there. Pa's very long coat was unsheared sheepskin in an orangey brown color which seemed to be a popular shade at the time. Ma wore her hair pulled tightly back from the face into braids which were wound into a tight pug well secured on the top of her slightly elongated head. She always wore a hat to church. When the weather was bad

she first wound a fascinator around her head and neck, then, pinning her hat securely to her pug and turning up her large fur collar, she was ready to withstand the strongest gusts of frigid winds. Once in the warmth of the wood stove-heated church she would remove the fascinator and replace her hat.

In those days the men sat on the right side of the church as you entered and the women on the left. Ma always sat in the second pew from the front and Pa sat in the corresponding pew on the men's side. We had no organ or other musical instrument to get the singing started in the right key, which the minister tried to do but did not always succeed. Sometimes the notes went so high or low that they needed to start over again. Ma had a loud clear singing voice and often kept the faltering singing going. Sometimes the church service would be a prayer meeting and the minister would call for volunteers to pray aloud. If there were no volunteers he would call upon members of the congregation by name. Everyone knelt on the bare pine floor usually facing the pews, backs toward the altar. Ma was frequently called upon to pray, but I don't remember ever hearing Pa pray in church. Most of the women played in timid trembling voices and I could never hear what they were saying, but when Ma prayed everyone throughout the church could hear her strong clear voice praising and thanking the Lord for his everlasting goodness and mercy, and calling upon him to justly punish the many who were wicked and sinful.

After church Ma usually invited the minister for dinner or supper and to stay overnight when the weather was bad. This invitation was accepted on numerous occasions. I had a number of older sisters who played the pump organ and sang. Ma praised and enjoyed their hymn singing but was not too pleased with some of the popular songs in their repertory. I loved to sing and endlessly repeated over and over again snatches of the songs I had heard. On one occasion when the minister was present I provided background music with an often repeated rendition of "My mother caught his eye and they got married on the sly, and now I have to call him 'Father'." As soon as the minister left I was collared by Ma's long slender hands and told in no uncertain terms what to expect if she ever heard me sing that song again.

We were a musical family. As I have already said, my sisters played the organ. Pa played the violin, as did my two brothers. They must have done quite well, since the boys were frequently asked to play at houseparties and barn dances. The Evangelical religion was strongly opposed to smoking, drinking and dancing, and it goes without saying that Ma would not approve of these excursions for my brothers. Having inherited some of their genes from their mother, the boys went ahead with plans to play at a Saturday night dance to the point of hitching the horses to the buckboard with their violins safely tucked under the seat. Before they could get into the buggy, Ma was at the horses' heads holding them firmly by the bridle. This was an unexpected impasse which obviously was not easily resolved. It was clearly a test of principles and wills and involved more than face or ego. The boys were in their late teens and Ma was in her late thirties and neither side could afford to capitulate. A quick jerk of the right rein and a flick of the whip sent horses and buggy in an arc to the right. The sudden action threw Ma off balance and to the ground away from the horses and buggy. She was not hurt physically, and according to her philosophy this was not a defeat but rather a victory for her. She had risked everything, including her life, to keep her sons from the clutches of Satan. Now it was in the hands of the good Lord to deal with as he saw fit.

It was this philosophy that kept her calm and serene, interested in life and interesting to others, and sane and happy throughout her long life.

FOR THE PRICE OF A HAIR RIBBON
Sister M. Susanna Neubauer, O.P.

It happened in Chicago, Illinois, in 1906.

My eldest sister was in need of a new hair ribbon. She had begged for it four or five times at least and each time my mother would say, "Child, I am sorry but we cannot afford it now." Then one evening my father heard the request and looking at her ever so kindly said, "Child, for the price of a hair ribbon I could buy a house." My mother looked at him and said, "Pete, do you really mean that?" To everyone's surprise the answer was: "Yes. I saw a sign in front of a little house on Elston Avenue at Clybourn—Name your own price."

From then on, things happened quickly and the next morning my mother was on her way to look into the matter. When she arrived at the scene, the sign was down, but not taken away. She made inquiries and was told that a young man had purchased the house for thirty dollars. Since the house had to be removed she wondered if the young man in question really wanted it, so upon inquiry, she located his whereabouts and to her delight was told that he would sell it. He made a small profit on it and seemed glad to have it off his hands. From there on, my mother's ingenuity was at work. She returned home to talk things over with my father. It was now his turn to be surprised. Her plan was to have the house moved backwards about four or five hundred feet to the edge of the Chicago River. A house mover had to be located. In those days many houses were being moved to make room for the building of large factories. When she contacted a mover, he wanted to know how far the house would have to be hauled. When told about three or four miles, he shook his head and said the price would be exorbitant. It would involve cutting streetcar wires, which in itself would be out of the question. She then told him of her plan to have the house put on a scow and sent up the river to Roscoe Street about three blocks north of Belmont Avenue. The house mover then remarked that he had never done that before and that it would be a big risk. She agreed on that point but said that she would take the risk. When he agreed to do the work, she returned home for a bottle of holy water. She sprinkled every room and prayed for the safety of all concerned. Then she said to the house mover, "Now let her sail."

Since the signatures of all who lived in the north 3300 block on Sacramento Street had to be obtained, our nearest neighbors' children knew about the house that would be "sailing on the river" and the entire Lutheran School at Belmont on the river was on hand to witness and cheer as it passed by. Two blocks north of the bridge the house was again transferred to land without mishap. Then another two blocks or so, and wires were cut for the first and only time to recross Elston Avenue. It still had another half block to go and in a very short time it came to its well-deserved rest. Much needed to be done to the interior and, with the exception of the plastering, my mother took care of that. The older children helped with the papering. All were happy as we now had a house of our very own.

The house is still in use and in good condition with a large spacious kitchen on the ground floor. Wall to wall carpeting is in evidence and a new plumbing and heating system in use. Two of my sisters are still living in this house we called home, and home it really was with seven children, parents and grandfather living together, with no mention of a generation gap any place along the line.

We had a home for the price of a hair ribbon.

PURPLE RIBBONS
Mabel Schroeder

The little white church stood proud and gleaming that Pentecost Sunday. The green branches placed on either side of the wide brick walk gave it a festive air. It was a beautiful June day.

The hushed moment just before the opening prayer was interrupted when through the open doors came the tiny figure of Tante Borsack, Grandpa's older sister. She wore her new rustly black dress, miniature lace cape and on her head the traditional black widow's bonnet of black straw and much lace.

The minister waited while she made her way to a seat near the front and seated herself next to Grandma Laper. As was customary in the Lutheran churches of that day, the men sat on one side of the middle aisle while the women and children sat on the opposite side.

The quiet church heard an audible gasp when Grandma Laper raised her head and beheld Tante Borsack's new bonnet. It was tied under her chin with a huge three-inch-wide purple satin bow. The streamers hung down to her waist.

The services began, but Grandma never once lifted

her head. Her cheeks were a mottled red and her mouth compressed into a straight line.

After the services the clan gathered at Grandma's house for dinner as they did on every festive occasion. The dinner was somewhat late because while Grandma changed into her second-best dress and starched white apron she read the riot act to Tante Borsack. Calm quiet Grandma almost screamed at her aged sister-in-law. How she had disgraced them all by wearing that big purple ribbon. It was brazen and like a woman of the streets to come to church dressed like a hussy.

The table conversation, after the prayer of grace, centered on that purple bow. The older women were outraged. The younger women, being more lenient, said everyone in the congregation knew that Tante Borsack was almost ninety years old and had been a good Christian all her life. The men were amused by all the to-do.

Grandpa Laper had a sparkle in his eyes and an amused quirk on his lips under the precise clipped moustache. Had anyone taken notice, he would have seen him patting Tante Borsack's hand under the table.

Grandma addressed herself to the whole group, asking what should be done about Tante Borsack's purple ribbons. Tante Borsack, in a decisive tone, answered her, "If I can't wear my new bonnet with the purple ribbons, I just won't go to church."

Uncle John rose to his six-foot-three height and settled the matter. What a commotion to make over an old lady who loved color. They all admired her beautiful purple gloxinias and all the brilliantly colored flowers in her garden. Let her wear her bonnet. They all must realize it was a Laper church, and with the exception of two or three families, everyone was related to everyone else. "Let Tante Borsack enjoy her new bonnet and let's forget about it and eat Grandma's good dinner before it gets cold."

Tante Borsack wore her purple ribbons every Sunday that summer. At the end of the summer she died peacefully in her sleep. As was the custom in the middle 1800s Tante Borsack was laid to rest in her best black dress and widow's bonnet. But Grandma Laper had her way at last. The purple ribbons were tucked into the bonnet and proper narrow black ones tied under the stubborn little chin.

Purple flowers predominated in the church that day, and most of them had lavender or purple ribbons attached to them.

Before the casket was closed, Grandma spied a generous section of purple ribbon peeping out from under the bonnet and nestled in the white hair above the wrinkled forehead.

Grandpa avoided Grandma's glance and with his handkerchief he wiped a tear (or did he cover up a triumphant gleam in his expressive eyes).

Later Grandma asked Uncle John about it, but she never did find out. Tante Borsack and her purple ribbons kept their secret well.

INSPIRATION FOR PRAYER
Roderick MacDonald

When I first saw the Bithac, I was riding with my father in our surrey, on our way home from a little town called St. Charles located about six miles from where we lived. The word Bithac, I was told, meant "little old lady" and originated in the north of Scotland.

She was terribly stooped; in fact, she was bent almost double. She was not tall and when she walked, her face didn't seem far from the ground. My father told me this was the result of a bad accident in a coal mine in southern Scotland.

When she appeared from behind a clump of weeds that were between us and a farm fence, something caught my eye and there she was and I was startled. She was looking sort of sideways at us with what seemed like a leer on her face. She yelled at my father—something in Gaelic—and he yelled back and she crossed the ditch and came and got in our surrey.

She was also on her way home from St. Charles and was carrying some supplies in a large sack. We drove her home a few miles beyond where we lived and she chatted like a magpie all the way.

Her family, two sons and one daughter, were married and gone. We knew her husband was killed in the Spanish-American War and it was the small pension from his war services plus her share of the proceeds from a farm share-worker that enabled her to carry on.

When she talked, her voice was almost as deep as a man's and had a noticeable, slight whistle in it, or maybe more like a squeak, somewhat like that made by a bagpipes when the player is trying to get them started playing.

She said she was now eighty-eight years old but felt much younger all in all; even with her facial scars and a deep squeaky talk, she seemed a most wholesome person. I got to like her at once.

A year or so after this first meeting, she died. In spite of no telephones, the word spread quickly and we knew the next morning. My father said, "Well, I'd better plan on being at the Bithac's tonight." We knew this was so, as he always was asked by the neighbors to lead in things such as church affairs, and he was the accepted leader at barn raisings and all affairs that needed a leader. The fact that he was deputy sheriff, I suspect, had something to do with it.

The call came and I was allowed to accompany my father to the wake, which was an established affair in that part of the country. The area was mostly Scotch-Catholic and was a long way from a church or a priest. The priest got around to saying mass and hearing confessions in our neighborhood about once a year and he tried to make all the funerals. My father was the most articulate man in our part of the county, so if a priest wasn't able to make it, my father could function first-rate as a stand-in, and often did.

When we arrived at the Bithac's home, there were a number already there and when we opened the door, a cloud of tobacco smoke met us in the kitchen part of the little house where most of the men were gathered and mostly all smoking. A neighbor lady friend of the Bithac escorted us into the part of the house used as bedroom and living room, where the Bithac lay in state. I got a surprise when I looked at her for she was lying flat on her back, not bent over at all. My father took a seat across from the bier, in front of several women who were seated on a long davenport opposite it.

When my father started the rosary, he knelt beside the bed where the Bithac lay. He had just about finished the fourth decade when I felt his foot against my knee, so I backed away a little. This happened several times and soon we were right at the door. By looking past him I saw the reason: the Bithac was sitting up, her mouth half open, her face turned towards us. I guess many saw this as I did.

There was a general rush to the door. In truth, the house was empty in less than half a minute. My father still was saying the rosary loudly and standing up, just outside the door. Just then a loud bumping noise started under the house and once in a while came a sound that was something like a wail. At this, despite my father's praying loudly, many started to run.

Those who remained were not paying much attention to the rosary, in spite of my father admonishing them that when saying the rosary they were in God's hands and nothing could hurt them.

Just then, though, a man went by on a horse, the horse at a gallop and the man shouting: "The devil is after you, you better get out of there!" At this, my father said in a loud voice: "Listen! Never mind praying anymore right now. The devil just went by in the form of Jack Brady, whom you all know as the prankster of this township. I hope God will forgive him for such a nasty trick as this."

My father then went to the side of the house, near the door, and pulled out a large block of wood, revealing a good-sized hole, and out jumped a very frightened dog from where it had been trapped beneath the house. From there, my father went to the back of the house near to where the Bithac lay, and from a window next to where she was lying, he pulled a length of clothes line that had been holding her but had been cut, allowing the corpse to sit up.

Around in front again, he showed this to those gathered and said: "Jack Brady won't have to go to confession for this. It will be a pleasure for me to tell the priest for him."

At this there was some laughter which seemed to relieve the strain. Then, Mrs. McCloed and some other neighbors went in and straightened things up a bit and, with the help of a couple of the men, soon had things looking OK. They then invited us in and we all had a fine midnight lunch.

MEET MY UNCLE BART
May Augustyn

The stiff pages of the old family album fell open to the middle section and there was the smiling face of my Uncle Bart. A dandy of the "Gay Nineties," his clothes were a perfect example of the times, and his manner was that of a "Man About Town." I've heard my mother tell how the men of the family sometimes snickered at his wardrobe and the things he did, but the women and children thought him a lovable authority, above reproach.

His picture always left us spellbound, as *he* had years ago. It was to this photograph that we turned first whenever the book was opened. Uncle Bart leaned gracefully against a wooden pedestal with his left arm resting on top of it, while his right hand nonchalantly fingered a heavy gold chain. The clip of this splendid chain fastened in a vest buttonhole. The two ends were draped across his ample expanse of waistcoat, coming to rest in small pockets on either side. A handsome gold locket formed a charm and occupied a conspicuous place in the picture.

One leg was crossed carelessly over its partner and a derby hat rested on the back of his curly black hair. His high button, toothpick shoes and tight trousers were the fad of the day, as were his puffed necktie and cutaway coat. But the most fascinating part of the whole picture was his long, black, wavy mustache, groomed until it shown like burnished metal. It was truly something to admire, and perhaps that is why his male relatives were a trifle jealous of this outstanding feature. His white skin was a marked contrast to his jet black hair and dark eyes.

The thrill of all thrills was when Uncle Bart reached into his vest pocket and drew out a quill toothpick. Then it was we forgot our manners and gazed with ever widening eyes at the things that toothpick could do. Finally it was carefully wiped and put away for another occasion.

The smell of a good cigar seemed always to cling to Uncle Bart, and the great smoke rings that floated lazily to the ceiling were always just out of our reach.

One of his greatest accomplishments was the vast number of songs he could sing. They would be called hillbilly tunes or folk songs today but they were tender and touching and we loved them. Small child that I was I cried plenty as he sang. The other members of the group often joined in the chorus, and when the evening was over all agreed they had had a fine time. Perhaps people today would find it hard to believe such evenings were fun, but they were. We could hardly wait for Uncle Bart's next visit.

Now after all these years the memory of his fashionable dress and gay manners flashes back to fill me with the love I felt for him. As Uncle Bart throws back his head and opens his mouth to sing he is with us again, and I'm happy to know you have met my Uncle Bart.

AN INCI-DENTAL CHILDHOOD
Herbert W. Kuhm

Some children are born with the proverbial silver spoon in their mouths; I teethed on a nickel-plated dental forceps. My father's dental office was in the front part of our home, and while some patient was groaning in the agony of parting with a molar, I was emitting my first meager yelp at coming into the world in a bedroom just down the hall. This was back in 1898.

The trauma of my childhood was hearing patients screaming from the excruciating agony of having a tooth extracted sans anesthetic. Only for multiple extractions was a general anesthetic administered, and then only by the neighborhood physician who came to my father's office with his apparatus for chloroform or ether. It was then I would palm my ears to mute the wailing.

Before the advent of local anesthetics, fear kept many from dental offices until their suffering was unbearable. My father, the late Dr. John Kuhm, an early Milwaukee dentist, told me of a husky coal-heaver who came to his office for an extraction. Belligerently threatening with a hammy fist, the feisty bruiser warned my father, who barely inched over five feet, "If you hurt me, I'll knock you through the window!" Unperturbed, my father placed a crown-setting mallet on his bracket instrument table, and ominously said, "If you make one move, I'll wallop you square between the eyes!" It was a case of brain over brawn. There was nary a peep from the cowed bruiser.

My father also related an embarrassing incident when no anesthetic was used. A young lady came to him one hot summer day, bustled and wasp-waisted in a white linen dress after the fashion of the late nineties. The torrid day, added to the heat induced by the bruting drill, caused the young lady to perspire profusely. When the ordeal was over, the Gibsonesque girl rose from the chair and to my father's chagrin, her dress showed a startlingly carmine-stained back and seat from his red plush upholstered chair.

Being the son of a dentist in those days could either

develop character or reduce one to sniveling paranoia. I was baited on the school grounds with taunts of "Your old man's a butcher!" or "Your pop's a horse doctor!" I soon learned I could not fight every bully spoiling to rough me up, and that to ignore them was the better part of valor.

My father's struggle to become a dentist was in itself a gritty saga of determination. At the age of thirty-eight, married and running a small tea and coffee store on Milwaukee's north side, he decided to take up dentistry. Mother took to tending the store during the daytime while he was at college; then he took over at night. With books and papers spread out over a counter, he would study between waiting on stray evening customers.

Upon graduation he sold the store and had my carpenter uncle build him a combined office and dwelling at Seventeenth Street and North Avenue, which was then still paved with tarred cedar blocks; fir wagons delivering coal, ice, or milk were horse-drawn. (Outside of the knife-sharpener's wagon with its foot-powered lathe, the most intriguing vehicle for us youngsters was that of the Little Sisters of the Poor, who paid visits to butchers, grocers and bakers, gratefully accepting handouts for their wards. It was a dinky windowless black box mounted on four spindly wheels, drawn by a nag equally spindly. We kids marveled to see the mendicant Sisters, always in pairs, fit their cumbrous starched headpieces into their cramped cubicle.)

Whereas the present-day dentist refers patients to exodontists, orthodontists, periodontists, endodontists, pedodontists and prosthodontists, and sends dentures, crowns and bridges to dental laboratories for processing, those early day dentists had to fulfill the concept of the "whole man," fashioning these products themselves. Dur-ing the busy fall and winter season my father worked at the chair on weekdays until about 8:00 p.m., came down for a light lunch which he ate leisurely while reading the *Germania Abendpost*, *Die Gartenlaube*, or *Fliegende Blaetter*, then went upstairs to his laboratory for several hours of mechanical work.

With most of my aunts, uncles and cousins gravitating to my father for their dental work, our home became the epicenter of the clan. Invariably they dropped in at our living quarters downstairs before their appointments for they never knew how presentable they would be after. In this clearinghouse of gossip, my mother came to hear most everything going on in the relationship, yet wisely chose not to add fuel to any low-smouldering feud between aunties or cousins. Her deftness at parrying prying questions was a lesson for both my sisters and me.

The coffee break is accepted routine in offices nowadays, but it was left to my father to invent the chicken break. Mid-morning and mid-afternoon he would feel the need for "the pause that refreshes." Excusing himself to his patient, he would doff his office gown, and go out to the backyard chicken coop that housed a dozen or so black minorcas, white leghorns and Rhode Island reds. He would check the nests for eggs, then give the cacklers a feeding of grits and ground shells. On Saturday mornings the coop became my domain to remove the week's accretion of guano with a putty knife and to change the nest straw. Each summer I had to paint its interior, much after the manner of Huckleberry Finn, with a calcimine paint called "whitewash."

In those days the north side of Milwaukee was so German that even the dogs used to bark in German. Some stores had signs for the benefit of the "foreigners" from the east and south side reading: "English Hier Gesprochen." Even the sign in front of my father's office was bilingual, reading "Dentist-Zahnarzt."

My early involvement in the life of a dentist did not deter me from following for fifty-two years in the footsteps of the man who must have inspired me. Obviously a case of "like father, like son."

MY CONTRIBUTIONS TO BUFFALO COUNTY
Otto Witte

I came to the city of Mondovi in 1903 to be a German clerk in a Pace and McGreggors store, which is now the Mahlum's Drug store. I was twenty or twenty-one years old. At the store I earned thirty-five dollars a month and when I was there for two years I received top pay which was sixty dollars a month. The store carried general merchandise, which consisted of clothing, material, dry goods, shoes and groceries. I lived in a boarding house on North Eau Claire Street. It was called "Aunt Toots." I had a room to sleep in and we had our meals in a dining room. I paid three dollars and fifty cents a week for this. The owner was a policeman in town. His wife ran the boarding house. It was later remodeled by Dr. P. B. Amunson into a hospital. I lived there until I married Ollie Gates in 1906.

In 1904 I thought there should be some entertainment or recreation so I decided to do something about it. I rented the upstairs of what is now the City Furniture Store, to open an opera house. I had a stage, complete with curtains, built with hired help. I borrowed the money without interest. Then I booked the best shows. I also put in a basketball court. I had it open at all times.

I only ran it for a couple of years—but people said it was a great success. I then sold it.

When Ollie and I were first married we rented a house in town. I then bought my first farm. It was located about one and a half miles west of Mondovi on County Trunk A. I had the house built before we moved onto the farm. It was nestled on the south side of a hill. We had eighty acres, on which I raised purebred Poland-China hogs for breeding. I would sell these hogs to my neighbors. The price of pork was then four dollars a hundred. At one time we had up to forty or fifty hogs. We also had about a dozen Jersey cows, chickens, turkeys, and a purebred collie dog.

When I came to Mondovi there was only one car in town. The next year there were six and each year after that they kept increasing. Cars were bought within the range of five hundred to a thousand dollars. I bought my first car in 1923. It was a Model T. The cars didn't go as fast as they do today, oh maybe forty miles per hour. In the wintertime the roads were not in shape for cars, so we used the horses, a buggy, a sleigh, and a cutter. We would take the cutter to town to do shopping. The roads were dirt and the county had a man who would grade them with a grader pulled by two horses. It often got awfully muddy, but with the horses you went right through it. I have had four new cars in my entire life. The first was a Model T which I bought new in 1923. The second was a Model A. I can't remember what the third was, but my last one was a 1961 Chevy which I bought new.

We stayed on the farm for about five years the first time. The farm was rented out then, but we later moved back. While on the farm I was the town treasurer of Mondovi.

After we left the farm we moved back to Mondovi

and I bought a confectionery store. I carried groceries and candies. The store was on South Eau Claire Street and the building still stands today as the Three Bears Bakery. I didn't have the store too long, just a couple of years. We went back to the farm again for a time.

In 1928 I sold Ford cars, trucks and tractors for a short time, but cars didn't sell because we couldn't get any cars due to the change from the Model T to the Model A. So to fill in for a job I started building roads out of native shale. As we were unable to get crushed rock, I opened shale pits with a gasoline-operated shovel, which I eventually purchased by paying three dollars a day until I paid for it. I started with seven trucks and seventeen men. I worked my company up to fourteen trucks and twenty men, also a horse-drawn grader. The men worked for thirty-five cents an hour. Then Buffalo County hired me in 1932 to be patrol superintendent because I could build better roads cheaper. We then started to use oil and blacktop. While I was Buffalo County Patrol Superintendent we lived in Alma for one year but moved back in 1935 when I quit the county. We then moved back to the farm.

From 1935 until 1955 I was on a few different farms. I would buy them and then rent them out. I also purchased lots in town and had some houses built, which I later sold at a profit. I owned one hundred and sixty acres of timberland in Eau Claire County. I had the timber cut and sawed and used this for my houses. I built one house on the corner of State and Vine streets. I sold it for six thousand dollars and it recently sold for fourteen thousand dollars. I also bought the Harvey School house for four hundred dollars and moved it to town on Vine Street. I started to remodel it when my wife died. I went ahead and finished it. I then sold it for twelve thousand dollars. I sold everything I could when my wife died because it was just me left and I didn't need it. I then moved to town for sixteen years. I retired at the age of seventy-two. I took trips downtown and played cards at my friends' homes.

I came to the American Lutheran Home in 1971. As a resident of the home I feed the ducks every day. They always come back and wait to be fed. I will often sit on the porch and smoke my pipe and reminisce of old times and of the mistakes I've made by changing jobs so many times. I have done so much in my life that it is hard for me to remember the correct dates and fit everything into place but I have a lot of good memories. I like the fresh air and I walk over town every day. Having been in Mondovi for seventy years I know everyone and they know me. I have a lot of friends and I enjoy them most of all. Everyone stops me on the street and says, "Hello Otto."

10 GYPSIES

FATHER MEETS THE GYPSIES
Ruth C. Lembke

Progress is not all pleasant. Sometimes pathos is a part of it. When my parents purchased our first automobile, a new Model A Ford, in 1927, it meant they had to sell Topsy, the buggy horse, to make room for the motorized vehicle. This was particularly difficult for my father. He loved Topsy as one of the family.

"George, why don't we take a trip to the Dells with our new car?" Mother ventured on the day that Topsy left and the car arrived. This was Mother's supreme sacrifice, for she didn't enjoy long trips of any kind. My sister Florence and I perked up, for we loved any excuse, as did Father, to go someplace—anyplace.

"Would you really like to go?" asked Father, beginning to warm to the idea. Mother's ruse to divert his attention from Topsy was working. Before long Mother was boiling water for tea, filling milk bottles with it, making dozens of jelly, peanut butter and New England ham sandwiches and washing raw carrots to take along. Florence gathered all the cookies she could find, for she was always hungry. Father assembled a kit of tools and patches for repairing tires. At five years of age, I was not that practical. I brought my doll.

"We must get to bed early tonight. We will get up at four o'clock tomorrow. It's a hundred and twenty miles to the Dells," Father's excitement registered in his voice. We dashed off to bed, but there was little sleeping.

The alarm blared out just as each of us had finally dozed off. Mother and Father bustled about. Breakfast was on the table in minutes and Father checked the luggage once more to see that the tent was tied securely to the running board. Still sleepy, Florence and I stumbled into the back seat. We were off in the darkness while everyone else was still in bed! The fresh cool air soon woke us up.

The first flat tire came around noon. We were near a schoolhouse with outdoor "plumbing" which was most welcome. Mother spread the tablecloth on the steps and brought out the lunch while Father jacked up the rear wheel and removed the tire and inner tube. I was fascinated by his skill. He let me hold the warm inner tube while he turned it to locate the leak. Every now and then he put a little spittle on the tube where he thought it was leaking. Finally little bubbles appeared in the spittle.

"There we are!" exclaimed Father as he reached for the patch. After lunch, when the patch had dried, Father put the tube back in the tire and pumped air into it. It looked like new again when he lowered the jack.

Late in the afternoon of that day, it began to rain. Florence and I were delighted because we liked excitement. Father stopped and we jumped out as he pulled the new side curtains from under the back seat where they were kept. Because they were new, we had to pull and stretch them to reach the buttons which for meant for each hole. It was fun to get inside again and feel cozy while the rain pelted outside. Of course we could not see out, the square isinglass windows were up too high. Though they were new the side curtains didn't fit tight and the rain dribbled in. Florence and I huddled closer together in the middle of the seat.

The shower passed, but we couldn't go.

"What's the trouble, George?" Mother sounded worried.

"The carburetor is wet. We'll have to wait for it to dry out," Father's response exuded confidence.

"Let's eat!" Florence suggested. Immediately Mother

opened a bottle of cold tea and wet sandwiches. Soggy as they were, we relished them.

After two more flat tires and another rainstorm we got to the Dells. We set up the tent and put up the cots to sleep on. Mother insisted on naps before we went to the ticket office and bought seating for the boat trip through the Dells of the Wisconsin River. The beauty was breathtaking. Stand Rock was my favorite. The ships were Father's. Mother liked the flowers and Florence the ice cream stand.

We slept well all night. We were so tired by now we could have slept on a rock. The next morning Mother woke early. She was eager to start home. I'm certain she could hardly wait to get home to her own bed. When the sun came up, we noticed that others were in the same tenting ground. The night before we were all alone. But the others were not in a tent. A colorful wagon stood close by. Two horses were tied to a tree. Mother's eyes grew big; her breath came in short jerks. She snatched Florence and me. We were on our way to look more closely at the pretty wagon.

"Gypsies!" she whispered into our ears. "Quick, get your father!"

"Gypsies!" gasped Florence and I. We had never seen gypsies, but we had heard all sorts of wild stories about them. They were supposed to steal everything from everybody. Once we heard that they even stole little children. Then it dawned upon me that I was a little child. I stepped closer to Mother and held on to Betsy tightly.

Father appeared in the tent opening. Mother, now speechless, pointed to the wagon and horses. Silently she formed the word "gypsies." In the gray light of early morning Mother's face looked paler than the white granite washbowl on the table.

"Let's get packed," directed Father, in a more decisive tone than he usually used. "It's time to go." He seemed to be ignoring Mother's fear, but he was only guarding his own.

In short time we were packed and ready. I was just a little disappointed, for we had not seen any gypsy.

"Get in!" ordered Father. We jumped into the back seat. The auto started on the third try. Father released the brake only to find the wheels wouldn't turn. We were stuck fast in the sand. Father got out and tried to push. He was a small man, but strong. Even all his strength expended wouldn't budge the new car. Florence began to bite her nails! Mother was next to tears and I squeezed Betsy until the sawdust came out of her insides.

All of us were so intent upon our predicament that we were unaware of the gypsies emerging from the wagon. They clustered about us. Startled, we looked up to see three dark-skinned men towering over Father and three gaily dressed women close behind them. I couldn't take my eyes off the women. One wore a red full long skirt with yellow and green shiny stripes and a bandana to match it, covering thick black shiny hair in a bun on her neck. One man had a wide sash of gold and another band of gold about his black hair. His smile showed very white and even teeth.

"Stuck?" he questioned as Father stood up.

"Yes," Father answered. His voice sounded like someone else's. "This sand is too much for these wheels."

"We help," the gypsy offered. Father and the three gypsy men pushed with all their combined might, but that Model A refused to move.

"We get horses. We pull." The three gypsy men went and hitched up the two horses. The women remained. They looked the car over and smiled at us. Mother wore her pasted-on smile which told us she was frightened. Florence began biting the nails on her right hand now. The gypsy with the bright skirt came close and touched my hair. I had red curls. She looked at the other women and said something in a language I didn't understand. She smiled. Suddenly I saw her as a beautiful woman not any different from my own mother. I smiled back. She patted me on the head. I can still feel that gentle touch.

Now the men had returned with the horses. They attached them to the front axle. The horses made short work of pulling the car out onto solid ground. The gypsies laughed.

Father hurriedly dug into his wallet to pay the gypsies.

"No! No!" They waved him off. "We like it."

Then the pretty woman spoke to the man. He turned to Father.

"She want curl from little girl hair," he explained. Father looked at Mother and Mother looked at Father. They smiled their own natural smiles and said, "Certainly."

From somewhere in her huge skirt the pretty gypsy woman brought out a small pair of scissors. She came to me, smiled into my face, lifted a curl and snipped it off. Then she bent over and hugged me. Mother relaxed and, pleased, smiled too. The gypsies stepped back and we started off. They waved until we were out of sight.

For a long time no one spoke. Each of us was undergoing a change of attitude—we were making real progress in the pleasantest of ways. At last Mother seemed to be speaking for all of us, "Aren't gypsies wonderful people!"

THE NIGHT THE GYPSIES CAME TO DINNER
Maurine H. Leischer

Moisture collected on the kitchen windows, shutting out the early dark as we prepared the evening meal. Mama was at the stove, turning the chicken over again and again as she fried it to a delicious tastiness. My two younger sisters were setting the dining-room table, while our grandmother, who was visiting us for the day, checked on their progress, wanting to be of help. I was just going to the pantry to cut the bread, when a loud demanding knock came at the kitchen door.

Mama, surprised at the unusual quality of the sound, turned and went to the door, but she had no more than touched the doorknob, when it was thrust open, and a gypsy woman, followed by a slightly smaller gypsy man, pushed their way into the kitchen.

Our little French grandmother gave a startled "Oh, my!" and shooing the girls ahead of her, fled to the living room where she sat facing the kitchen, big-eyed with fright. Apprehensively, I backed up to the pantry door to await what might happen, but Mama, slight of build but strong in character, faced the gypsies.

The gypsy woman gestured with an outflung hand. "Give us to eat," she said. The black eyes in her dark, alien face were intense in their demand.

Mama showed no hesitation at all, but motioning to a place near the door where they could put their bundles, calmly said, "Put your things right there and come and sit down. I'll get you something to eat right away. It's almost ready."

The gypsies held a little private conversation in their own language and placed their bundles by the door and then sat down at the table. The gypsy woman carefully arranged the folds of her dirty pink skirt as she sat down. It seemed to be very bulky. Her faded brownish shawl remained about her shoulders. The man, dressed in a green plaid shirt and brown pants, had neither cap nor jacket. It was very late in the fall for them to be out on the road in northern Wisconsin, for the gypsies who came to our small town every year had been gone for a month or more.

We had never fed gypsies before and had never fed any foot travelers in the house at all, but to look at Mama that night, you'd never have known but what she entertained gypsies every night of the week. Her calm attitude reassured me, and I started setting the table quickly, feeling that the sooner they were fed, the sooner they would be out of the house.

They sat so close to the table that I had to reach around them to lay their places. A smell of wood smoke and earth or leaves and many other unknown odors seemed to come from them in the warm room and to mingle with the smells of the steaming food on the stove.

The gypsy woman talked to the men and seemed to be telling him what to do but he only answered in monosyllables. Clearly she was the leader of the two. They didn't speak to us at all.

As soon as I had their places laid and the bread, butter, milk and jelly on the table, we put the hot food on. There was fried chicken, potatoes and chicken gravy, some late green beans cooked with bacon, and some of Mama's delicious home-canned corn.

They seemed particularly to enjoy the home-canned corn, and Mama refilled the bowl until they had finally eaten the whole quart. They had coffee, and ended the meal with jelly roll for dessert. Mama was noted for her

excellent jelly roll and I wanted these strangers to enjoy a real treat, so I had cut two good slices for each of them.

When they had eaten everything, they just sat and rested a few minutes. Then the woman picked up the silverware at her place and held it, handles down, resting on the table. She reached over and got the silverware from the man's place and added it to her collection. She followed this with the gravy spoon and the spoons from the vegetable bowls and finally took the small spoon from the jelly.

She moved the handful of silverware to the left, resting it a second, and then to the right, setting it down, and moving it again. I watched her, fascinated, wondering what she would do next.

Mama was watching her too, knowing that any second a lightning-swift move would carry it to some spot concealed in the folds of her heavy skirt and it would disappear forever. We waited.

Suddenly the man spoke. It was the first time he had volunteered any of the conversation between them, but he spoke with authority. It was only a couple of words, but the woman gave out something like a sigh and relaxed. She slowly opened her hand and laid the silver beside her plate. She carefully got up, rearranged her shawl, and they picked up their bundles. With the man's hurried "Tenk you, Lady," they slipped out the kitchen door into the night.

I hurried to the window and wiped away the steam so I could see which direction they were going, but all I could see in the light of that cold September moon was the sparkle of the frost at the edges of the wooden sidewalk boards.

In those late Depression days, there were many "tramps" on the road. Some whom Mama fed were men from the cities who were on their way to find relatives who lived on farms where they might stay and work for their keep.

In the spring there were always lumberjacks between jobs after the break-up of the winter logging camps. The men were always polite and offered to work, but Mama never required that of them.

She would ask them to sit in one of the chairs under the willow out in back of the house while she fixed something for them. Whatever we had in the house, she shared, for she had always believed in that verse that said: "For I was an hungered, and ye gave me meat: thirsty, and ye gave me drink: I was a stranger and ye took me in."

Even gypsies.

JUST PASSING THROUGH
Charlotte Knechtges

While I waited for the grocery man to fill my pitcher with scoops of ice cream, I listened to the men talking. "Oh, they're beggars and swipers all right but they never hurt anyone. At least not as far as I know. They do leave their mark, though. I'd get my stuff inside if I were you."

The farmer hefted his fifty-pound sack of sugar to his shoulder and left. The storekeeper turned to me, "Somebody having a birthday?" I squirmed in anticipation of the golden treat: "Mama." He put an extra dip into my pitcher. I handed him my eight hoarded pennies and flew out the door into the summer morning.

I stopped and looked both ways up and down the dusty street. "Always watch out for runaway horses," my mother cautioned me every time I went on an errand. I didn't see any white-eyed horses running amuck, but up the street where the town ended and the farms began I saw something else. I saw a caravan of gypsies.

I remembered them from other summers. The creaking wagons, the slowly walking horses driven by men with drooping moustaches, the young men on horseback, the heavy women plodding in their long skirts, the skinny-legged children, and the dogs—the dogs that barked.

Each year the gypsies passed through our town, coming in from the west, on their way to Madison. They camped overnight in Cooper's pasture on the eastern edge of town, beside the Six-Mile Creek. Their stay was brief because by the next day the town's lawman would catch up with them and move them on their way.

I ran home through the alleys and into the house, slamming the back door behind me. The kitchen smelled of hot crusty bread and freshly ironed dresses. "The gypsies are coming." My mother turned and looked at me. She put her flatiron back on the stove and said, "Run up and get your sisters. They're picking berries at Aunt Mary's. They're late now. Tell them to come home at once. Tell Aunt Mary the gypsies are here. Yell at her. Be sure she understands. Tell her to lock her doors. Then come home."

I ran up the hill and yelled at the shadow of a lady standing in her doorway, her white hair and white apron gleaming and the blue veins standing out high on her forehead. "The gypsies are coming. They are already on Main Street. Mama says to lock your doors." She heard and nodded. I ran to the berry patch. "Mama says to get right home. The gypsies are here." My sisters dropped their pails and ran with me. We could hear the dogs barking. The town dogs barked and the gypsy dogs barked back at them. We ran past a neighbor woman who hurried out her front door, wiping her hands on her top apron. "What happened? Your Aunt Mary sick? Did you tell the priest?" We shook our heads. "The gypsies are coming." She threw up her hands to heaven. We met old Grandpa Berschens, with his flowing beard and long white hair, on his way to the church to ring the Angelus at noontime. We shouted at him, "The gypsies are coming." He just hobbled on.

Mother was out in the yard. "First get those towels that are bleaching on the gooseberry bushes, then help me get the chickens in." She had already snatched the sheets off the clothes line and was flapping them at the protesting hens. We joined her with our towels and shooed them into the coop and hooked the door. "Pick the ripe tomatoes." Our two pet pigeons followed us to the garden begging to be fed. "Not now," I told them.

Mother ran to the smokehouse to take down a shriveled ham and a dried slab of bacon, leftovers from the days when my father was living. We hurried to help her. Her hands trembled as she tugged at the strings.

We had almost reached the porch when the first full toll of the Angelus rang out. Mother stopped. We all stood still, folded our hands and prayed our noon prayers with the bell in the background. Two strokes and a pause, two strokes and a pause, two more strokes and a pause and then the wild ringing of exultation. In the after quiet, an old gypsy woman and six children of varying sizes came toward us from around the house. She was fat with layers of clothes and toothless and dirty with smudges from her many campfires. Her wiry gray hair pointed in all directions. The children, their hungry eyes huge in their thin dark faces, mesmerized us. Mother stepped between us protectively, and the old woman said,

"Could you spaddige me a pidgie?" Our pet pigeons, proud in their white plumage, strutted close to us, pecking in the dirt.

"No," Mother answered quaveringly at first and then more firmly, "No." Suddenly the gypsy woman reached out and grabbed her hand. She uncurled the fingers. Bent low, the hand held flat in her own, she droned, "Trouble, trouble. Full of trouble. I see nothing but trouble." Mother snatched her hand away. "I'll get you some bread and butter for the children and then you must go."

We went with Mother into the house. She said to me, "Get the butter crock from the cellar." She pushed to one side the pitcher of melted ice cream on the table and took two loaves of bread from under the snowy dish towels spread over them, the bread she had been saving for the Sisters of St. Agnes.

She carried the loaves and the butter to the back porch in her apron and stretched out her arms full-length to hand them to the gypsy woman who stood waiting, her eyes darting to the chicken coop, on to the garden and back to Mother's face. The old woman wrapped the food in her ravelled gray shawl, and she and five of the children went down the steps, through the yard and out the gate. The other child ran on far ahead, dragging our ham and bacon behind him. We watched them go.

Mother turned and went into the kitchen, staring into her open hand as she walked. We followed her. She went to the wash basin and lathered her hand with the bar of Fels Naphtha soap that was on the bench. She rubbed and rubbed.

HALES CORNERS FAIR
Emily E. Hunt

A cloud of dust rose behind the hill. Harnesses jingled. "They're coming! They're coming!" The four children playing in the barn driveway raced toward the road. Each hid behind one of the great oak trees, for "Didn't you know that gypsies steal children?"

Peering out, they saw, first, a calico pony come racing over the hill, ridden by a dark boy about twenty. He wore khaki trousers, cowboy boots, a black shirt and a blue straw hat which was held on by bright red ribbons tied under his chin in a huge bow. Fourteen wagons followed. They were like old-fashioned delivery wagons but each was brightly painted blue, green, yellow or red. Designs, mainly of the sun, moon and stars, were superimposed upon the bright background colors. Each had an open back door. Suspended just below the door, across its full width, was a strong basketlike container heaped with all manner of belongings — pails, bedding, clothing and cooking utensils. Each wagon was leading a horse or two.

When the wagons reached the foot of the hill, the horses slowed to a walk for the long, level stretch of road in the front of the large farmyard. A vivacious dark lady with bright eyes, straight black hair and enormous golden earrings squatted in the back door of one of the wagons, chattering incessantly to the two little children who rode on top of the basket of belongings at her feet. She pointed out the farm children to them. The gypsy children giggled.

They were all on their way to the Hales Corners Fair. For this was the Friday before the first Monday of the month. Long before the turn of the century this fair had been held, regardless of the weather, on twelve "first Mondays" each year. For many farm people this was the highlight of the month. They met their friends and relatives from miles around and exchanged gossip and recipes for everything — from new ways to cook rhubarb to how to housebreak the dog. They also enjoyed looking for bargains, as did the hundreds of Milwaukee people who came regularly. These were, for the most part, wives of foreign-born working people who toiled in Milwaukee factories. There were never cannier buyers.

The gypsies camped Saturday and Sunday in a large woods on the edge of town. The men busied themselves training, grooming and carefully minimizing the faults of the horses they had brought to trade. They showed them to potential buyers who straggled into the camp from time to time. The women scattered over the town, each wearing a full bright skirt which reached the ground and which was held out by several equally full stiff white petticoats. They walked very rapidly, their eyes darting from side to side, evaluating the pedestrians. Choosing the more gullible ones, they would offer to tell a fortune for a silver coin.

Shortly before dawn vehicles loaded down with articles to be sold began to roll into the fair. The earliest arrivals had the best chance of getting the choicest spots on the square to park. First in was a large truckload of seed potatoes from Antigo. It had been in transit all night. Later in the season there would be a large truck or two from the south loaded with watermelons. The popcorn wagon pulled in and parked, as usual, in front of its owner's favorite tavern. The snake oil medicine man, big and burly, unloaded his bottles of medicine "guaranteed" to cure everything from corns to rheumatism. Finally, he took a huge, but harmless, sluggish snake out of a cage and draped it around his neck.

Then the farmers, who had had to do chores at home first, began to arrive. Feeder pigs, in lots from two to sixty, were plentiful. A man leading an obstreperous billy goat appeared and took his place. Two of the gypsies leading three horses found a place where they could tie them to a fence. These they would use as samples of what they had back at the camp in the woods. Pickup trucks with crates of chickens—stewing hens or fryers—were plentiful. One small boy was cradling a baby coon he hated to sell. In one truck a bushel basket with six small kittens, one of them coal black, was squeezed in among the crates of fowl. A skinny old farmer, needing a bath and clean overalls, was guarding a crate containing eleven guinea hens. "I'll get rid of them things, by gum!" he announced. "Good watchdogs? Ha! I don't need no watchdogs if a bat flies over or the moon rises."

There were cute goslings in baskets, muscovy drakes huffing and puffing, a calf or two, an old grey gander which tried to nip each passerby. There were eggs and more eggs.

Many card tables were set up. One was loaded with honey, another with crocheted articles that had been made since last fair day, and another had odds and ends — strange utensils, a few cracked dishes, a small wine press and some fruit jars. This last was tended by an older woman who had just broken up housekeeping.

A rawboned man with an untamed red beard, wearing dust-colored shirt and trousers was followed closely by a barefoot boy who was about twelve. The child wore no shirt and his chest and back were deeply tanned. His knickerbockers were without buckles and the legs hung loose halfway to his ankles. Both walked with an easy swagger, the boy copying every one of his father's movements. They could have come right out of Appalachia.

The Milwaukee customers began to arrive, each determined not to be cheated. Most of them were highly suspicious by nature. None were in the least bit bashful. "Youse! Get out of my way! I was here first!" was among the milder remarks.

"What! No brown eggs White ones is no good for cakes!"

"How much for the cow?"

"Eighty dollars, but she can be bought for less."

"Them eggs is too small. Don't you farmers ever learn nothing? You didn't leave them in the nest long enough."

A guinea hen escaped and flew cackling raucously to the very top of the old four-story hotel. "There! That's one I don't have to hear sass the moon tonight! Watchdog! Ha!"

A couple, the lady very large and aggressive looking, the man small and obviously henpecked, were selling potatoes, as were the people running the stand across the road from them. The woman was determined to make a sale to the customer, who was hesitating and eyeing the larger potatoes on the other stand. She screamed, "Yeah, maybe them that shows is a little bigger'n ours, but don't ever look at the ones in the bottoms of their bags."

A man, more than slightly inebriated, had bought thirty leghorn frying chickens. He had trouble counting out the payment, first cheating the seller, then cheating himself. Finally ready to leave with his new possessions, he began loading them into his shiny new station wagon loose. The seller was appalled.

"Hey" he cried. "Don't do that! Get some sacks or

some newspapers at least." The buyer drew himself up haughtily.

"You stay out of my business. It's *my* car, ain't it?" He finished loading and jerkily started the car. As the car pulled away the thirty chickens in the back flew up at once, hitting all the back windows in a flurry of white feathers. The beautiful, new, clean cushions in that car would not be the same, ever again!

The fair began to break up. The coal black kitten remained unsold. "We ain't goin' to take it home," said the lady of the house.

"Here, watch me," said her husband. He put it down on the path and stood back. A young couple with a toddling three-year-old boy approached. The little boy spotted the kitten.

He ran toward it calling, "Kitty, kitty, kitty!" He picked it up and cuddled it. The kitten started to purr.

"Put it down," his mother ordered.

He held it closer, saying, "No! My kitty!"

His father said, "Oh, let him have it! We'll find a place for it!"

The kitten's former owner, having gleefully observed all this, said, "Well Ma, it takes a man to do it. Now let's go home." He cranked their old Ford and off they went— among the last of all the people to leave.

Nearly everyone went home happy. The gypsies had sold five horses. The pockets in the bright skirts of the gypsy women contained many quarters which jingled as they hurried back to their campground.

The lady had finally found brown eggs so the cake she would make tomorrow would be "super."

The man who had brought the guinea hens would be able to sleep peacefully through the night without noisy false alarms.

The bargain hunters from Milwaukee would be able to gloat to their husbands at the supper table over the shrewd deals they had made, and just how much they had saved, and all by themselves, too

And the little black kitten was as happy as any of the others.

11 ENTERTAINMENT & HOLIDAYS

A GOOD SHOW TOWN
Mrs. R. E. Wolfgram

Viroqua is a Wisconsin city known widely as a "good show town" from the day it was incorporated as a village in 1866, to the present time. The oldest of its five thousand inhabitants will tell you the reason. In early days C. C. Brown opened a music store on North Main and Decker streets with an opera house on the second floor. His sons, Otto and Ben, were talented musicians. Ben played the piano, Otto was a trumpet player and a good magician. Ben booked early legitimate stage shows. Traveling troupes appreciated the fact the opera house was in the same block as Hotel Fortney, where they had lodgings during the one-week stay in Viroqua.

Otto and Ben were good salesmen—they sold pianos to area school boards. It happened occasionally that boards were slow in payments, and Ben and Otto found it expedient to go into the district and put on a show in the schoolhouse to help pay the bill. The schools had corners curtained off with sheets strung on wires to serve as makeshift dressing rooms for entertainers.

One winter night when Ben and Otto were putting on a show, Ben stepped offstage to make a quick change of trousers when he was surprised to hear loud laughter from the audience, when there was nothing on stage to warrant it. He glanced around, and found the curtain had parted and the audience was watching his quick change, revealing the red flannel underwear he wore.

Ben opened the first motion-picture show in Viroqua at the Air Dome, using a vacant lot across from the opera house. Admission was five cents to watch Kathleen Williams and William Farnum in a serial each Saturday night. Patrons sat on elevated seats. Ben opened the first indoor movie house, the Star on South Main, and crowds filled the place nightly. He continued to bill weekly show troupes. Children's matinees on Saturdays often played "Ten Nights in a Barroom" without complaints from adults. When the Dalrymple troupes presented "East Lynne" each year the women were happy. They supplied themselves with plenty of handkerchiefs to enjoy the death scene of Isabel Carlyle and the estranged husband. Some of the troupes gave away furniture on their last Saturday nights to lucky holders of tickets, which included the advertised sideboards, sofas, couches, and extension tables.

Rural residents were very good patrons. Show troupes vied for the chance to be in Viroqua during the annual September Vernon County Fair, which had been held since 1856. Home-talent shows were presented every winter, coached by Anne Hocking Smith from an eastern city. Gilbert and Sullivan's "Pinafore" was one especially liked.

Medicine shows set up on the street corners and enticed children to furnish skits, songs and dialogues to swell the crowds by offering five dollars for the best act. Marigene Lawrence and Myra Nelson appeared in the song "Where Oh Where Has My Little Dog Gone?" The winner was chosen by applause from the audience. The girls won easily, for their sisters, brothers and cousins ganged up in their behalf to cheer. The crowd had left when the girls went to collect the five dollars. They were told the sum had to be taken out in the medicines, ointments, linaments and salves before them. The eight-year-old girls were crestfallen but carried a conglomeration to ailing grandmothers and great-aunts. Medicine shows thereafter were not allowed to set up on Main Street.

Chautauqua appeared during the hot months, furnishing their own tents. They were welcomed and well patronized.

The Brooks Stock Company played in the opera house for several years, before providing their own tent shows on the Viroqua fairgrounds. When the Viroqua Masonic order built their Temple, which included the Temple Theater, Ben took over its management. He exemplified his faith in show patronage by building the Vernon Theater on West Court Street, to give the Viroqua area two theaters.

Harry and Lena Porter, who lived on the Maple Dell road in the rural area, were lovers of stage shows, scarcely ever missing a Saturday night performance at the opera house. One Saturday night, late in September, differed from all others and exceeded all expectations. They had attended the fair. Supper over, and chores done, they hitched up a single horse to the buggy, rather early, in the hope of finding a handy hitching post. Arriving at the opera house, they found all the hitching posts in use so Harry left Lena, while he sought the one hitching post in the dark alley behind the opera house. At the close of the show, Lena waited on the sidewalk for him, but he did not return and she could not imagine why. The crowd had left the streets and the troupe had gone to the hotel, but Harry did not appear. A chilly breeze had sprung up and she was becoming uncomfortable. Finally he appeared to tell her the distressing news — that the horse was gone, leaving only the buggy.

He told her also that he had been looking for the night-watch, Blinky Powell, to see if he could offer any information concerning the horse. Finally Lena saw Harry, Blinky and the horse coming down the middle of the road. Blinky was talking in a loud excited voice. A very nearsighted man, he had been given the nickname of Blinky, because of his habit of blinking. "You see," he said, "a bachelor from Round Prairie, who's a heavy drinker always comes into town Saturday nights, ties his horse in the dark alley, makes the rounds of the taverns, gets drunk, and leaves the horse standing all night. I saw the horse and buggy and decided to do something about it as I felt a heavy rain was in the air." Blinky explained, "I unhitched her, led her over to the Goodell livery stable, gave her a good feeding of oats and bedded her down for the night."

He was full of remorse and walked over to the buggy to assist Harry in hitching her up for the return home. The streets were deserted and no one witnessed the unrehearsed drama, or comedy — to which category it belonged, the Porters were not sure. One thing they were sure of was the fact they were hungry and the longer they lingered over the coffee cups the funnier the whole thing seemed and they laughed as they had never laughed at an opera house comedy. They had only compassion for Blinky. They wondered if they should compensate him for the bill at the livery stable, or not again embarrass him by mentioning it. After all, he had gone beyond his line of duty in compassion for a horse, even though it was the wrong horse.

They decided it was time to retire. There was to be a special program at the Methodist church they attended at 11:00 a.m. Sunday. They had purchased tickets for a concert at the opera house on Monday night and wondered what it would be like. Citizens like Harry and Lena Porter gave Viroqua the name of "a good show town."

SMALL TOWN CINEMA
Elizabeth I. Philleo

Are you of the nineteen-hundred vintage? If so, you witnessed the miracle of the silent film as it made its debut in the small northwoods towns in Wisconsin. It left its indelible mark on the memory of those who were fortunate to have been reared in one of our early lumbering towns.

The old opera house had set the tempo for small-town entertainment, but the advent of the silent film was the Seventh Wonder of the World! We all awaited the coming of Saturday night. My weekly allowance (five cents) was clutched tightly in one hand while the other was clasped by an ever-watchful adult who was to escort me to the show. Little girls always depended on an older neighbor girl for protection.

Even the trip across town was an adventure for a seven-year-old. In this era children never went downtown alone. The dangers that lurked between home and destination were inevitable—didn't I have to walk right past the livery stable with its easy, cussin' boys; and also the carefully curtained saloon? What I might hear or see as I passed this forbidden place with its steady clinking of glassware, and boisterous voices shouting from behind those green curtained windows was not fit and proper for a little girl.

The saloon-keeper's windows had the prettiest geraniums in town, and those ever-dusty artificial potted palms in the evil place's window somehow made it more fascinating than ever; but I was whisked past the place in a hurry.

Then, too, there were frequent runaways. Just last week the brewery team ran away, having been upset when that horseless carriage appeared on our Main Street again. Many were the warnings given to me as I started on my Saturday evening jaunt.

We walked the mile across town to the west side business district. Upstairs, over an old white frame building, was the so-called "picture house." With cautious steps I climbed the narrow outside rickety stairway as each board creaked and groaned under every footstep. Breathless, I entered a large, dimly lighted room. In the feeble flicker of the gaslights I searched for a seat. All but three of the wooden folding chairs were taken. Old Mr. Guildenhoffer sat dozing in one, and I soon learned why the rest were vacant! My nose told me, for Mr. Guildenhoffer was the village saloon-keeper's best customer.

Suddenly, an all too gaudy stage curtain was run by by means of a hand-operated crank and roller. Right before my eyes unfolded the "Wonder of the Universe." The customary request—"Ladies, please remove your hats"—was flashed on the screen. In those days you could hardly tell a hat from an umbrella unless it was daytime.

The pianist gave his all to a maudlin melody as the plot was introduced. Its theme was not for my young ears, but this didn't discourage me. It involved the old worn-out story of the innocent country girl seduced by the city slicker. As the plot thickened, it smacked of pioneer rowdyism. The heavy-bearded and bewhiskered characters raced across the screen. The village constable chased the imposters from pillar to post while our terrified heroine ran for her life. To further enhance the danger and tension, blank cartridges were fired backstage. All of this was accomplished with music from the tinny-sounding piano. As the tension increased, the musician improvised as best he could. He appeared to be somewhat limited, but jumped from the hesitant pattern of "Narcissus" to "The Moon Shines Tonight on Pretty Red Wing." As the constable pursued the villain, the pianist's fingers fairly raced across the keyboard to the exciting tempo of "Alexander's Ragtime Band."

Just at the height of a wild situation, the machine came to a halt with squeaks and snapping sounds. The gaslights were turned up while repairs were being made. A glance around the audience told us that the O'Leary twins, after much bawling, had finally gone to sleep. Mr. Guildenhoffer still snored loudly amid an aroma of malt and spirits. Momentarily his beady eyes peered over a bulbous nose, only to slip back into his usual stupor. Mr. Applebee had shifted his pampered, overgrown son to the other knee. A sleeping infant came to life with renewed vigor. Poor Mrs. Perkins was suppressing her sobs as she wiped her tearful eyes — hadn't her own dear Sadie left this very morning for the wicked city to seek employment?

I gasped for a breath of fresh air, but to no avail. The atmosphere hung heavy with the aroma of brandy and unbathed lumberjacks; and just a touch of the livery stable made me wonder if it were really worth it all.

In due time the machine was repaired, the musicians picked up the threads of a worn tune, the lights were dimmed and the miracle continued. The tension increased as the villain was again pursued. Blank cartridges stuttered backstage, and frantic little Myrtle Feetlebaum was helped back into her folding chair which had collapsed. Georgie Perkins choked on a peppermint, and Alex Smith dropped a bag of jawbreakers which accounted for his crawling around like a sand hog in order to pick up each precious morsel of sweets.

I was not without fear, but the mystery of the performance surpassed all anxiety. Finally our heroine returned unharmed, the villain was punished, and the picture came to an end. The pianist struck up a lively march, light was restored, and with much shuffling of heavily booted feet amid the clatter of unwilling folding chairs, we all surged toward the only exit. Again the stairs creaked and groaned as we descended to the boardwalk.

Tired, whimpering children clutched their mothers' skirts while an impatient father herded his family into the wagon. Old Dobbin, nervously pawing the ground, with harness wound several times around the iron hitching post, was glad to be homeward bound. Families called farewells to this gala evening, and as the nine o'clock curfew blew, only the metallic clatter of a saloon piano told you that life still went on in the little northwoods town.

LET'S GO TO WASHINGTON PARK, PAPA
Dorothy V. Walters

It's a summer Sunday afternoon in Milwaukee in 1914. What can a five-year-old do for amusement?

"Let's go to Washington Park, Papa."

As we walked toward that enchanting place, I bounced along with juvenile enthusiasm to keep up with my father's rapid stride.

One Sunday a German-American group was raising money to erect an equestrian statue honoring Baron von Steuben, who had played an important role as drillmaster for General Washington's army. To help finance the statue, which now stands near the park, gold-plated medallions were sold. A man approached us near the park entrance with a pitch for the Baron. Papa was apparently in favor of the project, because I acquired a medallion which was later useful for "play money."

Also near the park entrance an itinerant photographer had set up a little shelter in which he posed Sunday visitors. A postcard picture which he made of Papa and me shows a tall man with a dark moustache. He is wearing a gold cap, and is seated on a wooden bench. Perched on one of its arms, I project from the picture as a small, solemn child wearing a large hair ribbon, a black and white plaid dress, white stockings, and dark sandals.

As we entered the park, the hoarse "Aurh! Aurh!" from the sea lions' pool spoke of the zoo to come.

On the way to the animal enclosures I always observed my own rituals for visiting the park. There was the tantalizing moment spent in deciding which of the blue or red or yellow balloons I wanted my indulgent parent to buy for me from the vendor above whose grizzled head they floated on limber sticks. Finally, clutching a fragile blob of yellow by its stick, I walked into the park with papa.

As we came to the bridge which arched over a narrow channel between the two lagoons, we paused to watch the boaters rowing heavy, rented, wooden boats around in the muddy water. Steady and difficult to tip the white boats were; graceful they were not.

One of my rituals involved getting a tochold on the ornamental side of the bridge and leaning over to spit into the water. My mother, who occasionally took me to the park on a weekday, disapproved of this unladylike practice; but papa considered it a harmless activity. It was done to attract, momentarily, the brilliant flash of goldfish, which surfaced to investigate the disturbance of the murky water. They were so much bigger than the ones in a neighbor's aquarium!

Along the path just beyond the bridge was "my" bubbler. I mounted the concrete cube, about a foot in each dimension, which enabled me to get a drink of the refreshing water all by myself.

Another ritual involved a fat, black cannon, presumably from Civil War days, which was positioned on top of a low hill. I was lifted or climbed onto the cannon. Handing my balloon to papa, I slid down the smooth and sloping barrel of the war relic a few times.

"Now, let's go see the animals. I wanna see the polar bears and monkeys and all of them."

The path to the animal cages passed the refectory—so-called—where ice cream was sold. Papa's sweet tooth usually demanded a stop here for a nickel ice cream cone.

Because I was a city-bred child the zoo gave me a chance not only to see the polar bears, but also to meet in person Thornton W. Burgess's book characters: Jimmy Skunk, Reddy Fox, Blackie the Crow, and others.

Of course there were the more exotic mammals such as the limber and lively monkeys who would be climbing nimbly about or grooming one another; the pacing lions and tigers; the sinuous seals swimming in graceful arcs or posing beside their pool. Best of all were the elephants and the hippopotamus. To have the hippo surface from the depths of his pool and open his enormous mouth (easily of a capacity to take me in!) was the finest of all treats at the zoo.

Sometimes, the visit to the zoo was omitted in favor of other entertainment. There was a racetrack and grandstand at the northeast corner of the park. Once, a polo game was being played there. How swiftly the action progressed! How splendidly horses and men worked together! Sometimes there was harness racing. I didn't understand the fine points of the sport, of course, but the beautiful, fast-moving horses were fun to watch.

Another Sunday a soccer game was in progress. The ability of the players to knock the ball about with their heads impressed me with the idea that they were, literally, a hard-headed crew.

Papa and I never occupied seats in the grandstand. Perhaps he knew that my attention span was too short to make that worthwhile. So, we watched events from along the fence encircling the track.

Occasionally, Papa and I visited the park on a day other than Sunday. Came Independence Day and the park was the terminus for one of the many "Sane Fourth" celebrations provided for elementary schoolchildren in Milwaukee. Carrying stiff little American flags they marched, accompanied by self-sacrificing teachers.

"One, two, three, four, five, six, seven,

"All *good* children go to heaven.

"When they get there, hear them yell,

"M-i-n-e-r-a-l," chanted the Mineral Street School marchers.

"Ice cream, soda water, ginger ale, pop;

"Thirty-eighth Street School is always on the top," shouted the glorious Fourth celebrants from that school.

Boxes of mixed hard candies were supplied to the marchers as the parade ended.

How things have changed at Washington Park! There's a bigger, better zoo elsewhere. The racetrack is no more. A new, big, and busy Senior Citizens' Center serves the park's one-time child visitors and many others. I wonder if little girls and their papas go there on Sunday afternoons now and if so, what they do for amusement.

THOSE GOOD OLD DAYS OF WINTER
Lucille Boneske

Homemade entertainment was "the thing" back in the "good old days" of winter in the early nineteen-hundreds, when log cabins were still a common sight on the Wisconsin landscape and horse-drawn vehicles the only means of transportation. Parties and folk dances were plentiful in any community, and any occasion such as birthdays, engagements, weddings, quilting or feather bees, basket socials at schools, or housewarmings was reason enough to have one. Most young people enjoyed walking a mile or two in the crisp, starlit winter night to get there. Some couples came in one-horse cutters behind mettlesome, dashing steeds; others bundled up in bobsleds with hot stones or bricks at their feet.

Sometimes a "hayride" on a large farm sleigh would bring a group of ten or twenty young people and their elders, singing all the way, sometimes jumping off into the snow to get their circulation going again, arriving at the party rosy cheeked and breathless. Sometimes a young man with a cutter and a swift horse would catch up with the slower farm sleigh, dash alongside, extend a hand to grasp the hand of a young lady in the party, pull her across into his cutter, and dash away again, to the hoots and yells of the rest of the crowd. Young ladies vied for the attentions of young blades with swift horses!

Having arrived, the young folks adjourned to the parlor, where chairs had been placed against the walls, and the floor cleared of rugs or carpets. Games, such as The Needle's Eye, Blind Man's Bluff, or Button, Button, were soon in full swing. Our community was blessed with a concertina artist, and soon the young people were swinging in a merry square dance until the midnight lunch, which was passed around in baskets by the older folks, with plenty of hot coffee. Then the merriment resumed again.

The older women had set up their "bees," quilting or feather, in the big kitchen, where they could gossip as they worked, while the men played cards at another table. Sometimes the party was a basket social at the schoolhouse, where each young blade vied with the others to buy his particular young lady's basket, and woe to him if he let another win it. The best sport was bidding up the teacher's basket, especially if her "suitor" happened to be bidding for it! "Make him pay!" was the shout. Usually the good times lasted until two or three o'clock in the morning, when everyone loaded him or herself into the sleighs and started home.

Few roads were plowed in those days. After the first heavy snow the few cars that farmers owned were put in the barns or garages on the farm and raised on wooden blocks to take the weight off the tires. The radiators were drained, and the cars "rested" until the roads became passable again in spring. Often in May or June sinkholes appeared, deep ruts of mud through which cars had to be pulled by farm horses. One farmer near us had a deep sinkhole in front of his farm and made a tidy sum pulling cars through it with his big team of horses. At night he hauled barrels of water to the sinkhole to keep it soft. He was discovered, and ordered by the town board to haul gravel to the place until it was passable again!

The first heavy snow of autumn, a regular blizzard, struck during hunting season one year, and the hunters were literally "caught with their chains down." The snow was three feet deep in the road that passed our farm. My husband spent hours and wore out two teams of horses pulling cars through the big drifts. The hunt-

ers, cold and exhausted from shoveling and tramping in the cold and snow, were grateful for food and rest before going on again. Soon the big plows came through, but in a few days another blizzard filled the roads again, and made them impassable for days. The milk hauler with his strong team couldn't get through, so we had to use every available can and kettle in which to store the milk. The big plow finally came, pushing the snow ahead of it foot by foot, and building banks higher than the telephone poles! The milk hauler came behind the plow, but we had to carry the milk out to the road and carry all the empty cans back to the barn, until with much shoveling and our small snowplow we opened our driveway again.

It snowed so much that winter that the children walked to school on top of the drifts, looking down at the tops of fence posts barely visible below them.

We got our fill of buttermilk and buttermilk pancakes that year. When the milk hauler couldn't get through and we ran out of storage space, Dad separated the milk and we made butter, which was easy to store, and which kept well until we could sell it in the stores. How good the meals tasted, with plenty of butter in everything! There were always plenty of vegetables in the basement, both canned and stored. There were several kinds of canned and smoked meats and sausages in the basement and smokehouse, eggs and poultry in the barn. We were self-sufficient to a degree unknown today. We could quote the poet Whittier with understanding, when snow fell and blizzards howled:

Blow high, blow low, not all its snow
Could quench our hearth-fires ruddy glow!

Another small incident, very funny to the children, happened that winter. A pretty young schoolteacher boarded with us. Her boyfriend had a fast and spirited horse named Schnapps Charlie, and he would bring him to our place on Sunday afternoons and get him Friday evenings. One Friday Charlie was feeling particularly mettlesome. He pranced, shaking the bells on his harness merrily. Scarcely had the young teacher stepped into the cutter than Charlie started off with a spirited dash. Before the driver could curb him he was going at a gallop, the snow flying from his heels, making it almost impossible for the man to see where they were headed. A few rods ahead was the corner where they would turn to go home. The young man pulled with all his might, sawing on the reins, but Charlie had taken the bit between his teeth and would not be stopped by anyone! He took the corner at high speed, the cutter turned over, and man and lady rolled out into a big snowdrift, in true Jingle Bells style, while Charlie and cutter dashed off through the deep snow. A farmer coming from town saw what happened, leaped from his sleigh and caught the horse before he could do much damage to the cutter. He turned Charlie around and led him back to where the two people were emerging from the drift, looking angry and sheepish at the same time. They cleaned the snow off as best they could, got into the cutter, thanking the farmer gratefully, and drove off, with Charlie shaking his head and snorting as if to say, "Well, I almost made it that time!"

Yes, life could be fun in those "good old days" of winter, but it could be hazardous, too!

THE RAGAMUFFINS
Lois Tucker Pink

I meet few people nowadays who have ever gone ragamuffin. As far as I know, it was originally a Norwegian custom.

When I was a child the fun of being a ragamuffin during Christmas vacation was part of the social life in the part of southwestern Wisconsin where I was raised. That and the house parties were pleasant interruptions in the long, cold winters. Sitting around the parlor heater talking to my sisters and friends, while we warmed our feet on the shiny fender that encircled the black stove, could become boring even back in the early twenties. Some of our evenings were spent playing Flinch and Old Maid, but best of all were the evenings spent doing what we called "going ragamuffin."

A neighbor might phone and say, "There's going to be a moon tonight. Wouldn't it be a perfect night for ragamuffin!" But my family would often decide to go by ourselves and pick up someone on the way who wished to join us in the fun.

"You girls go up to the storeroom and find something we can all wear," Mother would say. Mother never threw anything away until it was worn out. Neither had her mother, so there were many possibilities for disguises in the boxes and old trunks we were allowed to rummage through. In the excitement I, the youngest, wasn't scolded for being underfoot. The smell of mothballs permeated the room as we shook out the clothes and chose our costumes for the evening. We couldn't afford to buy face masks so we improvised by cutting off the tops of Mother's old cotton stockings. We tied the tops together with a string, then cut holes for our eyes, nose, and mouth. It made a fine mask and a warm one. The more ridiculous we looked, the better. The important thing was not to look like ourselves when we gave our neighbors a surprise visit. I always dressed like a boy, and wore overshoes a size too long, because that was supposed to fool everyone.

My father never wanted to go along and made the excuse that someone had to stay home and "keep the home fires burning."

Walking on a crisp evening was more fun than riding in the old bobsled, so we usually went on foot to our nearest neighbor's house. My brother sometimes wore Dad's black horsehair coat which came past the calves of his legs. Mother looked like a fat little tramp in baggy trousers and a heavy jacket and stocking cap, and my two sisters sometimes wore long dresses and ridiculous hats. They all led the way while I tried valiantly to keep up. What a sight we must have been! The crisp snow crackled like dry kindling as our feet crunched down the hills and across the valleys. If the snow was freshly fallen and soft, I imagined we were an Indian party padding silently over the Wisconsin hills. When I fell behind, Mother would slow her steps to match mine and caution me, "Breathe through your nose, or the cold air will freeze your lungs."

We were never able to sneak up to anyone's door without the inevitable cow dog announcing our arrival. Every farmer around there who had milk cows also had a dog to chase the cows from the pasture to the barn at milking time. He either had a snug little house outside or was allowed to sleep behind the farmer's warm cook stove in the kitchen.

Our neighbor or his wife answered our knock at the kitchen door with a big grin, while their children peeked at us shyly from a safe distance. Ragamuffins were al-ways welcome in that neighborhood. We stamped our snowy feet on the porch, then crowded into the room where we stood on the brightly colored cotton scatter rugs everyone used to protect the linoleum rug. As soon as our boots were off, the fun of guessing our identity began. Sometimes it was easy, but we often fooled everyone for a while. Our hosts were usually too polite to peek under our masks, but stood back and looked us over thoughtfully until we started clowning. Soon we had everyone laughing.

It was even more fun if our hosts put on some old clothes and travelled with us to another neighbor's house. I recall walking long distances in one evening, often visiting several families.

The clothes we wore kept us warm while outside, but they were mighty warm inside the cozy kitchens. I was tempted to scratch as the perspiration trickled down my neck and back. It was a relief when we could remove our masks and coats. We were never allowed to leave anyone's house without having lunch. We ran off the calories (which we had never heard of anyway) going from one farm to another.

The number of ragamuffins diminished in my neighborhood in the late twenties. I was growing up and many of the young people had moved away. Our parents apparently did not have the energy anymore for such active entertainment.

The last time I went out ragamuffin was when I was eighteen years of age. One of my cousins owned a cutter and horse. He invited a friend and me to surprise neighbors to the north of us as we used to do. It was fun, but not the same without my family.

The best part of the evening was the ride home. The country road ran over hills and through the woods. There was only the muffled sound of the horse's hooves as the cutter skimmed over the snow. We were on a magic carpet carrying us away from old friends and simple pleasures as the beauty of the quiet woods fell behind us. But I remember feeling no sadness. My future was ahead, where I would always treasure the memories of being a ragamuffin.

THE CHRISTMAS I REMEMBER BEST
James A. Jones

Tonight I am repairing the hobbyhorse I rode for so many miles across the big kitchen floor when I was a little tyke and believed in Santa Claus. Its flowing mane is getting thin and the tail is entirely missing but I can fix both with some glue and jute twine. I already have added a few screws to its old aching joints. Maybe I should make a new pair of rockers too; these go clackety-clack like a flat wheel on a Pullman car, but it is getting late.

The old hobbyhorse is to be a surprise for my grandson on his second Christmas Day. He will be the third generation of Galahads to ride this noble steed.

Tomorrow when it is lighter and I can see to paint, I will add a new bridle and saddle. I think I will try red for the leather and gold for all the metal parts. That should look nice on a white horse.

It was seventy years ago when my mother received a letter from Aunt Kate in Chicago telling her that a box of presents from Santa Claus would arrive the day before Christmas at the railroad station two miles from our farm.

As Christmas Eve neared it seemed that Santa surely could not come to our house that night because the blizzard had lasted for several days. When the sun went down and the wind stopped blowing it turned bitter cold. I knew for sure then that I would have to wait to see Aunt Kate's presents.

My dad must have been a sentimental soul but I never knew it until that Christmas Eve. He could stick a pig and chop the head off a Plymouth Rock rooster and never blink an eye. Now I was beginning to understand him better.

Just before sundown he got ready to walk to the station. Drifting snow had covered the fences and was piled so deep that only the telephone poles showed to outline the highway.

He bundled up in his heavy horsehide overcoat and hung a gunnysack by a rope over his shoulder. When he put on his wool cap Mother tied her best knitted scarf around his head. That was when I saw him kiss her. Then he started off with a long stick to test the snowbanks and I watched from the bay window until his lantern was out of sight.

I fell asleep knowing that my dad would make it but I wondered about Santa Claus. If our farm team of dappled Percherons couldn't go four miles in the deep snow how could Santa get here from the North Pole?

I don't remember if I woke up when they were going to bed or if they were getting up on Christmas morning. What I do remember though is that Santa Claus had been there because my stocking hanging on the mantle was filled to overflowing, with an orange bulging in the toe and a candy cane hooked at the top.

Then I knew too that my dad had made it to the station because there under the balsam tree was the big box from Aunt Kate. In it was this hobbyhorse. It will be rocking strong again if I can get it repainted before Christmas Eve.

That was the Christmas I remember best—and I still believe in Santa Claus, because my dad was one.

THE CHRISTMAS HOLIDAYS, IN CHURCH AND ON THE FARM, IN THE 1890s
Elsie A. Schutz

It always began with the Christmas Eve program in church. Everyone attended, from the grandparents down to the babies.

When we were small, my dad would put the wagon box on the bob-sleigh and fill it with clean, fresh straw. He would throw a blanket over this and, after we were in, cover us completely with a quilt thrown over our heads. No one dared peek out; Mother was watching!

When I was old enough to sing and speak, I seldom missed a program. My grandfather taught me the German Christmas carols out of a book which he had brought with him from Germany. I still have it.

Our church was a rural German Lutheran, just across the corner from where my grandparents lived. There was always a giant Christmas tree down in the front on Christmas Eve. I can't remember any of my recitations, but I remember very clearly the first time my three-year-old brother spoke. He began as soon as he left his seat, "Susse, seliche, Weinachts zeit; kinder jubel, weit und breit . . . ." (Sweet Blessed Christmas time, joyful children far and wide . . .) By the time that he got to the front, he had finished, bowed and returned to his seat. No one had told him when to begin.

We also had songs rendered by the upper classes: "O Tannen Baum," which was a favorite; "Ihr Kunder Lein Kommet," now sung in English, as "O Come Little Children," "O, du Brohliche, O du Seliche," and others.

When the program was finished, every child received a sack with candy, nuts, and the inevitable apple.

By this time, the smaller children were tired, if not already asleep. There was still Christmas at home. I cannot remember what we did after church; I think everyone was ready for bed. But, when morning came, the "Weinachts Mann," Santa Claus, had been there, brought and decorated a small tree, usually set on a table so little fingers could not pull off the decorations. In our stockings we would find about the same as the night before, except this time it was an orange away down deep in the toe—precious, because Christmas was the only time that we could afford them.

Next morning, my dad would get up before it was light, start the fire and light the candles that were tied on the tree; and to wake us, he would sing "Am Weinachts Baum, die lichter brennen dann glanzed dass Fest Kind, lieb und schon" (On the Christmas tree the lights are burning and shines the Christ Child, fond and dear). I think that he enjoyed it as much as we did. Everyone would scramble out of bed, rush to the tree, grab their gifts and stocking and hop back into bed again. The wood fires had burned out during the night, and it was cold!

We usually had two gifts, one large and one small. For a girl there would be a doll, last year's was probably broken by now. If not, it received a complete outfit, down to bonnet and coat. The second gift would be a ribbon or some other small article. No one was particular; we enjoyed what we got.

The older ones would receive a garment, something

that was probably needed anyway: hand-knitted mittens or stockings, slippers or handkerchiefs, and maybe a book.

New Year's Eve, down would come the Christmas tree. The strings of popcorn, red candy cherries and strawberries would be divided. We rarely saved them for another year. The house was too small to hide anything from youngsters.

For the New Year, Mother would bake coffee cake with raisins. If there were apples, we would have an "Apfel Kuchen" (apple cake), raised doughnuts, and other delectable smelling goodies. By this time, the Christmas bakings would be eaten. Besides, if the pantry was well-stocked on New Year's Day, that would mean that there would be ample for the coming year (an old German belief).

That is the end of my story. Let it take you back into the 1890s, if you can remember that far. I hope that you will enjoy reading it as much as I did writing it. Auf Wiedersehen.

CHRISTMAS EVE 1897
Jessie Gaebele Bauer

I was born February 12, 1892, in Buffalo County, Wisconsin, on my grandfather Gaebele's farm near the town of Cream. By the time I was five, my parents had cleared land up on the bluff, three miles from Cream, and built their first house.

The Christmas Eve I remember best was a crisp, cold night in 1897. My older sister Lily, baby sister Selma, and I, Jessie, all had new dresses which Ma had sewed for us. She bundled us up and Pa tucked us into a straw-filled wagon box on a sleigh. There were hot bricks rolled in pieces of old blanket to keep our feet warm and a big featherbed over us. Baby Selma, wrapped in thick wool shawls, got to ride in Ma's arms.

Pa slapped the reins and the horses stepped out smartly. Bells on their harnesses sang "Ping! Pingle-Ping!" in rhythm with their steps. The runners squeaked in the packed snow. In the black sky, the stars looked close enough to reach.

After what seemed like a very long time, I struggled up from my cozy nest and called, "Aren't we almost there?" Pa pointed to a hill in the distance, to a row of lighted windows and light streaming from a doorway. It was the Herold church on the bluff. "Just a little while longer," he promised.

We drove through the churchyard to the long sheds beyond, open along one side. The horses could stand without being unhitched and, sheltered from the wind, could munch hay until the service ended.

Before we entered the church, I glanced warily to the left at the gravestones closest to the church in the little cemetery. They had the names of Ma's grandparents. I wondered if they would be watching our Christmas Eve.

It was good to feel the warmth from the two stoves on each side of the church, near the entrance. Pa found room for our bricks on one of them, so they would be toasty warm for our ride home.

The whole church smelled good. The odor of new varnish and of fresh cut pine boughs is still strong in my mind. The pews, the woodwork and altar, even the wood high in the ceiling, reflected the lights of the kerosene lamps, swaying gently on their long chains.

I held my breath! There at the front of the church was a glorious Christmas tree twinkling with dozens of white candles. Piled beneath were packages and small sacks. I knew there was a present for every child. On each side of the tree stood a church member, ready to replace any candles that burned down too low. But I didn't know that then; I thought they were guarding the presents.

After the program about baby Jesus, and the sermon, and the singing, the minister called out our names. Lily got a book. I got a beautiful doll with a china face and leather arms and legs that felt like skin. Selma was too little to unwrap a package, but she got a sack of candy and oranges, and Ma said, "She wants to share these with you and Lily."

Then the last name was called, the hot bricks were wrapped, and we fell asleep on the long ride home.

I was awake when we drove up to our house, but I pretended to be asleep because I liked to have my father carry me in. He came back for me. By that time, Ma had lighted the lamps and I could see Lily standing, speechless, staring at a box on the kitchen table. "What is it?" I wondered.

Pa took a wooden cylinder that had little metal pins sticking out all around it and snapped the roller into the front of the box. Then he began turning a crank handle, and as he turned, a bellows at the back puffed in and out. Little flat metal thumbs on the front of the box lifted up and down. It was playing a hymn called "The Old Rugged Cross."

Santa had been there while we were in church! He had left a music box called the Gem Roller Organ. There were a dozen of the little wooden rollers. All hymns.

We were sleepy, but eager, so Ma decided, "You can each play one song before you go to bed. There'll be plenty of time to play the rest tomorrow."

Then she helped us undress beside the big wood stove and get into our heavy flannel nightgowns and thick wool bed socks. I carried my new doll. Lily took the hot stove lid wrapped in a blanket. We scuttled up the icy stairway and huddled together under the featherbed with our feet on the lid.

What a wonderful Christmas Eve!

TRIPLE DUTY CHRISTMAS TREE
Sister M. Adrienne Downey, O.P.

Christmas at home was boundless joy for every small child in our large family. Our Christmas tree served as a shrine for our Bethlehem crib. It was a mothering shelter for the Holy Family and for our family. It drew all of us closer together each Christmas.

Mama and Papa had their own time scraping together enough cash to buy that tree but they managed somehow. I don't pretend to know how. And a week before Christmas the tree was set up in our living room awaiting the onslaught of the children who, each year "helped Santa Claus" decorate its branches.

The "helpers" had been busy for days stringing popcorn beads; making popcorn balls and sticking them together with homemade taffy; hoarding their scarce supply of pennies and buying candy cherries and candy strawberries which were conveniently joined in pairs for easy hanging on prickly branches; making paper cornucopias and filling them with Brazil nuts; resurrecting last year's decorations and the coveted "herald angel" and tinsel "star of Bethlehem"; carefully unwrapping the real clip-on candles, the fire hazard worry of my mother's Christmas season.

Now for the decorating. We all had a hand in it. What we lacked in artistic know-how we made up for in enthusiasm. I suspect the result was not an artist's dream but we youngsters loved it and this was enough for my mother. She could put up with *any* affront to her aesthetic sense if only each child of hers was given full vent to his particular creative inclination.

On Christmas Eve we gathered round our shrine and Mama, now relaxed and happy, sang ever so sweetly, "The angels sang in the silent night." We listened, enchanted. It was the highlight of our Christmas Eve.

Thus was ushered in two weeks of Christmas celebration. We children, released from school routine, abandoned ourselves to the carefree pleasures of the long vacation. The tree, shedding its needles copiously, stood its ground until "Little Christmas," January 6, the day set for its "raffle." Led by our oldest sister, we captured Papa's old derby and filled it with paper slips which accounted for every edible item on the tree.

All things in order, we invited our neighboring friends to the raffle. Everyone came and everyone received something: a stale candy cherry or strawberry, a cornucopia full of nuts, or a sticky, stale popcorn ball.

As the raffle progressed that tree became ever more forlorn and desolate looking. Finally, completely stripped of every adornment and of almost every needle, it stood as if waiting for even greater humiliations. Mama went to the kitchen and returned with choice bits of suet and strips of string. She gave each child a piece of suet and a string with which to decorate the tree once more. This done, we hauled the newly decorated tree to the back yard, propped it against the fence and watched the birds enjoy their Christmas feast.

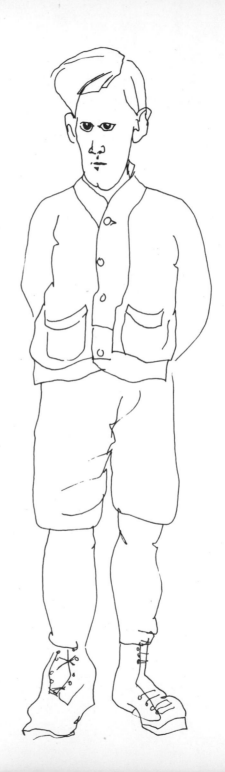

LIST OF CONTESTANTS, 1974-1975

Although some of the Yarns of Yesteryear contestants have been declared winners, in reality there are no losers. Each writer, through personal reminiscence or research, has contributed a unique block to the patchwork of living history. The emerging pattern is one of worth and beauty.

A

Gwendolyn Aaberg
Portage
Elizabeth Abbott
Marshfield
Hilda Abegglen
Racine
Ava Adams
Madison
Marguerite Adams
Milwaukee
Mildred Adams
Oxford
Pia Adkins
Madison
Jerry Ahrens
Two Rivers
Jennie Allds
Hillsboro
Margaret Allen
Baraboo
Esther Andersen
Eau Claire
Gertrude Anderson
Mosinee
Marie Anderson
Blair
Roberta Anderson
Kenosha
Esther Anding
Arena
Gladys G. Artingstall
Milwaukee

Mrs. Oswald Arzt
Kendall
Mrs. Clyde Atwell
Fond du Lac
May Augustyn
Fond du Lac
Wanda Aukofer
Milwaukee
Arthur Austin
Rio
Ethel Austin
Rio
Pearl Axelsen
Marshfield

B

Leo Bach
Berlin
Helen Backhaus
Waukesha
Reuben Backhaus
Campbellsport
Melba Baehr
Eau Claire
Mrs. Tom Bagan
Black River Falls
Benjamin Bailey
Friendship
Harry Baker
Oshkosh
Dorothy Balcom
Eau Claire

Harold Barkstrom
Brookfield
Arthur Barnhart
Menomonie
Berneice Barrett
Madison
H. T. Barry
Whitewater
Christine Bauer
Mondovi
Jessie Gaebele Bauer
Shell Lake
Yetive Baum
Colby
Ann Baumgard
Waukesha
Florence Beals
LaCrosse
Lenore Beck
Amberg
Sr. Mary Alfred Becker
Fond du Lac
Clara Bechtel
Waukesha
Eva Bell
Kenosha
Belle Bellile
Ashland
Nita Benedict
Waupaca
LaVerne Benson
Kenosha
Marie Benzie
Fond du Lac

Mrs. Esther V. Beran
Madison
Mrs. D. Berg
Eau Claire
Thea Berg
Milwaukee
Marie Berning
Cuba City
Richard B. Berres
West Bend
Estella Bhryn
West Salem
Jessie Biegemann
Waukesha
Nettie Blair
Manitowoc
Viola Blume
Waukesha
Esther C. Bock
Appleton
Hattie Bodenbach
Brookfield
Mary Knobloch Bodenburg
Phillips
Agnes Boehm
Phillips
Sr. M. Wilhelmine Boland
Baraboo
Justina Bolle
Menomonee Falls
Lucille Boneske
Athens
Della Bopf
Wausau

Leslie Borer
LaCrosse
Lucille Bork
Oshkosh
Rose Boutin
Eau Claire
Ardis Boynton
Beloit
Alice Brabant
Madison
Marian Brandt
Fennimore
Leona Braund
Pewaukee
Mrs. Joseph Breitweiser
Milwaukee
Clarence Brenenger
Galesburg
Thomas Brever
Rhinelander
Josephine Broadhead
LaCrosse
Agnes Brokaw
Muscoda
Glen Brossard
Columbus
Lucille Brost
Medford
Frances Brown
Neillsville
Frank E. Brown
Neillsville
Leslie Brown
Janesville
E.L.A. Bruger
Ladysmith
Fred Brunner
Durand
Arthur Scott Buchanan
Wisconsin Rapids

Francis Bucholz
Sheboygan
Theodore Buehler
Alma
Walter Buhrie
Kenosha
Henry Bujalski
Thorp
Marie Buritz
Manitowoc
Ruth Burmester
Reedsburg
Etta Burnett
Spencer
Edgar Buzzell
Delavan

C

Mrs. O.L. Campbell
Eau Claire
Hazen Canniff
Watertown
John Cappon
Madison
Laura Carlsen
Spooner
Bernita Carson
Madison
Ida Carstensen
Three Lakes
Benjamin Case
Milwaukee
Mrs. Albert Chamberland
Spencer
Mrs. Ernest Champeny
East Troy
Vernie Chapman
Portage

Esther Chlopek
Milwaukee
Helen Christiansen
Madison
Ruth Bunker Christianson
Frederic
Edwin Christenson
River Falls
Tena Christopherson
Wisconsin Dells
Rosalie Cicero
Racine
Dorinda Clark
Milwaukee
Myrtle Clark
Hancock
Erna Clark
Webster
Harvey Clausing
Cedarburg
Fred Cody
Racine
Catherine Coleman
Madison
Jerry F. Condon, Sr.
Mosinee
Alice Converse
Whitewater
Katy Cook
Loyal
Lester P. Coonen
Ft. Atkinson
Leota Correa
Kenosha
Lillian Cotter
Prescott
Edith Couey
Cadott
William Crapser
Madison

Edward Cronquest
Cadott
Florence Crump
Dousman
Alice Cummings
Endeavor
Laura Curtiss
Arkansaw

D

Mrs. Tillman Dahl
Cottage Grove
Elizabeth Dailey
Minocqua
William Daley
Milwaukee
Clara A. Damm
Racine
Anna Damp
Union Grove
Margaret Damp
Gillett
Barbara Darch
Madison
Sr. M. Eulogia Davies
Sinsinawa
Mary Day
Madison
Lottie DeHart
Elton
Mrs. Alvin Deischer
Prairie du Sac
Paula Delfeld
Brownsville
Amelia DeMarie
Spooner
Hazel DeMott
Westfield

Mabel Dencker
Sun Prairie
Ardis DeVoe
Rhinelander
Charles Dickson
Minong
Emma Dickson
Black Earth
R. J. Dietrich
Granton
Margaret Dillon
Janesville
Hazel Disch
New Glarus
Vada Dixon
Hustler
Esther Dodte
Neillsville
Gertrude Doherty
Almond
Mrs. Leonora Dohm
Sun Prairie
Ida Dokkestul
Eau Claire
Celia Dombrowski
Westfield
Mrs. Walter Donahue
Baraboo
Sr. M. Andrienne Downey, O.P.
Sinsinawa
Cleone Downs
Cuba City
James Drago
Kenosha
Hugo Drechsel
Milwaukee
Joseph Driscoll
Wauwatosa
Minny Drummy
Waupun

Bryan Dugdale
Platteville
Mrs. M.M. Dunn
Milwaukee
Rev. Lester Dunwiddie
Richland Center

E

Pauline Easterson
Eleva
Everdene Ebentier
Milwaukee
Erna Elliott
Springbrook
Alta Ellis
Madison
Gladys Elviken
Madison
Rose Engebretsen
New Auburn
Albert Engel
Madison
Mrs. Lawrence Engelhard
LaCrosse
Mrs. Ray Ensenbach
West Bend
Norma Erickson
Janesville
Mrs. Willie Erlandson
Lake Mills
Albert Esch
Edgerton
Anne Esch
Edgerton
Tillie Everson
Whitehall

F

Alma M. Fabisch
Beaver Dam
Edna Farrell
Kenosha
Esther Farrey
Platteville
Dorothy Feeney
Spooner
Bernadette Feisst
Madison
Sr. Claude Feldner
Fond du Lac
Marie Felze
Sheboygan
Kathryn Fenlon
Milwaukee
Erna Fenton
Shawano
Harlo Ferris
Wild Rose
Ben Finger
Madison
Florence Fischer
Lannon
Edith Fleming
Park Falls
Henry Fleming
Janesville
Alvina Floistad
Scandinavia
Leda Fofford
Saxon
Margaret Follstad
Madison
Sr. M. Remberta Ford
Sinsinawa
Evelyn Francis
Evansville

Mary Frels
Madison
Harry Friedman
Milwaukee
Jack P. Fritz
Rhinelander
Alma Fromm
Hamburg
Anastasia Furman
Oshkosh

G

Peggy Galbraith
Schofield
Ted Gall
Madison
Elaine A. Gardner
Racine
Eva Garner
Verona
Eugene Gauger
Wautoma
Mary Geimer
Green Bay
Charla George
Gleason
Pansy Gerlach
Madison
Mrs. Olga L. Gest
Sun Prairie
Mrs. Melvin Getlinger
Rudolph
Wilhelmina Geurink
Wausau
Winifred Gibbons
LaValle
Arthur Giere
Galesville

Rena Gilbertson
Strum
Gertrude Gisch
Milwaukee
Mary S. Glavin
Milwaukee
Mary Gmoser
Milwaukee
Mrs. Edward Goerke
Waukesha
Irving Goessl
Curtiss
Laura Good
Rice Lake
Gladys Goodburne
Milwaukee
Mary Gort
Eau Claire
Olive Goth
Madison
Edith Gotz
Pittsville
Doris Graham
Augusta
Wilma Greene
Madison
Edith Gregarson
Chetek
David Griffin
Eau Claire
Julia Grosse
Appleton
Viola Grueneberg
Wausau
Irene Grunden
Madison
Theodore Gundlach
Oak Creek
Howard Gunderson
Eleva

H

Alice Hackett
Lake Geneva
Lorenz Hackbarth
Tomah
Emily Hadley
Kingston
Katherine T. Haefliger
Janesville
Helen Haefmeyer
Waukesha
Helen Hahn
Milwaukee
Margaret Hall
Richland Center
Frank Halloran
Gays Mills
Ellouise Halstead
Union Grove
Sr. M. Candida Halm
Racine
Mrs. Carl Halvorson
Crandon
Georgianna Hamilton
Evansville
Christine Hansen
Fairchild
Laura M. Hansen
Rhinelander
Mrs. Clara Hanson
Deerfield
Mrs. Mildred S. Hanson
Eau Claire
Evelyn Hapke
Gleason
George H. Harb
Madison
Helen Haroldson
Mt. Horeb

Marie Harris
Argonne
Elva G. Hart
Milwaukee
LeRoy Hartz
Merrill
Elmer Harvey
Oshkosh
Viola Haskins
Green Bay
Arnold R. Hatch
Eau Claire
Margaret M. Hawig
West Bend
Lucy Hawkins
Kimball
Martha Hayes
Wausau
DeLorr A. Hayward
Green Bay
Emma Heath
Phillips
Cecelia Hebal
Stevens Point
Lawrence Hebal
Stevens Point
Stanley Held
Alma Center
Dorothy Helmke
McFarland
Eugene T. Helmuth
Rhinelander
Marie Hemner
Altoona
Doris Henke
Eau Claire
Winfred Herberg
Mayville
Cecelia Herreid
Madison

Teeda Herreid
Madison
Elizabeth Herritz
Baraboo
Helen Herschboeck
Waukesha
Leo Hershberger
Manawa
F. M. Hessler
Hayward
John Higbie
Jefferson
Marie Hilbert
Green Bay
Wanda Hile
Madison
Carlton Hill
Schofield
Helen Hill
Schofield
Gilbert Hillestad
Rio
Pearl Hillman
Shell Lake
Emma V. Holden
Marshfield
Vera Hollibush
Stoughton
Gertrude Holtman
Kenosha
Margaret Holzman
Waupaca
Mildred O. Homuth
West Bend
Amy Honeyager
Waukesha
Evelyn Hoppe
Columbus
Martha Hoppe
Waukesha

Alvina Hosely
Wausau

Mabel Howard
Wisconsin Rapids

Eva P. Hougum
Stratford

Jack Houston
Manitowoc

Mildred Huber
Madison

Dorothy Huehnerfuss
Wausau

James Hughes
DePere

Lydia Humphrey
Albany

Emily E. Hunt
Waterford

Russell Hustad
Madison

I

Mrs. George Israel
Marshfield

J

Dolores Jack
Bagley

E. Louise Jackson
Pardeeville

Sigurd Jacobsen
Milwaukee

Mrs. Clarence Jacobson
Hixton

Loreen Jacobson
Madison

Myrtle Jahnke
Pepin

Mrs. A. Jank
Sheboygan

Ardalia Janko
Medford

Steve Jankovitz
Milladore

Edith Jens
Stoughton

Ellis Jensen
Kenosha

Agnes Jepsen
Madison

Gladys Jepsen
Milwaukee

Mrs. John Jewell
West Bend

Amie Johnson
Tigerton

Hattie Johnson
Cashton

Isabel M. Johnson
Milwaukee

Jean-Page Johnson
Oconomowoc

Maud Johnson
Rhinelander

Tekla Johnson
Brule

Toni Johnson
Milwaukee

Abbie Jones
Holcombe

Cecilia Jones
Janesville

James A. Jones
Rosendale

Mrs. Leslie Jones
Holcombe

Mildred Jones
Baraboo

Mabel Jonkel
Baraboo

Jennie Erb Joos
Verona

Doris Jorgensen
Milwaukee

Mrs. John Julius
Fond du Lac

Adelaide Jungemann
Arlington

Dorothea Jurgensen
Gays Mills

K

Gwendolyn Kaltenbach
Potosi

Thomas Kammerud
Blanchardville

Mrs. Otto Kangas
Milwaukee

Paul F. Karberg
Madison

Emma J. Kauffman
Neillsville

Esther Keilholtz
LaCrosse

Lillian Kelling
Walworth

Beatrice Kelly
Tomahawk

Louise Kerr
Holmen

Helen Kessenich
Spring Green

Mrs. Reinhart Kieper
Antigo

Lydia Kimball
Madison

Jay E. King
Madison

Ruth Kingsbury
Madison

Marion Kirkland
Algoma

Muriel Kleczka
Brookfield

Julia Klein
Milwaukee

Ida Klemm
Manitowoc

Hobart Kletzien
Madison

Lucille Klockow
Franksville

Josephine Budzisz Klotz
Milwaukee

Mary Klune
Neillsville

Henry Knaff
Port Washington

Olga Knapp
Bear Creek

Charlotte Knechtges
Madison

Helen J. Knight
Dalton

Kathleen Knutson
Redgranite

Mrs. Otto Koberle
Middleton

Gertrude Koch
Madison

Harold Kolb
Kenosha

Mrs. Oscar Kollath
Seymour

Mrs. Raymond Kraemer
Marshfield

Marie Kramer
Eastman
Mildred Kreager
Madison
Rose Kreuger
Madison
Helen Kronberg
Green Bay
Thelma C. Kroske
Brookfield
Anne Krueger
Green Bay
Mrs. Lester Krueger
Cochrane
Violette Krueger
Hazelhurst
Mrs. Ralph Kundert
Monroe
Ida Kuehnast
Stevens Point
Herbert Kuhm
Wauwatosa
Sr. M. Celeste Kunkel
Racine
Ottillie Kunkel
Neillsville
Mrs. Hubert Kurkowski
Menasha
Edna Kvalheim
Soldiers Grove

L

Martha Laffin
Wausau
Agnes Landwehr
Watertown
Charlotte Lanham
Danbury

Mary Lanphere
Beaver Dam
Mildred LaPort
Spooner
Gerelda Larsen
Neillsville
Charles Larson
Port Washington
Ruby E. Larson
Menomonie
Lucile Lauper
Hollandale
Evelyn Leach
Saukville
Frieda M. Lease
Oregon
Martin Lee
Hayward
Ida Lefevre
Green Bay
Mrs. Harry P. Lehman
Madison
Harry P. Lehman
Madison
Maurine H. Leischer
Oak Creek
Ruth C. Lembke
Sussex
Elda Lemmen
Eau Claire
Mrs. Albertus Lemmenes
Waupun
Edith Leppla
New Berlin
Sr. Laurina Levi
LaCrosse
Catherine Lewis
Fond du Lac
Blanche B. Lindblad
Ashland

Albert Lindow
Chili
Loie Lipka
Marshfield
Jennie Long
Sayner
Paul Looker
Crivitz
Agnes Lorenz
Fond du Lac
Sr. M. Lorenz
Sinsinawa
Laura Louthain
Waukesha
Isabel Lowe
Washburn
Anna Lucia
Westboro
Marguerite Ludwig
Racine
Eva Lundahl
Lake Geneva
Eva Lundall
Elkhorn
Barbara Lunenschloss
Madison
Iva Luther
Poynette
Ellen Lyons
Birnamwood

M

Hazel Maas
Adams
Roderick MacDonald
Madison
Helen M. Machovec
Hillsboro

Nora Mackley
Adams
Arthur H. Maegli
Milwaukee
Margaret Maier
Racine
Aurelia Malik
Milladore
C. E. Maloney
Pound
Vivian Malueg
Clintonville
Agnes Mann
Racine
Margaret Manser
Waukesha
Frances W. Mapp
Wauwatosa
Sr. Maristella Anne
Stevens Point
Mrs. John Marshall
Gillingham
Henry F. Martin
Iola
Portia Martin
Richland Center
Ethel F. Mates
Kenosha
Helen Mather
Milwaukee
Lue Mattern
Kenosha
Eunice Mattakat
Evansville
Mae Matthes
Viola
Elizabeth Matthew
Middleton
Hilda Matthies
Wauwatosa

Edith M. Mattke
Baraboo

Ruben Mauer
Fennimore

Ruth Mayer
Thorp

Daisy McAdams
Racine

Florence McConochie
Colgate

Mary McCrorey
Hixton

Agnes McDaniel
Eau Claire

George A. McDermid
Strum

Hazel McDonald
New Glarus

Elizabeth McGowan
Poynette

Geneva McKay
Madison

Elsie May McKee
Verona

Alice McKenzie
Appleton

Ada McKnight
Stoughton

Evelyn McLean
South Byron

Leone Mech
New London

Lorraine Meffert
Waunakee

Roy R. Meier
Ogema

Sr. Paulina Meis
Fond du Lac

Blanche Mendl
Deerbrook

Jerry C. Mendl
Deerbrook

Bess Meredith
Rhinelander

Marie W. Merkel
Wausau

Isabelle Mertens
Withee

Irene D. Messman
Two Rivers

Mrs. Fred P. Meyer
Cable

Marie R. Meyer
Eau Claire

Emily Milan
Twin Lakes

Marjorie Miley
Sheboygan Falls

Charles H. Miller
Milwaukee

Mrs. Chester Miller
LaValle

Helen B. Miller
Kenosha

Sabrina Miller
West Salem

Frances Millin
Lancaster

Mrs. George Mitchell
Sun Prairie

Goldye Mohr
Madison

Lola Monroe
Shullsburg

Clarice L. Moon
Delavan

Lillian Morey
Iron River

Alvin H. Morgan
Kenosha

Eleanor Morgan
Kenosha

Mrs. E. M. Morgan
Scandinavia

Leslie Morris
Madison

Delyla Mortag
Wauwatosa

Mrs. K. Moseler
Two Rivers

Dorothy M. Moser
Muskego

Mrs. Kenneth Mosher
Gotham

Mrs. Leonard Mosiman
Cochrane

Elma Mots
Milwaukee

Mark Movrich
New Richmond

Auguste Mueller
Wausau

Ida J. Mueller
Oshkosh

Ottilie Mueller
Wausau

Cyrilla Muller
Dodgeville

Ruth Myers
Madison

N

Emma Nefzer
Beaver Dam

Catherine Neilson
Racine

Esther Neiswender
Waupaca

Irene Nelezen
Crivitz

Mrs. Art Nelson, Sr.
Downing

Mary R. Nelson
Waupaca

May Nelson
Park Falls

Nellie Nelson
River Falls

Sr. M. Susanna Neubauer, O.P.
Sinsinawa

Dorothy Newmann
Algoma

Edna Nielsen
Racine

Cecelia Nieman
Muskego

Elva Niemi
Ogema

Margarette Nienaber
Madison

Josephine Nixon
Ontario

Mrs. John Novak, Sr.
Deerbrook

Pearl E. Nysse
Plymouth

O

Emma Olson
West Sturgeon Bay

Eva Olson
Stoughton

Mona B. Olson
Chippewa Falls

Ruby Olson
Racine

Edward J. O'Neill
Cuba City
Jane M. O'Neill
Cuba City
Anna P. Onsrud
Stoughton
Rae Onstine
Prairie du Sac
Carl Opelt
Neillsville
Augusta Ormston
Grantsburg
Esther Oslage
Rothschild
Dorothy Osner
Portage
Mae E. Ott
Chili
Catherine Otten
Milwaukee
Floyd Owen
Rhinelander

P

John Parker
Hartland
Johanna Parris
Milwaukee
Magdalene Patterson
Superior
Florence Patton
Lake Geneva
Adele V. Paulson
Stevens Point
Viola M. Paulsen
Amherst
Marjorie Paulson
Milwaukee

Mrs. Martin Paust
Columbus
Lucille Peller
Kenosha
Mrs. R. A. Penn
Hazelhurst
Helen Peschel
Madison
Florence A. Petersen
Racine
Mrs. Alfred Peterson
Mt. Horeb
Arnold Peterson
Ashland
Bessie Peterson
Siren
Mildred Peterson
Lodi
Ruth Phelps
Oconomowoc
Elizabeth I. Philleo
Wisconsin Rapids
Charlie Phillips
Waukesha
Mary J. Phillips
Sun Prairie
P. C. Phillips
Sun Prairie
Gwen Pickney
Milwaukee
Mrs. Nick Pier
Racine
Grace Pierce
Manitowoc
Margarete Pierce
Neillsville
I. A. Pietrzak
Stanley
Lois Tucker Pink
Union Grove

Gladys Pippenger
Phillips
Dora Polanski
Bloomer
Alonzo Pond
Minocqua
Dorothy Pond
Minocqua
Greta L. Potter
Superior
Katherine Power
Green Lake
Hilda Prahl
Milwaukee
Josephine Prasser
West Allis
Ralph C. Pratt
Green Bay
Beulah Mae Puariea
Plover
Ed Pudas
Iron River
Margaret Putz
Waukesha

Q

Mrs. Fred C. Quaden
Waukesha
Emma Qualmann
Hustisford
Alice Quigley
Green Bay
Esther Quinn
Columbus
Lillian Quinn
Wausau

R

Irene Rademacher
Stanley
Edna Rand
Richland Center
Reinhold Rayeske
South Milwaukee
Mary Fran Readinger
Dodgeville
Blanche Reed
Beloit
Lois Reine
Wausau
Leone Remington
Kenosha
Martha Renk
Sun Prairie
Grace Rentmeister
Fond du Lac
Frank Revie
Merrill
Mrs. Clarence A. Rhode
Neshkoro
Clarence Rhode
Neshkoro
Carl H. Rhody
Ogema
Florence Richards
Rice Lake
Charles W. Rippey
Fond du Lac
Thora Rishel
Phillips
Elizabeth Risser
Madison
Hilbert Roell
Fredonia
Mae H. Roets
Milwaukee

Dorothy Root
Fond du Lac
Elmer E. Root
Fond du Lac
Anne C. Rose
Mondovi
Mildred M. Rosenthal
Fond du Lac
Malcolm Rosholt
Rosholt
Flora Rossdeutscher
Richland Center
Louis Roth
Madison
Mrs. Cecil Roundy
Portage
Florence Ruka
Milwaukee
Mrs. Roy Rule
Mineral Point
Emma Rupp
LaCrosse
Herman A. Rusch
Milwaukee
Dulcye Rush
Madison
Edna Russell
Tomahawk
Harold Russell
Janesville
Henrietta L. Ryall
Kenosha

S

Roger R. Sacia
West Bend
Mrs. Fred A. Sager
West Bend

Genevieve St. Clair
Fox Lake
Norman Sainty
Eau Claire
Iona Sallander
Madison
Grace K. Samuelson
Sturgeon Bay
Phil Sander
Kenosha
Glen Sandmire
Stanley
Mrs. Glen Sandmire
Stanley
Mrs. Harry Sarb
Westfield
Cora Sasman
Madison
Josephine Sauer
Wauwatosa
Leone Schaaf
Mineral Point
Cecilia Schaden
Manitowoc
Emil J. Schaefer
Madison
Laura Scherer
Combined Locks
Elsie Schmidt
Rib Lake
Irene W. Schmidt
Oak Creek
Jean B. Schmidt
Siren
Leona Schmidt
Marshfield
Leona J. Schmidt
Winter
Ruth Schmidt
Merton

Emily Schoechert
Madison
Mrs. Norman Schoenoff
Menomonie
Herbert Schollmeyer
Germantown
Jennie T. Schrage
Whitewater
Dorothy C. Schrader
Evansville
Edna Schram
Mishicot
Grace Schroeder
Spooner
Mabel Schroeder
Fond du Lac
Thelma M. Schroeder
Warrens
Virginia Schroeder
Horicon
Leone Schultz
Fall Creek
Alice Schulze
Brillion
Harriet Schumacher
Combined Locks
Mrs. John Schumacher
Combined Locks
Ellsworth Schutte
Wausau
Elsie A. Schutz
Portage
Marguerite Schwandt
Wautoma
Evelyn Schwebke
Beloit
Maurice Scribner
Waterloo
Kenneth Searles
Union Center

Mrs. Clarence Sedbrook
Lancaster
Joseph L. Seiler
Algoma
Mrs. Herman Semingson
Eleva
Mrs. Jens Serum
Nelson
Mrs. Albert J. Servais
Cochrane
Evelyn Seybold
Appleton
Fern Shannon
Cazenovia
Lois Sheehan
Madison
Nell Shellman
Suring
Beryl Sheridan
Kendall
Florence K. Shodron
Milwaukee
Julie Rath Sholem
Wauwatosa
Helen Sieber
Plymouth
Esther Siebert
Milwaukee
Dick Sigl
Marshfield
Casmer Sikorski
Stevens Point
Marie Silbernagel
Rib Lake
Anne Simley
Madison
Robert Sitton
Verona
Violette Skindingsrude
Whitewater

Clara Skott
Middleton

Flora Smith
Winneconne

Joseph Smith
Madison

Helen C. Smith
Evansville

LaVerne Smith
Richland Center

Roberta A. Smith
Kenosha

Sylvia Smith
Sparta

Teresa Snorek
Richland Center

Amy Sollie
Ashland

Mrs. E. R. Sommer
Neshkoro

A. M. Sontag
Milwaukee

Blanche Sorenson
Bruce

Mrs. John Sorley
Brown Deer

Henry C. Spear
Beaver Dam

Genevieve Spielbauer
Cudahy

Vera Springer
Elmwood

Laura Stachoviak
Schofield

R. R. Stanley
Menomonee Falls

Mary Agnes Starr
Madison

Helen Stashek
Milladore

Geraldine Stavrum
Cable

Esther Stein
Sheboygan

Clara Steinberg
Oshkosh

Eva Mae Steiner
Pardeeville

Hazel Stenseth
Verona

Florence Stern
Hiles

Blanche R. Stevens
East Troy

Mrs. Myron Stevens
Madison

Grace Stone
Madison

Anne Stubbe
Madison

Clara Stuewer
Bonduel

George Suchy
Waukesha

Esther J. Sullivan
Williams Bay

Paul Suminski
Milwaukee

Virginia Sutter
Owen

Violet Swanson
Plover

Cal Swenson
Waupaca

T

Pearl Tagatz
Darlington

Irma Taylor
Endeavor

Clifford Tellefson
Cambridge

Gustave Telschow
Fountain City

Edith Tennant
Arena

Harold Tesch
New Berlin

Edith Tesser
Wisconsin Dells

Kathryn Theiler
New Glarus

William C. Thies
Reedsburg

Lorenzo Thomas
Montello

Mrs. Bert Thompson
Kenosha

Earl W. Thompson
Richland Center

Hilda Thompson
Richland Center

Mrs. Marshall Thompson
Milwaukee

Ruth S. Thompson
Richland Center

Henry Thurber
Platteville

Samuel H. Thut
Madison

Mrs. J. L. Tibbetts
Shawano

LaVerna K. Tinkham
Ripon

Elmer Tonsfeldt
Siren

Louie Tornowske
Patch Grove

Clara Torrison
Reedsville

Sr. M. Carola Towne
Fond du Lac

Mabel Traiser
Appleton

Marie Traut
Poynette

Anna Trowbridge
Milladore

Leila Tubbs
Cross Plains

Lydia Tukalek
Rice Lake

Maude Tullis
Evansville

Selma Turner
Westby

Mary Tutkowski
Milwaukee

U

Harold F. Uehling
Waupun

V

Amarette Van Epps
Beloit

Herschel Van Gilder
Birchwood

Frances Vannix
Tomahawk

Angeline Van Putten
West Allis

Mrs. Marwood Veale
Kenosha

Mrs. Frederick Viken
Stoughton
Gladys Vincent
Park Falls
Cora Voltz
East Troy
Ivan B. Von Berg
West Allis
Gladys Vorpagel
Grafton

W

Mrs. Leonard Wagner
Galesville
Monica Wagner
St. Nazianz
Josephine Waldenberger
Onalaska
Elizabeth Wallace
Burlington
Tom Wallace
Burlington
Fern Walsh
Wisconsin Rapids
Eleanore Walter
Milwaukee
Margaret Walter
Lake Geneva
Mrs. Wilbert Walter
Rio Creek
Dorothy V. Walters
Milwaukee
Elizabeth Warner
Madison
Alda Warnkey
West Bend
Edna Weaver
Stoughton

Olive Webster
Lyons
LeRoy Weeden
Oconomowoc
Hazel Weiland
Eau Claire
Mrs. William Weimar
Coon Valley
Mrs. John M. Weiss
Sun Prairie
Hazel Welch
Superior
William C. Welch
Minong
Elsie Weller
New London
A. H. Wellnitz
Lac du Flambeau
Berkeley J. Wells
Ashland
Irma K. Wells
Oakfield
Isobel Welter
Solon Springs
Ethel Werderitch
Madison
Alice Werndl
Hayward
Gene J. West
Wautoma
Edith Westbury
Madison
D.I. Wherritt
Plover
Elaine White
Madison
Rhoda White
LaCrosse
Mrs. C. R. Whitney
Colby

Marion A. Whitworth
Mondovi
Lauretta Wieland
Pewaukee
Norman Wilbert
Kohler
Marie Wilcox
Racine
Beatrice Wilkins
Marinette
Mrs. O. R. Wilkins
Madison
Anne E. Williams
Green Bay
Pearl G. Williams
Middleton
Ada F. Williamson
Poynette
Helen Willmes
Racine
Warren Wilson
Medford
Grace M. Winkler
Hiles
Mrs. Arno Wipperman
Plymouth
May Wirkuty
Neillsville
Otto Witte
Mondovi
Elsie Wittenberger
Genoa City
Helen Witz
Waukesha
Evelyn Wolfe
Kenosha
Mrs. R. E. Wolfgram
Viroqua
Louise B. Wolfgram
Milwaukee

Sylvia Worden
Plover
Anna Woyjcikowski
Milwaukee
Gertrude H. Wright
Milwaukee
Sr. Kathleen Wright
Sinsinawa
Walter R. Wright
Columbus
Emily Wurl
Wauwatosa
Bernice Wurtz
Kenosha
Ted Wurtz
Kenosha

Y

Addie Yaudes
Madison
Alexa Young
Madison

Z

Lucille Zais
Stanley
Estelle Zukowski
Thorp
Sr. Jane Zurbuch
Fond du Lac
June A. Zwickey
Appleton